JUDAISM
THE WAY
OF HOLINESS

SOLOMON NIGOSIAN

First published 1986
Second Impression 1987

© **Solomon A. Nigosian 1986**

British Library
Cataloguing in Publication Data
Nigosian, Solomon A.
Judaism: the way of holiness
1. Judaism
I. Title
296 BM561
ISBN 0-85030-560-8
ISBN 0-85030-429-6 Pbk

Crucible is an imprint of
The Aquarian Press,
part of the Thorsons Publishing Group

Printed and bound in Great Britain

To
The invincible Armenians and Jews
who survived
the unparalleled horrors
of time.

CONTENTS

ACKNOWLEDGEMENTS

APPRECIATION is expressed to the following publishers and authors for permission to quote from copyrighted material.

W. M. Abbott, ed., *The Documents of Vatican II* (Guild Press, New York).

J. A. Brundage, *The Crusades: A Documentary Survey* (Marquette University Press, Milwaukee, Wisconsin).

I. Epstein, *Judaism* (Penguin Books, Harmondsworth, England).

M. N. Kertzer, *What Is a Jew?* (The World Publishing Co., H. N. Abrams, Inc., New York).

L. Roth, *Judaism: A Portrait* (Faber and Faber Publishers, London).

A. Schwarz-Bart, *The Last of the Just* (Martin Secker & Warburg Limited, London).

Weekday Prayer Book (The Rabbinical Assembly of America, New York).

The publishers would like to thank Genut Audio Visual Productions for their help and advice in selecting illustrations.

INTRODUCTION

WHEN Michael Cox, Editorial Director of the Aquarian Press, asked me to write a book 'for the general reader' on Judaism, intimidated as I was by the magnitude of the project, I agreed to write it for the following five reasons: my upbringing in the Middle East; my association with Jewish neighbours; my understanding, as an Armenian, of the Jewish people; my academic studies in the religion of ancient Israel and my professional interest in Judaism as a historian of religion. Each of my reasons requires some elaboration.

The first twenty-three years of my childhood and adolescence were shaped by the social, political and cultural milieu of pre- to post-World War II Alexandria, Egypt. Native Egyptians, Arabs, Ethiopians, South Africans, Jews, Armenians and all types of Eastern and Western Europeans lived in this sunny and beautiful Mediterranean seaport of Alexandria. Egypt itself (particularly the cities of Alexandria and Cairo) was, in the true sense of the world, multicultural and multilingual. Politically, the country was a semi-independent state, ruled by a monarchical system of government administered jointly at all levels by British and Egyptian officials. The towers, spires and portals of mosques, churches and synagogues shared the skyline of most cities and villages. Thus, I was exposed to Jewish, Christian, and Muslim religious traditions from a very early stage in my life.

I received my primary and secondary education in two of the leading British private schools for boys established in Alexandria. Enrolments represented miniature world communities—Muslim, Christian, and Jewish sons of leading dignitaries, rulers, professionals, and the economically well-

to-do class. Different cultural customs and religious traditions became familiar, commonplace characteristics of everyday life as a result of the religiously mixed character of
classmates and friends who were my companions during all
my years of school life. My close associations—sharing
meals, games, or studies—with my Jewish and Muslim
classmates taught me to respect their cultural traditions and
religious values.

My earliest and most vivid recollections of Jewish life and
religion are of our next-door Jewish neighbours in Alexandria. Their son, René, and I lived and grew up together in the
same neighbourhood for over fifteen years. We played
together, we went to parties together, we went to the beach
together, we loved to stroll the streets together, we went to
movies together and we had all the fun that kids and boys of
our age enjoyed. But still something separated us.

Raised in a strict Orthodox Jewish home, René was not
allowed to eat in our house. He attended the local Jewish
school and studied the Torah to prepare himself for the Bar
Mitzvah. Almost every Friday night after sunset (the start of
the Sabbath) I was asked to turn on the lights in our
neighbour's house, a request that puzzled me for years until I
came to understand the significance of the service I performed for them.

René constantly talked of Palestine, the Holy Land, which
he and his family often visited and hoped to see restored to
the Jewish people as a national homeland. Through René and
his family I received my first impressions of Judaism—of
Torah, of Holy Land, of kosher, of Sabbath, of circumcision,
of Bar Mitzvah, of Yom Kippur, of Rosh Hashanah, and
many other religious practices and feasts.

The next important factor that shaped my sympathy for
Judaism is my Armenian roots. I am constantly reminded of
the close parallels in the history and destinies of the Jews and
the Armenians. I shall select only a few for purposes of
illustration.

Both Jews and Armenians are of ancient stock and have
held a kingdom for a brief period in history. Both peoples
have lived, and many still live, far from their ancestral
homeland, dispersed throughout the world. Both have
suffered at the hands of foreign rulers. Both survived the

vicissitudes of time while other nations perished. Both celebrate the historical struggle for freedom of conscience and religious worship as a national holiday: Hannukkah among Jews, Vartanantz among Armenians. Both experienced, in the twentieth century, the incredible crime of genocide: the Armenians at the hands of the Young Turks during World War I and the Jews at the hands of German Nazis during World War II. Both have re-established their national state in their respective ancestral homeland: the Soviet Socialist Republic of Armenia since 1921 and the independent State of Israel since 1948. Thus, as an Armenian I believe I am well aware of and particularly sensitive to the issues that are of utmost importance to Jews.

So far I have described the purely subjective influences that shaped my understanding. My formal, academic studies represent objective justification for my interest in Judaic traditions.

The area of concentration that I chose for my undergraduate and graduate studies at the universities I attended in Canada was Ancient Israelite Religion. This is the period of Biblical Judaism, as compared to the period of Talmudic Judaism or to the period of Modern Judaism. Fortunately, my instructors represented both Jewish as well as Christian experts, thus providing me with an insight into the entire topic from at least two points of view, to which I trust my former teachers will concede I have done sufficient justice in the following pages to compensate them for their labours.

For the past thirteen years my academic interest and professional career have centered on the history of religion, from a global perspective. This means that, as a historian of religion, I critically analyse the global role and function of each religious tradition, whether it has survived to the present day or has become extinct. The survival and role of Judaism in the entire scheme of the history of religion is, in my opinion, sufficiently fascinating to communicate to anyone unfamiliar with it.

These five factors, then, are the primary reasons why I wished to write on Judaism, though Michael Cox knew nothing of this when he accepted my submission. And yet, a crucial question remains to be answered: can I as an 'outsider', or rather as a non-Jew, locate and take the measure of, as it were, the heart and pulse of Judaism? Although in the last analysis it is the reader who must judge, yet I believe I can. For, although in one sense I am an 'outsider' (as a non-Jew), in another sense I am an 'insider' (as an Armenian), who can identify with the historic lot of Judaism. In other words, I stand in a very unique position: I am able to view events from both a subjective as well as an objective perspective.

Thus, my overall objective in this book is to present a distinctive religious tradition, that of Judaism. There are some thirteen million Jews, who live in all parts of the world, though not all of them are pious adherents of their religion, nor are they unified in their interpretation and practice of their religion. It is not my intention to present a historical account of the Jewish people around the world, far less to record their contribution to human civilization. There are enough books that have done that.

My primary aim in this book is to penetrate into the *spirit* of the unique, thriving religious tradition of Judaism as understood in its multi-faceted forms by its millions of adherents. Far from presenting merely a skeleton, I wish to put across to every reader the idea that the life-blood of Judaism is 'holiness'. It is impossible to penetrate into the mind and spirit of Judaism without a proper understanding of this Judaic concept of 'holiness'.

To call something or someone 'holy' means primarily that the object or the person is related to what is 'divine'. In other words, that which is 'holy' is 'set apart' because it belongs to divinity. The importance of Judaism lies precisely in this notion of the 'holy': a 'holy' God, a 'holy' people, a 'holy' land, a 'holy' book, and 'holy' observances. These five— God, People, Land, Book, and Observances—belong to the Divine. They form an indivisible entity in Judaism.

A quick glance at the list of contents will indicate that the five chapters correspond to the five 'holy' characteristics of Judaism. Each chapter starts with an appropriate biblical or Talmudic passage that sets the stage for understanding the proper significance of what constitutes a 'holy' element. Biblical and Talmudic excerpts are either my own translations or quoted from two separate sources: *The Holy Bible*, New York: Thomas Nelson and Sons, 1952; and I. Epstein

(Ed.), *The Babylonian Talmud in English*, 36 vols., London: Soncino Press, 1935-1953. Then follows an explanation, in some detail, of the subject matter in each chapter. A final chapter, 'Reflections', briefly charts my personal assessment, as a historian of religion, of the role and survival of Judaism in the global context of the history of religion. In my opinion, in this present age no religious tradition can be defined or understood in isolation and in terms of its teachings, practices, and institutions alone. Its role, contribution, and function in the development of the religious consciousness of human civilization is as important a factor for its survival as the relevance of its teachings, institutions and practices. This entire book, then, is a presentation of the origin and development of a particular religious movement—Judaism—that was capable of surviving the vicissitudes of time.

I am indebted to numerous scholars who, over the years, have shaped my thoughts, and this is quite evident throughout this book, both in the main body of the text as well as in the sources of quotations. Also, I am deeply grateful to two people who were directly involved throughout the preparation of this volume: Patrick Trant and Debbie van Eeken. Their persistent helpful interest and their invaluable advice were a constant inspiration and encouragement in bringing this book to fruition. Finally, I wish to thank my ever-understanding wife for her magnificent support of an author attempting the impossible.

S. A. NIGOSIAN
Toronto, Canada

1

HOLY GOD

God, where shall I find Thee,
Whose glory fills the universe?
Behold I find Thee
Wherever the mind is free to follow its own bent,
Wherever words come out from the depth of truth,
Wherever tireless striving stretches its arms towards perfection,
Where men struggle for freedom and right,
Where the scientist toils to unbare the secrets of nature,
Wherever the poet strings pearls of beauty in lyric lines,
Wherever glorious deeds are done.

Reconstructionist Prayer Book

God Is

In the beginning God created the heavens and the earth.

Genesis 1:1

THE very first sentence of Jewish Scripture affirms God's existence. Unlike Christian theologians and philosophers, Jews require no proof. God simply is. The existence of the universe and the existence of the Jews affirm the existence of God. God is acknowledged as the source of all beings and the rationale for the enduring survival of Judaism.

To be sure, some modern Jews (including some Israelis) see themselves as members of just another nation or ethnic group. Their allegiance to the Jewish people, attested by their acts of self-sacrifice, is no less committed because it is secular rather than religious, but it stands in stark contrast to the traditional self-perception of the Jewish people. For them, God, not national identity, is central to their lives and to their destiny. Jews, then, predicate God's existence not only on the universe and all that is in it, but fundamentally on their very existence as a people. God is central to them—their *raison d'être*.

This unequivocal acceptance has not, however, precluded the development of various theological concepts of God. On the contrary, Jewish theology assigns various interpretations to the character and attributes of God, but only as limited, human attempts to define the unfathomable totality and immutability of God.

The human mind, according to Jewish understanding, cannot fully encompass God. In other words, God remains hidden from the human mind. But He manifests Himself in two areas: in nature and in human activity. Several quotations from Jewish Scripture serve to illustrate these beliefs.

And God said to Moses: '*Ehyeh-Asher-Ehyeh.*' And He said: 'Say to the children of Israel, *Ehyeh* sends me to you.'

Exodus 3:14

And he [Moses] said: 'Show me Your glory . . .' And He [God] said: 'You cannot see my face; for no one can see me and live . . . 'Behold there is a place by me where you can stand upon the rock; and while my glory passes by . . . I will cover you with my hand until I have passed by, then I will take away my hand and you can see my back, but my face cannot be seen.'

Exodus 33:18-23

Do you not know? Have you not heard?
Has it not been told you from the beginning?
Have you not understood from the foundations of the earth? It is He who sits above the circle of the earth, and its inhabitants are like grasshoppers; who stretches out the heavens like a curtain, and spreads them like a tent to dwell in; who brings princes to nothing and makes rulers of the earth as nothing.

Isaiah 40:21-23

Who is like the Lord our God . . .?
He raises the poor from the dust,
and lifts the needy from the ash heap,
to make them sit with princes,
with the princes of his people.
He gives the barren woman a home,
making her the joyous mother of children.

Psalm 113:5-9

The first two quotations illustrate the conviction that one can never know fully what God is. The last two infer that whatever insights about God lie within the compass of human understanding they come mainly through His manifestations as Creator and Ruler of the totality of nature, including human beings. These are the conclusions of scholars. Their justification is as follows.

The first quotation from Exodus affirms the Self definition of God. *Ehyeh-Asher-Ehyeh* is usually translated as 'I Am Who I Am', or 'I Am What I Am', or 'I Will Be What I Will Be'. The word *Ehyeh* derives from the Hebrew root word *hayah*, which means 'life', 'being'. The same root is also the antecedent of the word, or name, YHWH—the four letters of the ineffable name of God, never pronounced by Jews. Basically then, the Self definition of God as *Ehyeh-Asher-Ehyeh* is understood to mean that God is a BEING—an Absolute, Immutable Being, but beyond human comprehension. And this is precisely the reason that Jews refrain from articulating the word YHWH lest, by naming the undefinable, they diminish His Being and reduce it to human level. Consequently, wherever the word YHWH (normally pronounced Yahweh) occurs, Jews pronounce it *Adonai*, meaning 'the Lord'.

The second quotation tells how God denies Moses the privilege of seeing Him face to face, on pain of death, but invites Moses to view His back. The point of the story is quite clear. No one is capable of fully knowing what God is, and yet no one can fail to recognize His presence. In other words, the Jew knows that God exists, that God is; but the Jew also knows that God is partly hidden and therefore beyond human understanding.

A vivid analogy of this divine paradox is attributed to Joshua ben Hananiah, a prominent rabbi of the first century. The story goes that he was challenged by a high ranking potentate of the period.

'I want to see your God,' said the Emperor to Rabbi Joshua ben Hananiah.

'You cannot,' replied the Rabbi.

'But I insist,' repeated the Emperor.

The Rabbi's response was to point up to the blinding light of the noonday sun. 'Look into the sun.'

'I cannot,' answered the Emperor.

'If you cannot look at the sun, which is one of the servants who stands in the presence of the Holy One, praised be He,' said the Rabbi, 'then is it not even more evident that you cannot see God?'[1]

This paradox, belief in God's existence on the one hand and acceptance of God's incomprehensibility on the other, is further expressed by leading Jewish thinkers. Moses Maimonides (1135-1204), the most famous Spanish Jew, writes in his *Guide of the Perplexed* that 'God's existence is absolute . . . It includes no composition . . . We comprehend only the fact that He exists, not His essence [i.e., we comprehend only that He is, but not what He is].'[2]

Similarly, Hermann Cohen (1842-1918), founder of the Neo-Kantian school at Marburg, maintains in his *Religion of Reason from the Sources of Judaism* that, while every partial knowledge of God can lead a person towards a new knowledge of Him, yet God is forever removed from a person's grasp. The same assertion appears in the *Zohar*, the basic textbook of the Kabbalists (mystical sects), edited by the thirteenth-century Spanish mystic Moses de Léon: 'The Holy One, praised be He, is transcendent in His glory, He is hidden and removed far beyond all ken; there is no one in the world, nor has there ever been one whom His wisdom and essence do not elude, since He is recondite and hidden and beyond all ken . . .'[3]

The third and fourth quotations, from Isaiah and Psalms, affirm the creative acts of God. To Jews, the universe is neither self-created nor eternal. That is to say, the world and all that it contains is not the product of chance or of the accidental collocation of atoms. God is the source of all life, who created this world, including human beings, and who actively intervenes in daily events. Everything that happens in nature is a testimony to the sovereignty of God. Thus, for Jews, God is not merely a Creator, but a purposeful one. And since God's works of creation serve to testify to His dominion, pious Jews praise God with gratitude and reverence every morning:

Praised are You, O Lord our God, King of the universe.
You fix the cycles of light and darkness;
You ordain the order of all creation,
You cause light to shine over the earth.
Your radiant mercy is upon its inhabitants . . .
Praised are you, O Lord, Creator of the heavenly bodies.[4]

And in the evening:

Praised are You, O Lord our God, King of the universe.
Your command brings on the dusk of evening . . .
You order the stars in their heavenly courses.
You create day and you create night . . .
Praised are You, O Lord, for the evening dusk.[5]

Jews see the reality of God revealed in all the forces and wonders of nature (Psalm 29:3-10), as well as in all human activities (Psalm 139:7-10). But such a view of God has not escaped the criticism of sceptics. From the earliest times they have cited the book of *Qoheleth* (Ecclesiastes) to justify or explain their reservations. From its initial note to its conclusion, the sweeping statement of the author of *Qoheleth* is that everything in this world, including human life, is 'vanity of vanities.'

The English rendering of 'vanity' for the Hebrew term *habhel* is somewhat misleading. *Habhel* literally means 'breath' or 'vapour', and figuratively, therefore, implies impermanence, transitoriness, worthlessness. Thus, the conclusion reached by the author of *Qoheleth* after a long process of investigation is that all existence is impermanent, transitory and worthless. Does he then deny the existence of God? The sceptics think so. They accept his pessimism at its face value. Believers do not. The significance they place on his conclusion is that an understanding of life, let alone God's purpose in life, lies beyond the reach of mere human intellect.

The mainstream of Jewish thought has never wavered in its firm conviction about the existence of God. This conviction is, perhaps, best summed up by the founder of Hasidism, Rabbi Israel Baal-Shem-Tov (1698-1760). He concluded that one can know God from three sources: faith, thought, and tradition.

There are two sorts of persons who believe in God. The one believes because his faith has been handed down to him by his fathers; and his faith is strong. The other has arrived at faith by dint of searching thought . . . But he who combines both kinds of faith is invulnerable. That is why we say 'Our God', because of our searching, and the 'God of our fathers', because of our tradition.[6]

This firm belief in God's existence is reiterated most emphatically throughout the centuries both by Jewish philosophers and non-philosophers. Saadia ben Joseph al-Fayyumi (882-942), philosopher, a native of Egypt, and Head (*Gaon*) of the Jewish Academy in Sura, Babylonia, writes the following in his *Book of Beliefs and Opinions*:

. . . the Creator has existed since eternity, that is a time when none of the things created were connected with Him or related to Him . . . the Creator . . . existed alone, when there was as yet no such thing as place . . . no such thing as time . . . all creatures are God's creation and handiwork . . . because originally there existed nothing outside of Himself.[7]

That's the philosophical proposition or premise. Dogma, regulations, and religious law reflect it and flow from it. They represent the non-philosophical consequences. The following is a sample typical of rabbinic piety reflecting the same premise.

The day consists of twelve hours.

During the first three hours, the Holy One, praised be He, is engaged in the study of Torah. During the second three He sits in judgement over His entire world . . .

During the third group of three hours, He provides sustenance for the entire world . . .

During the fourth, He sports with Leviathan . . . (according to others) He teaches schoolchildren.[8]

Every pious Jew, then, accepts the reality of God as a fact. God is!

God Is One

Hear O Israel, the Lord our God, the Lord is one.

Deuteronomy 6:4

The proclamation that God is one is a religious affirmation, not a philosophical declaration. Jewish teachings throughout the ages speak with one voice about the One-ness of God. These teachings assert that above and behind all seen and unseen phenomena is the one God. It is a declaration of 'monotheism', a term which is derived from two Greek words, *monos*, meaning One, and *Theos*, meaning God.

But Judaism asserts more than just that. It proclaims the unity and uniqueness of God, characteristics which are axiomatic in Judaism for they exclude whatever tends to obscure the idea of the One and Unique Being of God. Indissolubly bonded to this concept is the belief in the destiny of Jews as bearers of this truth. More about that later.

The One-ness, or unity, of God is not asserted in any metaphysical sense, since metaphysics is a philosophical exercise, not a religious affirmation. Nor is the claim intended to mean that God is only the God of the Jews, and not of other people, since that is contrary to the universalism inherent in Judaism. Like the later Islamic proclamation—There is no other God beside God—the Jews affirm that there is only one God, and none other beside Him and that this one and only God is the God to whom Jews pay absolute homage.

Thus, all dualistic theologies (like the Zoroastrian), or trinitarian ones (like the Christian), or polytheistic ones (like the Hindu), are seen by Jews as direct denials of this Judaic theology of the one and only God. This one God created one world, created one man as the progenitor of mankind, and established one universal norm, law, or standard known as Torah to govern morals.

Inseparably associated with this monotheistic doctrine of the one-ness or unity of God is the doctrine of the uniqueness of God. God is, in the Talmudic expression, *ha-geburah*, the omnipotent. His power has no limit. All the forces of nature are the immediate work of His hands and subject to His will, just as all human activity is under His absolute control.

Linked to this unique, divine attribute, is yet another one. God is *shekhinah,* omnipresent. 'There is no place,' say Talmudic teachers (teachers of Jewish civil and ceremonial law) 'without *shekhinah.*'[9] This does not mean that God is limited by the world, or coextensive with creation, or identical with it. What it does mean is that God is made manifest in the flowers and animals of the field, running water, and the heavenly bodies, but they do not become, by virtue of *shekhinah*, objects of adoration themselves as they do in the pantheistic Hindu universe in which God is everything and everything is God. *Shekhinah* attributes to God the power to extend His providence over the entire universe and to transcend it—to stand above and beyond it.

Indivisible from this doctrine of transcendence in Judaism is the doctrine of divine incorporeality. God is pure spirit, free from all limitations of nature or matter, space or time. He is the everlasting, the eternal. And this leads to yet another unique divine attribute: God is omniscient. Even the innermost secret thoughts of human beings cannot be concealed from Him.

The majestic order of the heavens (Psalm 19:1; Isaiah 40:26; Amos 5:8), the gifts of human speech and hearing, all testify to the existence of an all-knowing, all-seeing and all-hearing providence (Psalm 94:9). Thus, God's omnipotence, omniscience, and omnipresence guarantee the fulfilment or triumph of His ultimate, universal purpose. That purpose is nothing less than the universal recognition of the One God and of His one moral law for all. Nothing can in any way circumvent this ultimate realization.

This doctrine represents much more than an intellectual abstraction. Its implications have resulted in the most significant consequences affecting both Jews and non-Jews alike. Two recent events suffice as illustrations. One was the Jewish holocaust perpetrated by the Nazis (1933-1945). The other was the establishment of the state of Israel (1948). Both events are discussed in their appropriate contexts later on. Here, they serve to illustrate the fulfilment of God's universal purpose from a Judaic perspective. The transition of the Jewish people from the status of victim to victor represents the assurance of God's concern and the realization of His goal.

This link between doctrine and consequences is the factor which carries doctrine beyond the confines of an intellectual abstraction. According to Jewish theologians and philosophers, the scholars of Judaic traditions and beliefs, humans are judged by God according to their 'works' not according to their 'faith'. The observance of the Torah, not dogma, is the main requirement enjoined on adherents of Judaism. In the last resort, the Talmud exhorts—'Better that they abandon Me, but follow My laws . . .'[10] As long as a Jew observes Jewish laws, doubt or even disbelief in God is not entirely inadmissible. The converse, however, is not true. No one who believes in God but abandons Jewish law is considered a religious Jew. To put it differently: action as the expression of faith is more proper than faith as the source of action.

These tenets required no elaboration in a closed community, but in the day-to-day encounter of differing cultures and religious traditions, Jewish apologists felt compelled to justify Judaic doctrines and ideologies in terms that made sense to non-Jews. Judaic affirmations about God, however, were not always understood in the same way, nor were they even given the same emphasis among Judaic philosophers and mystics. Biblical, Talmudic, and rabbinic statements on the nature of God remained relatively fluid until Moses Maimonides (1135-1204) started the 'dogma' controversy in Judaism.

A distinguished student of Jewish Law and Talmud, a reputable physician, and a leading thinker of his day, Maimonides' achievement was to synthesize biblical revelation with neo-Platonic Aristotelianism. His monumental work, *Guide of the Perplexed*, is regarded as one of the world's classics. He also wrote extensively on medicine, philosophy, and Jewish Law. It is in his *Commentary on the Mishnah*, that he enumerated his creed—a list of thirteen basic principles, or articles of faith, which he identified as obligatory for every faithful Jew. Although subjected to prolonged debate and severe criticism, Maimonides' list of articles of faith was finally documented as an explicit credo. Today it is sung as a prayer-hymn at the conclusion of the synagogue prayer. Here is an abstract of the creed:

1.   Belief in the existence of a Creator and Providence;
2.   Belief in His unity;
3.   Belief in His incorporeality;
4.   Belief in His eternity;
5.   Belief that to Him alone is worship due;
6.   Belief in the words of the prophets;
7.   Belief that Moses was the greatest of all prophets;
8.   Belief in the revelation of the Law to Moses at Sinai;
9.   Belief in the immutability of the Revealed Law;
10. Belief that God is omniscient;
11. Belief in retribution in the world and the hereafter;
12. Belief in the coming of the Messiah;
13. Belief in the resurrection of the dead.[11]

Encapsulating Judaism within such a neat creed has occasioned embittered controversy. Pietists were, and still are, unimpressed by Maimonides' brilliant answers about the nature of God. In fact, many pious Jews found Maimonides and other philosophers presumptuous, inadequate, and unequal to the task of investigating the truths of Jewish faith. This is best expressed, perhaps, by the Spanish rabbi Hayyim ibn Musa (1390-1460).

In my youth I heard a preacher preach about God's being one and one only, in a speculating manner—in the manner of philosophers. And he said many times over that if He were not one only God, then this and that would necessarily follow. Thereupon a man rose . . . and said: 'Misfortune came upon me and mine at the great disaster in Sevilla [Pogrom of 1391]. I was beaten and wounded, until my persecutors desisted because they thought I was dead. All this have I suffered for my faith . . . And here you are, dealing with the traditions of our fathers in the manner of a speculating philosopher, and saying: "If He were not one only God . . ." I have greater faith in the tradition of our fathers, and I do not want to go on listening to this sermon.' And he left the house of prayer and most of the congregation went with him.[12]

Some modern Jewish philosophers also feel uncomfortable with the systematization of Judaism by Maimonides. For instance, Leon Roth writes: 'Thus Maimonides with his systematic mind, though with the best will in the world, thrust men out of Judaism instead of keeping them in; and thrust them out by virtue of a definition, which, by laying down a boundary (and a boundary not of religious practice but of intellectual belief), put many plain people on the wrong side.'[13]

Indeed, 'plain people' were not the only Jews to balk at a codified dogma. Jewish exegetists also deny that the acceptance or rejection of beliefs (as distinct from practices) is fundamental to Judaism. The concepts implied by terms such as 'belief', 'fundamental', 'acceptance', or 'rejection' are alien to Judaism. The relevance of 'dogma' to Judaism is a subject of endless controversy. The words 'belief' and 'faith' are, according to Jewish critics, synonymous with a logical proposition. Faith, to such critics, is seen as the root or source of precepts, rather than as a summons, a call to action, a command. Judaism requires something other and more than 'dogma'. It requires 'works'. And the performance of works is not equivalent to, nor a substitute for, the acceptance of a proposition. Works are axiomatic to Judaism, even if their nature or quantity is disputed.

To fulfil moral obligations and to perform religious duties, then, is to assert the one-ness of God. He is 'God of gods and Lord of lords, the great, the mighty and the terrible God' (Deuteronomy 10:17). Judaism prescribes in great detail how one ought to live, not what one ought to believe. No attempts are made in the Bible (Old Testament) to offer philosophical explanations for God's omnipotence, omniscience, and omnipresence. The only assertion the Bible makes is that God is and that He judges human beings, in particular His own people, who are morally responsible for all their deeds.

Behold, I set before you this day a blessing and a curse: the blessing if you obey the commandments of the Lord your God . . . and the curse, if you do not obey the commandments of the Lord your God.

Deuteronomy 11:26-28

To *obey* God is to assert God, to assert His existence, sovereignty, and one-ness.

God Is Moral

His work is perfect, for all His ways are just.
A God of truth without iniquity, just and right is He.

Deuteronomy 32:4

Judaism teaches that those who love God and keep His commandments benefit from the love, mercy and grace of God. Those who disobey His commandments only reap His anger and justice. The paradoxical relation between divine compassion and kindness on the one hand, and justice and judgement on the other, is recognized in Judaism. God's moral attribute of justice is offered as ample justification for fearing God, while God's moral attribute of love or compassion is reason enough for loving God. Divine mercy and divine justice are the two primary attributes which govern God's dealings with human beings. But they are in no way thought of as two separate characteristics. Judaism asserts that the God of justice is the God of mercy, one and indivisible. In other words, the dual moral nature of God is one.

Thus, God combines power, justice and judgement with mercy, kindness and love. In other words, divine justice and divine mercy are complementary aspects of God's character. For human beings this is a contradiction, but for God, it is not. To Jews, God is the sum total of justice and mercy. A rabbinic commentary explains it this way: if the world were governed strictly on the basis of God's justice, then nothing would survive; if, however, the world were governed on the basis of God's mercy alone, then the sins of humanity would engulf it. For a proper moral balance, God maintains the world with justice and mercy.[14]

Divine mercy mitigates the effects of divine justice; divine judgement is tempered by divine kindness. These two complementary aspects of God find expression in the biblical writing of two prophets, Amos and Hosea. To Amos, God is a righteous God who expects His chosen people to reflect the divine image of justice and righteousness in their daily activities. To Hosea, God is a loving and merciful God, in spite of the infidelity of His chosen people. But it was left to the prophet Isaiah to capture these two divine aspects in the description of the 'holiness' of God. 'Holy, holy, holy is the Lord of hosts,' proclaimed Isaiah (Isaiah 6:3). Similarly the author of Leviticus adjured his readers to pattern human life to conform to God's moral character of holiness: 'Be ye holy, for I YHWH your God am holy.' (Leviticus 19:2).

Among adherents of Judaism, God's holiness is the attribute that separates Him from the natural and physical and establishes His transcendence over everything other than Himself. Creation itself attests to God's will. There is a cosmic order in the physical world, but there is also a moral order rooted in God, for He is the source of both orders: physical and moral. Thus, divine holiness fulfils itself in the quality of mercy and justice. Divine justice imposed on the disobedient or the guilty is tempered with divine mercy in expectation of the penitence of the guilty. Obedience, on the other hand, promotes positive responses. God bestows more than such obedience might justify.

This Jewish understanding of the moral character of God is, perhaps, best stated in its traditional setting. God reveals Himself to Moses as a 'merciful being, gracious, slow to anger, abundant in loving-kindness and truth, keeping mercy to a thousand generations, forgiving iniquity and transgression and sin; but who will by no means clear the guilty, punishing the iniquity of the fathers to the third and fourth generations' (Exodus 34:6-7). That is the Judaic concept of holiness.

The adjective 'holy' is so frequently applied to God that He is often called simply, 'the Holy One'. The Hebrew word for 'holy' is *qadosh*. The basic meaning of the root is to be 'set apart', from everything that is ordinary, unclean or profane. In time, the Hebrew word for 'holy' assumed the meaning of 'divine' or 'wholly other'. When the prophet Isaiah uses the epithet the 'Holy One of Israel', the phrase refers primarily to the divine majesty and greatness of God. But Isaiah is quick to declare that the Holy One of Israel is also the Creator to whom humans look for help (Isaiah 17:7). Thus, the holiness of God has a dual meaning. On the one hand, it signifies the unapproachability, the awesomeness of God, and on the other the beneficence, the mercy of God.

Another moral characteristic closely associated with the holiness of God is the 'jealousness' of God. 'For you shall worship no other god', states the Bible, 'for the Lord, whose name is Jealous, is a jealous God' (Exodus 34:14). This means that God will not tolerate any other god besides Him (Exodus 20:5), and that no other god or human being may share His glory (Isaiah 42:8; 48:11). In fact, the jealousness of God is like a devouring fire (Deuteronomy 4:24), and is associated with His judgement and punishment (Zephaniah 1:18; Nahum 1:2). This divine wrath is a moral characteristic of God. It is a divine indignation, a proper moral reaction, arising from an offence committed against divine majesty. Offending God is tantamount to open rebellion.

But the jealousness of God has also a positive side, namely profound concern for the well-being of His chosen people. This is clearly expressed by the prophet Ezekiel: 'Thus says the Lord God: Now will I bring again the captivity of Jacob, and show mercy to the whole house of Israel, and will be jealous for my holy name' (Ezekiel 39:25). Hence, the duality of God's nature is apparent in two of His moral characteristics: holiness and jealousy. They are fresh aspects of God's nature that match the same opposite moral tendencies: wrath, justice and judgement on the one hand, and love, mercy and patience on the other.

The tension that exists in the concept of the duality of God's nature is expressed with particular force in the sayings of the prophet Hosea, where he describes God in debate with Himself as He resolves whether or not to punish His chosen people.

> How can I give you up, O Ephraim?
> How can I hand you over, O Israel?
> My heart is turned within Me,
> My compassion grows warm and tender.
> I will not execute My fierce anger,
> I will not destroy again Ephraim,
> For I am God and not man,
> the Holy One in your midst . . .

> Hosea 11:8-9

This same conclusion about the dual moral nature of God is also expressed by modern Jewish theologians. Here, for instance, are the words of Franz Rosenzweig (1886-1929): 'God the Lord is simultaneously the God of retribution and the God of love.'[15]

In recognizing the dual moral character of God, Judaism confidently asserts that God's power and justice will be exercised with love and mercy. This duality is expressed in the designation of God as 'Father' and as 'King'. In their prayers of petition or thanksgiving, Jews address God as 'our Father our King.' God as 'King' is all-powerful and majestic, who created the world and rules it, and who judges all human beings justly. God as 'Father' is all-loving and merciful, who waits, even till their moment of death, for people to repent and to return to Him. In judging the world, God as sovereign is fully aware of human frailties and consequently deals with them kindly, as a father who knows the weaknesses of his children.

If God is the creator of the world and is the basis of all morality, then how and why does evil exist? This question strikes at the heart of Jewish thinking since Jews have suffered great atrocities, especially at the hands of European Emperors, adherents of Christianity, and Nazi leaders. Evil is of two types: natural and man-made. Earthquakes, disastrous floods, diseases and death have natural causes. War, torture, murder and injustice, for instance, are man-made. Both types of evil raise the same question: who or what is the source of evil?

The Jewish Bible states unambiguously that everything, good or evil, results from God.

> The Lord kills and brings to life;
> He brings down to Sheol and raises up.
> The Lord makes poor and makes rich
> He brings low and also exalts.
>
> I Samuel 2:6-7

> I am the Lord and there is none other.
> I form light and create darkness,
> I make peace and create evil,
> I the Lord do all these things.
>
> Isaiah 45:6-7

See now that I, even I am He;
and there is no god beside me.
I kill and I make alive,
I wound and I heal . . .

Deuteronomy 32:39

Judaism teaches that God is the creator of both good and evil. At no time has Judaism insisted that the faithful attempt to know the full nature of God. The only condition required of adherents is righteous and holy conduct because God's nature is righteous and holy. It is true that Jewish tradition recognizes Satan as the mythical symbol of all the evil forces in the world. There are a number of references to Satan in the Bible, but it is doubtful if Jews ever took these references literally, except perhaps for a brief period before the Christian era. The book of Job, for instance, characterizes Satan as a real adversary. But a number of distinguished rabbis frankly concluded that the book of Job was nothing more than the product of some ancestor's imagination to be accepted as fiction.

Again, certain Jews who lived under the domination of the ancient Persians (Iranians) believed, like the Zoroastrians, that there were two great forces in the world: the God of Light and the God of Darkness. Satan was then equated with the God of Darkness and blamed for all the evils, wickedness and calamity in the world. But such ideas were ultimately rejected as alien to Jewish tradition.

So too was the belief that Satan was associated with the evil impulse which prompts humans to evil actions. It is a notion that has never taken deep root in Judaism. And while references to Satan still persist in some Jewish prayer books (in the Orthodox and Conservative prayer books), these references are simply regarded as figures of speech.

What, then, is the answer to the origin and existence of evil? Judaism readily admits that this most difficult question is, by definition, unanswerable. For God is, by definition, infinite, above nature and beyond human reasoning or understanding. Thus, human beings, who are finite and within nature, cannot comprehend God and His ways. This enigma is beautifully stated in Jewish tradition: *lu yadativ hayitiv*—If I knew Him, I would be Him.

This does not mean, however, that Judaism excludes evil as a divine attribute. The possibility is implied in the acknowledgement that the God of Judaism is the God of both mercy and justice, a single and indivisible aspect of His moral character. Human understanding of the origin and existence of evil does not add or subtract an iota from God's moral character. Morality consists in fulfilling divine demands, not in satisfying one's rational faculty.

God and History

> He makes nations great and He destroys them,
> He enlarges nations and leads them away.

Job 12:23

One of the most significant tenets of Judaism relates to God's intervention in human affairs, particularly as it applies to the unique relationship between God and His 'chosen' people, the Jews. To the Jews, God's presence is, unquestionably, implicit in the natural realm of the universe and explicit in His disclosure of His more intimate divine presence, primarily in human history. Although a somewhat similar insight was and is held by some ancient and modern groups, Jews believe that their history stands in a unique relationship with God, a belief that has markedly affected and fashioned Jewish life-styles and modes of existence. Regardless of this view that God directs history on behalf of His chosen people, such partiality in no way limits God's love and intervention in the affairs of the entire human race. The universal love of God is revealed in 'His love for the stranger' (Deuteronomy 10:18).

Judaism is the religion of history. It asserts that God controls history. God created the world, including human beings, so that everything that happens to people, including the Jews, happens because of divine providence. In other words, Judaism affirms the disclosure of divine sovereignty in creation as well as in human history. The conviction that the course of human action is rooted in a confrontation with the divine, not as an abstraction, but as a person, is particularly compelling in the case of the Jewish people. In fact, history provides the clue for understanding Judaism.

History provides Jews with evidence of two important, interdependent kinds: it represents a disclosure of God's purpose and a manifestation of human inability to live in accord with God's purpose. Even Jews themselves, who are the chosen people of God, failed—and still fail—to fulfil their obligations to God, resulting in divine retribution within history.

This basic view emerges from very early times, as evidenced in the biblical texts, and for centuries thereafter has provided the incentive and rationale for Jewish survival. Jewish prophets, philosophers, poets, mystics and others, all in one way or another sought to affirm or to deny the sovereignty of God in human history. Their emphases varied. At times their differences were profound, but their writings and sayings have not in any way diminished the confidence of the faithful in asserting the providence of God in human history.

The classic contradiction of theistic faith is quite evident and accepted in Judaism. God is omnipotent, and yet humans are responsible for their actions. God is omniscient, anticipating events, and yet humans have a free will. God controls and rules human destiny, and yet humans are morally responsible for their choices. Any misdeeds committed by humans will be judged by God.

Judaism cannot be defined in terms of Christian theological categories or of any other philosophical systems. Catechism is alien to the essence of Judaism. And yet there is an immanent logic within Judaism that sooner or later becomes evident to the careful investigator. What becomes quite striking in Judaism is that its faith is not grounded on theological dogmas or metaphysical speculations, but on divine-human actions.

The story of God's continual activity in history, and particularly in the history of the Jewish people, starts with God as creator of the natural order, including humanity. The biblical stories of the Garden of Eden, the Flood and the Tower of Babel, all point to the rebellious and disobedient nature of human beings. Then a particular family, namely Abraham (followed by his son Isaac and grandson Jacob), is identified from among all humanity, or 'chosen', by God for a specific divine purpose: the establishment of peace and well-being in this world and among mankind. Jews, therefore, believe that, as descendants of their ancestors Abraham, Isaac, and Jacob, they stand in a unique relationship to God—a relationship confirmed or ratified by a mutually binding agreement, a special 'covenant' between God and the Jewish people (Exodus 6:2-8). This covenant required from the Jews obedience to the Torah, not simply for the benefit of the Jewish people but also for all mankind.

The subsequent history of the Jewish people, specifically as recorded in the Bible, represents the outcome of tension created by rebellion or obedience in response to the changing historical context. The years of slavery in Egypt, the Exodus from Egypt, the revelation of the Torah received on Mount Sinai, the wandering years in the wilderness, the establishment of a kingdom in the promised land, and then the exile, all affirm the divine-human encounter within history.

To non-Jews, this relationship represents a paradox. God made a covenant with a particular people, namely the Jews. But God's love is universal, and He cares for all mankind. In Judaism, this particular-universal aspect of divine providence is not thought of as contradictory. On the contrary, it is thought of as an enhancement of human solidarity. How is this to be explained?

Jewish polemicists and non-Jewish commentators have sought to explain the so-called uneasy tension in God's universal-particular sovereignty without signal success. From the perspective of Jewish faith, these two sovereign aspects are not two sets of contradictory assertions. Rather, both are true as a description of Judaism since neither is true without the other. Thus, on the one hand, Judaism makes the claim that God chose a particular people from among all the nations for the task of applying the strictest obedience to the Torah as an instrument for enhancing the well-being of all humanity. On the other hand, Judaism asserts that God's universal love and care will lead mankind to the day when all shall know that the Lord is One.

The covenant with God binds the Jewish people in a unique way. The Jews are to experience God's nearness to a degree greater than that of all other peoples because they are a 'holy nation'. They are never to be abandoned by God since they are His 'own possession'. They are to be led by the mighty acts of God to the 'promised' land. Ultimately, they are to be the instrument for the redemption of the entire human race. But, in return, God expects from His chosen people absolute obedience to His statutes as ordained in the Torah. This includes loyalty and obedience to the Torah in every aspect of human behaviour, from the most private to the most public. If His chosen people disobey the Torah, and sin, then God will judge them with stricter standards than those applied to other people. But in no way will God ever put His chosen people utterly aside and seek a new group. For the covenant God made with His chosen people is an everlasting one, and God as God cannot break a covenant.

Several important passages in the Bible confirm these terms of the agreement. Here are two for purposes of illustration:

If you obey My voice and keep My covenant, You shall be My own possession among all the peoples, for all the earth is Mine, and you shall be to Me a kingdom of priests and a holy nation.

Exodus 19:5-6

I am the Lord your God who set you apart from other people . . . Be holy unto Me, for I the Lord am holy, and I separated you from other peoples that you should be Mine.

Leviticus 20:24-26

To be God's chosen people is both a privilege and a responsibility. It is a privilege in that choice confers merit and distinction. As a responsibility it explains the untold tragedies borne by the Jewish people. But why did God choose this people rather than some other people?

Several attempts have been made through the ages to defend and explain this Jewish religious concept of singularity. It is a concept increasingly subject to attack. Some forms of Zionism and a number of modern Jewish theologians have sought to

abandon this problematic view. Thus, for example, interpretations of Zionist theoreticians who break with tradition betray
the influences of both socialist ideas and of political nationalism.
Other Jewish thinkers have borrowed (from romantic nationalism) such ideas as the 'genius' of the people. Mordecai Kaplan
(1881-1984), the leading American Jewish thinker and founder
of the Reconstructionist group, rejected the idea of singularity
among the nations. After the establishment of the State of
Israel, some Jews insisted that the idea of singularity was an
impediment to the maintenance of a normal existence among
the nations of the world.

In spite of the difficulties consequent on the notion of divine
election there are many Jews who continue to affirm it. To
such, Judaism is inconceivable without the concept of chosen-
ness. Their justification is based on the traditional biblical view
which ascribes this divine choice to the unknowable love of
God, not to any innate merit of the Jews.

The Lord your God has chosen you to be a people for His own
possession out of all the peoples that are on the face of the earth. It was
not because you were more in number . . . but it is because the Lord
loves you and He keeps His oath which He swore to your fathers . . .
Deuteronomy 7:6-10

The founder of Neo-Orthodox Judaism, Rabbi Samson
Raphael Hirsch (1808-1888), is counted among those who
affirm the classical notion enshrined in Judaic tradition. His
words express the sentiments shared by many:

Because men had eliminated God from life . . . it became necessary
that a people be introduced into the ranks of the nations which
through its history and life, should declare God the only creative cause
of existence, and the fulfillment of His will the only aim of life.[16]

Again, Abraham Isaac Kook (1868-1935), who became the
Chief Rabbi of Palestine in 1921, reassured the Jewish people of
their divine election, and the holiness of the Jewish faith and of
the land of Israel. Here is an excerpt from his words:

This people was fashioned by God to speak of His glory; it was
granted the heritage of the blessing of Abraham so that it might
disseminate the knowledge of God, and it was commanded to live its
life apart from the nations of the world. God chose it to cleanse the
whole world of all impurity and darkness . . .[17]

And, finally, the ending of one of the Jewish prayers expresses
the deep traditional conviction of many faithful Jews:

> You, O God, are the Source of salvation;
> You have chosen us from all peoples and tongues.
> You have drawn us close to You;
> We praise and thank You in truth.
> With love do we thankfully proclaim Your unity,
> And praise You who chose Your people Israel in love.[18]

And yet, Judaism asserts that this special covenantal relationship
between God and His people does not in any way negate the
universal rule of God. In fact, it is precisely this universalistic
position that underscores the particular relation. To emphasize
or neglect one of these relationships in favour of the other is to
distort the way most Jews see themselves and non-Jews. In no
way can the reality of their special status as God's divine elect
separate Jews from the universalism of God in the fulfilment of
His ultimate purpose for all mankind. Yet, humanity is neither
expected nor obligated to live within the jurisdiction of the
Torah. Their responsibility provides only that they accept the
divine covenant made with Noah.

Noah is seen in Judaism as the ancestor of all mankind, to
whom God made a promise after the Flood: that his descendants
would never be utterly destroyed.

God spoke to Noah and to his sons saying: 'Behold, I establish My
covenant with you and your descendants after you . . . never again
shall all flesh be destroyed by the waters of a flood, neither shall there
be a flood to destroy the earth . . .'

Genesis 9:8-11

Thus, the rabbis made this covenant with Noah the basis of

their theory regarding the religious status of non-Jews. It forms the basis of rabbinic teaching which stipulates that all people know what God wants of them. But as the story of Noah immediately makes clear, humanity regularly violates its covenantal responsibilities to God. According to rabbinic tradition, these responsibilities comprise seven basic obligations: not to profane God's name, not to worship idols, not to commit murder, not to steal, not to commit adultery, not to be unjust, and not to cut limbs from living animals.[19] People do not need to be Jews; they need only keep the commandments of Noah. The rabbis acknowledged that pious non-Jews could be as fully righteous in the sight of God as the Jews themselves.

The Covenant with Abraham and his descendants the Jews is then seen as a reparation for the sinfulness of humanity. This in no way annuls the covenant God made with Noah. Rather, both covenants are essential and indicate God's complete sovereignty in human affairs.

Judaic Theology

Rules of Conduct

> Be holy, for I the Lord your God am holy.
>
> Leviticus 19:2

Knowledge of God, of all His divine attributes, or even of instances of His divine intervention in human affairs is not a requirement of Judaism. Neither is perfection, which lies beyond the capacity of mere humans to attain. The strongest demand Judaism invokes from adherents is righteous conduct patterned on the divine holiness of God. In other words, recognition of God's holiness imposes an obligation on every Jew to live a life of high moral standards which are documented in meticulous detail in the Torah. Obedience to the models specified in the Torah constitutes *imitatio Dei* or, in the rabbinic phrase, the imitation of attributes of God.

Thus, Judaism does not prescribe asceticism as a condition of conducting a moral life. In no way does Judaism advocate the renunciation of the world—of the here-and-now—as the highest spiritual goal, let alone the ideal path to piety. The spiritual vocation of a Jew is to hallow life—to elevate tasks of

the everyday world to their highest level of religious significance, so that they reflect nothing less than the divine unity of
all being.

This emphasis on individual conduct is a dominant characteristic of Judaism which has also shaped the distinctive Judaic
doctrine governing human beings. Judaism defines human
beings as a combination of two different elements: an earthly
body and a heavenly spirit. Yet these two, body and spirit, are a
unity representing a form of life superior to any life on earth. A
human being is endowed with worth and dignity surpassing
any other form of life in God's creation. Though people are
products of the earth—weak, frail, insignificant and fated to
revert to dust or ashes—they are also heavenly spirits, created in
the image of God and endowed with divine characteristics. This
dual but united component of the individual is explicitly
expressed by the Psalmist in the Bible:

When I behold the heavens, the work of Your fingers, the moon and
the stars which You have established; what is man that You are
mindful of him, and the son of man that You care for him? Yet You
have made him a little lower than God, and have crowned him with
glory and honours.

Psalm 8:4-5

Throughout succeeding centuries, rabbis have elaborated on
this combination of human characteristics—the animal or
bodily traits and the divine or spiritual. Like an animal, a person
eats, drinks, excretes, multiplies, and dies. But as a divine
entity, a person communicates, reasons, anticipates events,
invents, improvises, and contributes towards the fulfilment of
God's purpose in establishing peace, justice, and righteousness
on earth. Thus, according to the tenets of Judaism, body and
spirit are united in order to create the highest form of earthly
life: the righteous (holy) person. This means that unlike other
creeds, Judaism rejects the notion of conflicting dualism. The
notion of a pure spirit housed or even caged within an impure
body is foreign to Judaism. There is no dichotomy or paradox
in Judaism between matter and spirit, between the finite and the

eternal, the earthly and the heavenly. On the contrary, the earthly and the heavenly are viewed in harmonious relationship one with another.

Then the Lord God formed man of dust from the ground and breathed into his nostrils the breath of life; and man became a living being.

Genesis 2:7

So God created man in His own image, in the image of God He created him; male and female He created them.

Genesis 1:27

Human beings are then created in the likeness of God. Artists and sculptors have certainly accepted Scripture at its face value and invested their images of the divine with prophetic features—eyes, nose, flowing beard, and voluminous robes. Nevertheless, the link between the human and the divine, according to the Judaic tradition, has more substance than physical similarities. The link, in Judaic terms, is made manifest in human dominion over the world (Genesis 1:28-30) and in human imitation of God's divine, moral character.

This human imitation of divine attributes, then, demands fear, respect, love and servitude. This is clearly stated in the Scripture:

And now, Israel, what does the Lord your God require of you, but to fear the Lord your God, to walk in all His ways, to love Him, to serve the Lord your God with all your heart, with all your soul, and to keep the commandments and statutes of the Lord . . .

Deuteronomy 10:12-13

The appropriate human response to fear and love is obedience. For God is sovereign, spiritual, eternal, while the individual is weak, temporal and finite. It is, therefore, fitting for a person to recognize and acknowledge dependence on God as a prere-quisite to imitating Him. To trust in one's own strength is tantamount to rebellion against God (Psalm 52:5-7; Isaiah 14:13-15; Jeremiah 17:5). Not only is this a sign of pride but an act of blasphemy in making oneself equal to God. To rely upon human strength is to abandon God.

Proper, ethical conduct in Judaism demands a life of dependence on God. To depend on God means to live according to the statutes of God. And what are God's statutes? To emulate divine justice and righteousness.

He has showed you, O man, what is good; and what the Lord requires of you: to do justice, and to love kindness, and to walk humbly with your God.

Micah 6:8

Biblical prophets as well as Jewish rabbis and philosophers reiterate the same theme, that the fulfilment of justice and righteousness is the only conduct that God deems appropriate from His people.

It was this theme, expounded by biblical prophets, that, in less than two centuries, was chiefly responsible for moulding and shaping the religious and moral character of Judaism. So deeply concerned were these prophets with the shortcomings of the social systems, institutions, and practices of their time, that they fearlessly condemned them and in no uncertain terms pronounced the impending doom of God's people. No amount of religious formalism, they said, was justified in relieving the conscience of Jewish society or of mitigating the consequences of tolerating oppression, cruelty, and injustice. Here are the stern words of two prophets, Amos and Isaiah:

Thus says the Lord . . .
'I hate, I despise your feasts,
and I take no delight in your solemn assemblies.
Even though you offer Me burnt offerings
and cereal offerings, I will not accept them . . .
I will not look upon them. Take away from Me the noise of your songs; to the melody of your harps I shall not listen. But let justice roll down like waters, and righteousness like an ever-flowing stream.

Amos 5:21-24

'What to Me is the multitude of your sacrifices?' says the Lord; 'I have had enough of burnt offerings . . . I do not delight in the blood of bulls . . . When you come to appear before me . . . Bring no more vain offerings . . . New moon and sabbath and the calling of assemblies—I cannot endure iniquity and solemn assembly. Your new moons and your appointed feasts my soul hates . . Even though you make many prayers, I shall not listen . . . Cease to do evil; learn to do good; seek justice; correct oppression . . .'

Isaiah 1:11-17

Among Jews, then, ethical and moral obligations are more important than ceremonial religiosity. Therefore these moral obligations are more properly expressed in social behaviour than in forms of worship. In fact, true piety in Judaism is equated with righteous conduct. The righteous person, in contrast to the wicked, fulfils certain duties towards God and certain duties towards neighbours. The wicked live without God, are proud and defiant, hot-headed and foolhardy. The righteous, however, are subservient to God, wise, strong, responsible, and thoughtful.

That God is the ultimate ground for all ethical conduct is unambiguously stated in Scripture: 'You shall be holy, for I the Lord your God am holy' (Leviticus 19:2). A rider to this general principle qualifies the love of one's neighbour: 'You shall love your neighbour as yourself' (Leviticus 19:18).

A life of holiness is a life to be lived in this world in association with other human beings: neighbours. Initially the word 'neighbour' referred primarily or even exclusively to other Jews. *Love your neighbour* was an injunction that implied a call to a kind of national solidarity. Indeed, throughout the ages Jews were, and still are, extremely conscientious in caring for one another in all aspects of life. The strenuous and unremitting efforts of modern Jewish agencies to help needy Jews through-out the world reflect this most ancient tradition of loving one's neighbour.

Among Jews, this love of neighbour is a legal, binding obligation upon every Jew, not simply a generalized moral ideal. It is an imperative command with its roots in a divine purpose: to set an example for all humanity. In the words of the founder of Neo-Orthodoxy, Samson Raphael Hirsch (1808-1888): 'Every son of Israel is a priest, setting the example of justice and love . . . spreading true humanity among the nations.'[20] Holiness is expressly linked to the maintenance of justice and the self-denying expression of love.

The consequences of ethical actions are, among other rewards, prosperity and happiness. Such tangible consequences include numerous progeny, wealth, victory over enemies, success in all endeavours, integrity, and peace. A righteous person, then, is a blessed, prosperous person who has a peaceful life and is favoured by God. The wicked, by contrast, invite the wrath of God, pain, suffering, and calamity.

People get what's coming to them is not a thesis that supports close scrutiny. Though it represents a traditional outlook, it has not escaped unchallenged (Psalm 73:1-14 and Jeremiah 12:1-2). In practice, pain and destitution are not literally interpreted as the wages of sin, and the author of the book of Job illustrates that the facts of life disprove the theory: the righteous often suffer and are overtaken by tragedy while the wicked frequently prosper and lead happy lives. But Job clearly makes the point that true piety needs no outward proof of success, since, no matter how incomprehensible God's rule may seem to be, He is still righteous and rules the world righteously.

Thus, the traditional values expressed in biblical times are echoed throughout the ages in Judaism. In summary, God is omnipotent; no one understands His ways. To pass judgement on God's ways or to question His righteousness is to be guilty of scandalous presumption. He has chosen a people for a specific role: to achieve the redemption of mankind through the exemplary life of His chosen people. From this perspective, Judaism requires from every Jew a life of obedience to God as instituted in the Torah. Moral principles are as essential to the faith of Judaism as ceremonial observances. The religious practices of the Jew are God-given. Imitating God's righteousness in all aspects of one's daily social life is devotion to God. In the words of the twelfth-century Spanish-Jew physician, Judah Ibn Tibbon:

My son . . .
If the Creator has mightily displayed His love to you and me, so that Jew and Gentile have thus far honored you for my sake, endeavor

henceforth so to add to your honor that they may respect you for your own self. This you effect by good morals and by courteous behaviour . . . Let your countenance shine upon the sons of men: tend their sick, and may your advice cure them. Though you take fees from the rich, heal the poor gratuitously . . . Thereby shall you find favor and good understanding in the sight of God and man. Thus you will win the respect of high and low among Jews and non-Jews . . .[21]

Sin and Repentance

There is not a righteous man on earth who does good and never sins.

Ecclesiastes 7:20

The quotation from Ecclesiastes voices a conviction echoed in I Kings 8:46 and is repeated at the graveside as a postscript to every Jew's life. The concept of sin in Judaism is equated with the debasement of human nature, not simply a rebellion against God. To be sure, sin is the rejection or evasion of God's ordinances, but the more serious transgression is the wrong done to other humans. Sins committed against God may be expiated by true penitence, prayers and piety, whereas sins committed against human beings can only be atoned for by redressing the wrong, by winning the forgiveness of the victim.

Judaism differs radically from Christianity on the doctrine of sin. Unlike Christian theologians, Jewish scholars have made no attempt to derive from the story of Adam and Eve in the book of Genesis any theology that reflects the 'fallen' nature of mankind. According to Judaism, God implanted in all of His creation, including human beings, an inclination to both good and evil. This inclination is called *yetzer* in Hebrew, which means 'the drive'. And this is precisely what is stated in Genesis 8:21, 'The *yetzer* of man's heart is evil from his youth.' It was his *yetzer*'s proclivity to evil rather than to good which prompted Adam to transgress against God's command. As Adam possessed it, so do all human beings possess this *yetzer*; and if this drive can influence human beings to do evil, it can equally influence them to do good. Control of this influence, factor, or agent is, in the Judaic tradition, synonymous with freedom of choice or will.

To put it differently, Judaism, unlike Christianity, holds that within every person, including Adam, there is the drive to do right as well as to sin. All humans commit sin as Adam did but not because of Adam. There is no concept in Judaism of 'original sin', or of 'a fall from grace'. Adam's death was a consequence of his sin, but no one dies on account of Adam's sin. Each individual dies because each person sins.

There are several terms in Hebrew that imply a hierarchy of sin. One of them is *het*, which literally means 'missing the mark'. This term is used in Jewish confession on Yom Kippur, when sins against other human beings are penitently admitted before God. *Het* does not imply deliberate intent but lack of judgement or zeal or effort. *Aberah*, on the other hand, is a Hebrew term which means 'transgression', and is used in reference to 'stepping out' of the boundaries God has set in the Torah. It implies intent and a degree of deliberation.

The question that evades unambiguous solution is why God endows human beings with the capacity for evil in the first place. Judaism offers little in the way of direct explanation. Instead, Jews are admonished against attempting to understand the inscrutable will of God but to apply themselves to redressing or atoning for the wrongs they commit against God and their neighbours. 'The Torah is the only remedy for the impulse to evil,' said the mystic Moses Lezatto (1707-47), 'Whoever thinks that he can be helped without it is mistaken and will realize his error when he dies for his sins'.[22]

To be sure, the Jewish concept of sin has grown and changed through the centuries. To ancient Jews—that is, Jews in biblical times—sin was the violation of a taboo. This constituted an offence against God and required an appropriate sin-offering in the form of animal sacrifice. But gradually, over the years, the concept of sin came to mean the inability to live up to the teachings of the Torah—the failure of people to meet their full responsibilities as Jews, that is, as God's chosen people.

Yet the effects of sin are not irrevocable. Though humans are free to sin and suffer its consequences, they are also able to repent and do good. The Bible and rabbinic Judaism use the Hebrew term *teshuvah*, meaning 'returning', to identify the act of repentance. The true penitent can thus return to God and be reconciled with Him.

Let the evil man forsake his way and the wicked man his plans, and let him return to the Lord and He will have mercy upon him.

Isaiah 55:7

I do not desire the death of the wicked man, but that the wicked man return from his evil way and live.

Ezekiel 33:11

The last day of the ten days of penitence following the Jewish New Year is known as Yom Kippur, or Day of Atonement. It is one of the two Holy Days of Judaism and is marked by twenty-four hours of fasting and prayer. The prayer which runs through the entire service on Yom Kippur reads as follows:

> For the sin which we have committed against
>   Thee under stress or through choice;
> For the sin which we have committed against
>   Thee in stubbornness or in error;
> For the sin which we have committed against
>   Thee in the evil meditations of the heart;
> For the sin which we have committed against
>   Thee by word of mouth . . .
> For the sin which we have committed against
>   Thee by exploiting and dealing treacherously with our
>   neighbour . . .
> For all these sins, O God of forgiveness,
>   bear with us, pardon us, forgive us![23]

The distinguishing mark of a human being, according to Judaism, is the ability to make a choice between obedience and disobedience to God. This is considered to be an ethical choice and is viewed by Judaism as a tension between two impulses: to do good or to do evil. Every single individual, Jew and non-Jew, is party to a covenant and has to choose between obeying or disobeying divine sovereignty. Judaism is not predicated on a life entirely free from sin; but neither does

Judaism condone mere intellectual brooding and handwring-
ing—mere remorse. The tragedy in yielding to sin is that one
sin leads to another until the individual is removed further and
further from God. The road back demands action, not
introspection—restitution, not prayer. Judaism therefore prescribes two options against sin: repentance, that is returning to
God from where one strayed; and, conscious effort to avoid
sinning by close acquaintance with the Torah and strict
adherence to all its terms and conditions.

Thus, the rationale for obeying the Torah is the assurance
that it authentically represents divine favour. To obey the
Torah is tantamount to obeying God. Judaism is not overbur-
dened by metaphysical speculation about sin. The context or
setting for tracing sin to its source is human life itself.

Humans are sinful from their time of conception (Psalm 51:5)
and are therefore vulnerable to all the evils life may hold. Sin
arises from the corrupt soul or 'heart', the centre of one's being.
For the heart is not so much the seat of the intellect as of the
will. As a sinner, then, a person is at odds with the Creator. The
essence of sin lies in the depths of a person's being, not in
isolated acts of transgression. And the sin of an individual
involves everyone associated with that individual. Sin is viewed
as so dreadful a sickness that only God is able to offer His grace
as an antidote.

If humans are incapable of escaping the taint of sin, is it
reasonable to conclude that they ought not to be held
responsible for it? No, not according to the tenets of Judaism. In
the first place, sin is considered basically as the consequence of
an act of misdirected or perverted freedom and therefore
attributable to no one but the perpetrator. In the second place,
God urges the sinner to repent (literally 'return') and to forsake
wickedness. In other words, sinners are not misguided inno-
cents. They know what they are doing.

'As I live,' says the Lord God, 'I have no pleasure in the death of the
wicked, but that the wicked turn from his way and live. Return,
return from your evil ways, for why will you die, O house of Israel?'
                                                              Ezekiel 33:11

God holds all people, Jew and non-Jew, to account for their sins, but the Jews are (more than any other people) answerable to Him. Their sin is all the greater because of their Covenant with God and because of their intimate knowledge of God's will. Sin is, therefore, to the Jew, a personal affront against a holy and righteous God. And as long as the sinner remains in sin then the sinner is subject to the wrath of God. God judges the guilty by imposing retribution: pain, misery, and ultimately death—death in a spiritual as well as a physical sense.

By Judaic definition, a sinner is someone who embraces wickedness as a way of life, not the infrequent transgressor. A God-fearing person, then, qualifies as a righteous person, even though that person may occasionally fall into sin. The reason is quite clear. The basic attitude of the righteous is rejection of sin, whereas of the wicked, it is defiance of God.

Only a change of mind, a feeling of remorse and rejection of sin, constitutes repentance in Judaism. One may recover the mercy and favour of God by renouncing sin and returning to Him. Genuine repentance leads to obedience to God and to His statutes as instituted in the Torah. The following prayer recited silently by a penitent Jew expresses this awareness more accurately than anything else:

> Our Father, bring us back to Your Torah;
> Our King, draw us near to Your service;
> Lead us back to You truly repentant
> Praised are You, O Lord, who welcomes repentance.
>
> Our Father, forgive us, for we have sinned!
> Our King, pardon us, for we have transgressed . . .
> *The Eighteen Benedictions*

Suffering

You only have I known of all the families of the earth; therefore I will punish you for all your iniquities.

Amos 3:2

God, do not tell me why I suffer, for I am no doubt unworthy to know why; but help me to believe that I suffer for Your sake.

Hasidic Prayer

Human suffering, whether deserved or undeserved, has always been a preoccupation of compassionate people, but among Jews it has a special significance. The reaction of most Jews to suffering is more than a personal, external reflection of anguish. It expresses also their mental image of God.

Since the Jewish faith speaks of a just and righteous God, who rewards the pious and punishes the wicked, the Jewish mind is tormented by the irreconcilable discrepancies arising from this doctrine and human experience of God in His government of nations. The discrepancy, bluntly stated is, Why does God allow the righteous to suffer at the hands of the wicked?

Many passages from the Bible represent the efforts of Jewish thinkers to come to terms with doctrine and history. The problem is that doctrine, or theology, applies human reasoning to interpret divine acts, which, by definition, lie beyond mere mortal limitations. In the earliest stage of Judaism, biblical authors showed no particular inclination to identify the origin of human suffering. Nor were they interested in distinguishing between physical and mental suffering or suffering imposed by nature and by people. They simply inquired into the reason and purpose of suffering. In line with other religious traditions, they interpreted suffering as a divine punishment for wickedness and sin. So firmly convinced were these biblical authors of the moral order that guided the destinies of individuals and nations, that God's swift retribution on the disobedient and wicked was an outcome they expected and approved.

Some, however, expressed impatience when God's wrath fell so far short of expectations that the wicked prospered (Jeremiah 12:1-4; Habakkuk 1:2-4; Malachi 3:7-15). Others interpreted Jewish calamities and sufferings as indications of God's righteous indignation at the wickedness and sin of their forefathers, including their monarchs (I Samuel 22:18; I Kings 21:20, 22, 29; II Kings 21:10-11).

Still, the fundamental question remained: Why did the righteous suffer, if there was a moral order governing the universe? It continued to plague and challenge the minds of serious but sceptical thinkers who persisted in their search for answers.

The author of the book of Job, for instance, resigned himself to the incomprehensibility of the wisdom of God. For, after all, he seems to ask, who established the world and its moral order? Was it God or human beings? The conclusion, he implies, does not leave us much the wiser, but who are human beings, anyway, to assume that they can rationalize and understand divine acts?

Others found satisfaction in the idea that God would, sooner or later, vindicate the cause of the righteous (Psalm 22:19-20; 31:9, 21; 55:22; Proverbs 10:2-3). For, after all, they might point out, a thousand years in God's sight are just as a day (Psalm 90:4).

But none of these solutions could satisfactorily explain the expulsion of the Jews from their homeland in the sixth century BC. Suffering associated with exile and dispersion had a profoundly traumatic effect. One was a feeling of vengeance born of hopelessness:

By the waters of Babylon, there we sat down and wept . . .
How shall we sing the Lord's song in a foreign land?
O daughter of Babylon, you devastator!
Happy shall be he who requites you with what you have done to us!
Happy shall be he who takes your little ones and dashes them against the rock!

                                                    Psalm 137:1-9

Another effect was a sense of betrayal and violent recrimination against God for neglecting His people:

You cast us off and abased us . . .
You made us turn back from the foe;
and our enemies have gotten spoil;
You made us like sheep for slaughter,
and scattered us among the nations.
You sold Your people for a trifle
demanding no high price for them.
You made us the taunt of our neighbours
the derision and scorn of those about us.
You have made us a byword among the nations . . .

All this has come upon us even though we have not forgotten
   You or been false to Your covenant . . .
Wake Yourself up! Why do You sleep O Lord?
Awake! Do not cast us off for ever!
Why do You hide Your face? . . .
Rise up, come to our help.

Psalm 44:9-26

The search for the meaning of exilic suffering led, in Judaism, to some far-reaching and fundamental conclusions. In the first place, Judaism demonstrated itself proof against any compromise on the nature of God, in spite of His inscrutable ways. In the second place, Judaism accepted the suffering and persecution of the Jewish people as a divine test, not as the result of corporate disobedience and sin. As a chosen group, a particular people, and a minority, the Jews were tested to show their loyalty and strength to their faith. This gave the 'ungodly' nations (the Gentiles) the opportunity to show a spirit of 'godliness' in dealing graciously with the Jews. If the nations failed, their failure was attributed to their own shortcomings in spiritual attainment and to thwarting divine will.

Very closely related to this notion is the parable of the Suffering Servant in Isaiah 53. The implication is quite clear: the steadfast faith of the sufferer sets the example from which all future generations may learn and profit. Guilt is not an inherited trait like blue eyes. It is the consequence of individual action and therefore a personal responsibility. One accepts suffering as a test of faith—a test which imposes discipline required of an exemplary life.

It is remarkable that with all their experience of suffering, the Jews are possessed of an invincible optimism. In fact, the suffering and the restrictions such as ghetto life endured by Jews served to bring out the best qualities in Judaism. For instance, the emphasis on self-help and on mutual support among Jews might have weakened in the absence of the horrors and consistently recurring predicaments in which they have found themselves in history.

The determination of Jews to adhere with singular steadfastness to their faith in the face of all sorts of tragedies and persecutions attests to this attitude of invincible optimism. It is an optimism exemplified by the Jewish philosopher Baruch (Benedict) Spinoza (1632-1677). When the innumerable exemplary lives of Catholic martyrs who had died for their faith were cited to him as a justification for his conversion to Catholicism, Spinoza's reply was that no people in the world other than the Jews could count among their number as many martyrs who had suffered death and unspeakable torture rather than compromise their beliefs. Thus, in the long history of suffering, Jews enhanced their genius for survival and unquenchable optimism through the searing flame of their faith in Judaism.

This faith emerged from the deep covenantal conviction of all Jews in the ultimate fulfilment of divine purpose, no matter what the consequences. There is an old story that illustrates this unbreakable bond quite vividly. When a contagious disease on board his ship threatened the lives of crewmen, the Captain disembarked all his passengers on an open shore. Among them was an exiled Spanish Jew with his family. Hunger and climatic exposure killed his wife and children, and just before his own death he cried out loud: 'Master of the worlds, know this for sure that I am a Jew and I shall remain a Jew no matter what else you may bring upon me.'[24]

Since suffering is the constant, recurring national condition of Jewish history, a Jew might be forgiven for asking whether, perhaps, God has abrogated His covenant with His people. And yet, the unparalleled will to live in the face of all atrocities and shattering experiences indicates, *ipso facto*, the invincible faith of the Jewish people. The image that comes to mind immediately is of the three young men in the book of Daniel. So furious was King Nebuchadnezzar with Shadrach, Meshach and Abednego for not worshipping the national gods, that he threatened to cast them into the burning fiery furnace. Their answer was: 'O Nebuchadnezzar, . . . if it be so, our God whom we serve is able to deliver us from the burning fiery furnace . . . but if not, be it known to you, O king, that we will not serve your gods . . .' (Daniel 3:16-18).

But if God does not deliver His people from suffering, from genocide and extermination, how does Judaism survive such assaults on the credibility of a covenantal faith? There seems to be ample justification for unbelieving Jews, since any human endeavour to explain God's 'purpose' theologically or to reason it philosophically is bound to fail. Regardless of apparent paradoxes, many Jews continue to believe, with an invincible determination, the basic tenets of Judaism. Jews who retain such an undying faith affirm that all people, including Jews, are accountable to a transcendent God of justice, whose thoughts and acts are incomprehensible. So long as God exists, all events in history are willed by Him and have a meaning. Respect and obedience to this God is the proper human response—the only response. Such affirmation, however, does not absolve all Jews from the horrors and perplexities attendant on their beliefs. Tribulation reinforces their faith, which must be retained at all costs for the sake of the redemption of all humanity.

The realization of this goal—the redemption of humanity—coincides with the Jewish understanding of the Messianic age. But until it dawns, and despite all suffering, the Jew survives as a living witness to God's divine plan and purpose.

The Messianic Age

And it shall come to pass in the end of days that the mountain of the house of the Lord shall be established as the highest of the mountains . . . and all the nations shall flow to it, and many peoples shall come and say: 'Come, let us go up to the mountain of the Lord, to the house of the God of Jacob, that He may teach us His ways, and that we may walk in His paths.'

Isaiah 2:2-3

Behold, the days are coming, says the Lord, when I will raise up for David a righteous scion, and he shall reign as king, and deal wisely, and execute justice and righteousness in the land.

Jeremiah 23:5

The Jewish concept of the coming of the Messiah and the establishment of the Messianic Age represents, among Jews, the final goal of history and the ultimate fulfilment of divine purpose. But this vision of the Jewish Messiah gives rise to two conflicting interpretations. One is the age-old belief in a Messiah who is a human being (not a divine being such as the Christian Messiah), possessing extraordinary attributes, such as an ultimate degree of righteousness, great wisdom, and superior powers of leadership. This individual is seen as a descendant of the 'House of David', who would redeem mankind and establish a 'Kingdom of God' on earth by provoking a social revolution that would usher in an era of perfect peace and justice on earth. The other interpretation is of very recent origin. It sees the Messiah not as an individual redeemer, but as all peoples collectively, who, by their own acts and by attaining the highest level of enlightenment, will ultimately usher in a paradisical era of peace, justice and kindliness on earth. Orthodox Jews hold to the former persuasion while Reform Jews are of the latter. Both interpretations, however, deserve closer scrutiny.

Jewish tradition since the days of the prophet Isaiah (eighth century BC) envisioned the coming of a Messiah as a person of royal lineage with national antipathies and political aspirations. The Hebrew word *mashiah* literally means 'the anointed one' and originally referred primarily to the biblical Jewish kings. The basic form of the title 'the anointed one of the Lord' (sometimes also 'Mine anointed' or 'His anointed', according to context) appears in the Jewish Bible and designates King David (II Samuel 19:21; I Samuel 2:35; Psalm 84:9; 89:38, 51).

Thanks to the efforts of King David, who ruled in the ninth century BC, the Jewish concept of kingship or royalty became the model on which a Messianic figure was based. Characteristics of the ruling king that were cherished or admired or venerated were transferred to the future ruling Messiah. Consequently, court style and royal forms and phraseology gradually developed into a Messianic ideology. It is, therefore, not surprising that the so-called 'Royal' Psalms (Psalm 2, 18, 20, 21, 45, 72, 101, 110, 132) came to be interpreted as Messianic statements. This King-Messiah is spoken of as the 'begotten-son of God' (Psalm 2:7), who will secure for his people the blessings of God (Psalm 72:6, 16); who will provide law and justice (Psalm 72:1-4, 12-14), righteousness and peace

(Psalm 72:7); who will defeat all enemies (Psalm 2:8–12); and who will rule over the whole world forever (Psalm 2:8; 21:4; 72:5, 8–11).

Similarly, the sayings of the biblical prophets were projected into the distant future, when God would send His Anointed, the Messiah, to establish, for all time, God's kingdom under the Covenant. The prophet Isaiah predicted (around 732–722 BC) the impending birth of the Messiah as an event of double portent: the punishment of King Ahaz, including the people of Judah; and salvation for the faithful remnant (see Isaiah 7–9). In the words of Isaiah: 'The Lord Himself will give you a sign; behold a virgin [young woman] shall conceive and bear a son, and shall call his name Emmanuel' (Isaiah 7:14). And then Isaiah confers on this child the coronation titles:

For unto us a child is born, to us a son is given. And the government will be upon his shoulder, and his name will be called: 'Wonderful Counselor, Mighty God, Everlasting Father, Prince of Peace.' Of the increase of his government and of peace there will be no end upon the throne of David, and over his kingdom, to establish it and to uphold it with justice and righteousness from this time forth and for evermore.

Isaiah 9:6–7

The prophecies of Micah regarding the expectation of a Messiah have strong affinities with that of Isaiah. This Messiah is presented on the one hand with mysterious intimations, as one 'whose origin is from old, from ancient days' (Micah 5:2), and, on the other hand, as a descendant of David, the Ephrathite (Micah 5:2; I Samuel 17:12). Moreover, Micah expects the reign of the Messiah to be representative of God and universal in extent (Micah 5:4).

To the prophet Jeremiah, the Messiah is a representative from the line of David, who is to rule wisely, and to execute justice and righteousness (Jeremiah 23:5). To Ezekiel, the image of the Messiah is again linked with the lineage of David (Ezekiel 34:23–24), whose reign will be a sign to all the people in the world that God is with the Jews and that the Jews are His chosen people. To put it in the words of Ezekiel: 'I the Lord

their God, am with them, and that they, the house of Israel are
My people' (Ezekiel 34:30; cf. 37:28).

Finally, two more prophets, Haggai and Zechariah, predict
an imminent Messiah. Both of them saw Zerubbabel, a
descendant of David, as God's governor and the long expected
Messianic ruler (Haggai 2:23; Zechariah 6:9-14). Then, there is a
passage added to the book of Zechariah (whose date and
authorship is disputable) which presents an impressive image of
the Messiah. Here the Messiah is pictured as a humble king
riding an ass (instead of the symbolic royal horse), who is
nevertheless triumphant in establishing universal peace:

Rejoice greatly, O daughter of Zion!
Shout aloud, O daughter of Jerusalem!
Lo, your king comes to you; he is triumphant and victorious, humble
and riding on an ass . . .
and he shall command peace to the nations; his dominion shall be from
sea to sea, and from the river to the ends of the earth.

Zechariah 9:9-10

The Messianic expectation of the biblical prophets extended
over the centuries into the mainstream of Jewish faith. But
before tracing the development of the Messianic concept in
post-biblical times, let it be clearly understood that at no time in
Jewish thinking or teaching was the Messiah conceived of as a
supernatural being, much less as a God or as a Son of God
empowered to forgive sins. From biblical times to the present
day, Judaism has represented the Messiah as a mortal leader,
who will be instrumental in restoring: Israel to its ancient
homeland; the whole of humanity to its proper social and moral
life; and the universal reign of God on earth, and in the lives of
mankind.

Regardless of whether the Messiah is conceived of as a being
of flesh and blood who will appear in person to preside over this
world's arena (as Orthodox Jews believe), or as corporate
humanity itself collectively enlightened and redeemed (as
Reform Jews believe), both schools of thought subscribe to the
same scenario that will signal the dawning of the Messianic
Age:

- the return, to their promised land of inheritance, of Jews scattered all over the world;
- the universal abolition of social and moral discrimination, unrighteousness, and immorality;
- a societal order of truth and peace;
- a universal religion by which all people advance in knowledge of and in everyday contact with the one and only God, known for centuries to the Jews.

Only when these conditions are realized will God's purpose on earth achieve ultimate fulfilment.

In other words, devout Jews hold that this world is God's world, chosen by Him to become the scene of a divine order in which truth, peace, and goodwill towards human beings reign supreme. This constitutes the quintessence of the Jewish conception of the Kingdom of God. It is the key to an understanding of Judaism in all its varied and even foreign or unfamiliar forms. It is also sharply at variance with Christian or Islamic visions of the same kingdom.

Judaism does not elevate the Kingdom of God to a celestial pedestal high above all struggles, pains, tears, hopes, and ambitions. On the contrary, the Kingdom of God, for Jews, has a terrestrial and social setting. It is destined for creation here on earth by humans under divine direction, rooted in all the complexities of human failure and achievement. In the fullness of time there will no longer be war and destruction in the world. Mankind will enjoy peace and prosperity. The challenge implicit in understanding the wisdom of God and obeying His commandments will become a universal incentive.

A New Testament or Christian Messiah of divine or heavenly origin, predestined to suffer and to die on behalf of all mankind, is inimical to the Judaic tradition. There are superficial similarities. Judaism developed, in post-biblical times, the idea of a suffering Messiah and even of one subject to death by violence but, though the concept was a source of controversy, it was never associated with atonement or with Christ's unique redemptive mission on the cross. Argue as they might, all Jewish scholars were unanimous in asserting that suffering and death, if they were to be part of the destiny of the Messiah, would be a consequence of establishing the Messianic Age not representative of the sacrifice of God personified or anything like it.

There is little unanimity on the timing of such events. Some, like the Apocalyptic writers, attempted to document infinity like a calendar. Others insisted that only God could know the day and the hour. Some rabbis advocated penitence and absolute obedience to the Torah as measures calculated to hasten the coming of the Messiah. Others dismissed such conjecture as irrelevant to the timing of the Messiah's coming.

The one constant among variables of expectation and conviction is unremitting and enduring hope. After the destruction of Solomon's Temple in AD 70, rabbis looked forward to an earthly Messiah, a scion of David, who would end the rule of 'pagan nations' over the Jewish people and inaugurate an age of peace and justice. Their expectation is best expressed in the prayers they included for daily recitation in Jewish worship:

> Sound the great shofar to herald man's freedom;
> Raise high the banner to gather all exiles . . .
> Have mercy, O Lord, and return to Jerusalem, Your city . . .
> Re-establish there the majesty of David, Your servant . . .
> Hasten the advent of the Messianic redemption;
> Each and every day we hope for Your deliverance . . .[25]

Thus, one of the innermost strengths of Jewish survival is belief in the vision of the Messianic Age. It is a conviction about the future: the coming of the Kingdom of God on this earth; the restoration to Jews of their ancient homeland, including its ancient glories and greatness; and the enthronement of the one and only God among all nations.

Successive generations of Jewish rabbis, philosophers, and mystics longed for the speedy arrival of the Messianic redemption. In fact, for over twenty centuries the pattern throughout the history of Judaism remained constant. Messiahs came and Messiahs went, always gaining the support of the masses but never capturing the credence of rabbinic authorities. Each time, the leading exponents of Judaism concluded that the time for the coming of the Messiah had not arrived.

It is not surprising, therefore, that in modern times the vision of an individual Messiah has given way for many Jews to the hope for a Messianic Age. The origin of this concept is credited to the rise of Reform Judaism in the nineteenth century which led to a number of changes, including the traditional concept of a Messiah. Some of these changes look, in retrospect, like harbingers of modern Zionism. Moses Hess (1812-1875) advocated Jewish nationalism as a form of Messianism. In his view, the Jews were the Messianic people capable of discharging their divinely assigned task of ushering in universal social justice, human co-operation and permanent peace, if only they were able to return to their ancestral homeland.

Inspired by this Messianic tradition, Abraham Isaac Kook (1868-1935), the first Chief Rabbi of Israel, associated the universal Messianic ideals of justice and righteousness with the Jewish national movement. In his view, God's Messianic people were synonymous with the Jewish nation which 'exerts holy influences by her very existence. Many hate her, many persecute her, but none can deny her existence, and her existence will never cease influencing human thought and cleansing humanity from its dross.'[26] Similarly, David Ben Gurion (1886-1973), the first Prime Minister of Israel, declared in 1957: 'The ingathering of the exiles, that is the return of the Jewish people to its land, is the beginning of the realization of the Messianic vision.'[27]

Besides the specifics of this Messianic vision there is another Jewish concept of more ambiguous, less definite proportions: the concept of the World to Come. Little is said about this concept in Judaism, except that it represents life after death—the ultimate bliss to which all Jews aspire. The justification for saying little else about the World to Come, is that the Talmud warns against any formulations, stating categorically that 'No eye has seen it.'

By contrast, the emphasis placed on the Messianic vision in Judaism is this-worldly. It represents a preliminary stage in progress toward an ultimate, divine resolution, culminating in the World to Come. Thus, an individual's failures and achievements in life reach a climax or culmination in the World to Come.

Judaic Scripture also makes reference to an intermediate vindication of all righteous Jews. At some point during the Messianic Age, the righteous Jewish dead are to be resurrected to share in the fulfilment of the Messianic vision: life in its perfect form in the Kingdom of God, here on earth. This Kingdom, no matter how long it is destined to endure, is not permanent but fated to come to an end. The resurrection of the non-Jewish dead is deferred, then, to the end of the world. Of these non-Jews, the unrighteous are judged and doomed. The righteous are transformed in order to share in the World to Come.

Although in the past, concepts associated with heaven, hell, Satan, angels and resurrection were topics of speculation and debate in Jewish theology, today they are relegated to a status of minor importance among leading Jewish thinkers. Pain and anguish have been so much a part of their history that there seems little point in speculating about the possibilities of everlasting torture, infernos or similar horrors in the afterlife.

Jewish faith affirms the immortality of the soul, an immortality whose nature is only known to God. Beyond that, Judaism has little to say about the afterlife. Concepts of heaven and hell are not interpreted in any literal sense. True, there exists the idea of *gehinnom*, a term which implies a temporary punishment limited to a sentence of twelve month's duration.[28] Judaism is not invested with multiple scenarios of ultimate human destinies. They are left in the hands of God.

Angels, too, have played a minor role in the celestial Judaic pantheon. In biblical times, angels simply meant 'messengers' of God. It was only later that they were given form and substance as special creatures serving as specific messengers of God. Later still, there developed the idea of 'guardian' angels. Today, Jewish thought recognizes angels as endowed with minor roles and possessing an inferior position to God.

Similarly, the notion of Satan, adopted from ancient Iranian beliefs in the sixth century BC, assumed several forms in Judaism. Dualism (belief in a power of evil dedicated to the overthrow of whatever is noble or good) and fear of demonic forces were among the strongest forms of belief associated with Satan. But here, too, Satan was always subservient to God. At no time in Judaic tradition has Satan featured as anything but a loser. Satan no longer has any role in modern Reform, Conservative, or Reconstructionist Judaism and only a minor role in Orthodox Judaism which affirms that ultimate power rests in God alone.

The doctrine of resurrection is not central or dominant to Judaism even though it has a long history. It is a history that dates from the prophet Daniel (sixth century BC?) who stated: 'many of those who sleep in the dust of the earth shall awake, some to everlasting life, and some to shame and everlasting contempt' (Daniel 12:2).[29] Jewish opinion on this doctrine is sharply divided between those who believe it and those who do not. By and large Orthodox Jews subscribe to the doctrine of the resurrection and Reform and Conservative Jews do not.

Judaism is not a religion distinguished for its preoccupation with a life or existence after death. The basic concern and longing of most Jews is for the Messianic Age which constantly inspires them to work for the establishment of the Kingdom of God on earth. They see it as a logical fulfilment of all human aspiration for Jews and non-Jews alike. In the words of Hermann Cohen (1842-1918):

The future, which the prophets have painted in the symbol of the Messiah, is the future of world history. It is the goal, it is the meaning of history . . . The realization of morality on earth, its tasks and its eternal goal, this, and nothing else is the meaning of the Messiah for us . . .[30]

2

HOLY PEOPLE

For you are a people holy to the Lord your God, and the Lord has chosen you to be a people for His own possession, out of all the peoples that are on the face of the earth.

Deuteronomy 14:2

It was not because you were more in number than any other people that the Lord set His love upon you and chose you, for you were the fewest of all peoples; but it is because the Lord loves you, and is keeping the oath which He swore to your fathers . . .

Deuteronomy 7:7-8

You shall be to Me a kingdom of priests and a holy nation.

Exodus 19:6

The Patriarchs

And the Lord said to Abraham:

'Go from your country and your kindred and your father's house to the land that I will show you. And I will make of you a great nation, and I will bless you, and make your name great, so that you will be a blessing. I will bless those who bless you, and I will curse him who curses you; and by you all the families of the earth will bless themselves.'

Genesis 12:1-3

IF indeed all the families of the earth have blessed themselves by Abraham, they have, by and large, chosen strange ways of doing so. The record suggests that the families of the world were more often prone to demand conformity than acknowledge any favoured status. Jews and Judaism have survived assimilation and proscription since the beginning of recorded history. It is one factor which makes the Jewish people quite unique. Who are they? When, where, and how did they originate in history? Why do they consider themselves to be 'chosen' and 'holy'? Why have their traditions proved durable?

No single definition is broad enough to encompass all Jews. Strictly speaking, they are not a race. Most Jews are white Caucasians, but there are black (Falasha) Jews, Chinese Jews, Japanese Jews, and Indo-Mexican Jews.

Jews do not represent a nation in the full sense of the word. Jews in Israel proudly refer to themselves as a nation, but there are no national ties that unite all Jews throughout the world. Israel is a Jewish nation as Great Britain can be said to be a Christian nation and Iran an Islamic nation. True, most Jews share a sense of kinship—the legacy of a common history, a vast literature, and a sense of common destiny—but there are many Jews (like the Irish and Italians) who feel more at home in Brazil or Canada than they do in Israel, Ireland, or Italy. Jews represent no particular nation any more than Christians do.

Are Jews a religious group of people? Certainly a vast number of Jews adhere rigidly to their age-old faith and tradition, but there is also a large segment of Jews who have totally eliminated religion from the way they live.

Perhaps the most appropriate definition of the Jewish people is still the biblical one: *Beth Yisrael*, the House of Israel. The name implies family, a sense of kinship expressed in custom and practice, a sense of filial obligation and duty even amidst quarrels and conflicts, and a sense of experiences shared, all of which have linked the Jewish people in a common tradition. The father and founder of this common tradition of the House of Israel is none other than Abraham nominated and elected, so to speak, by his God.

Judaism affirms that God's choice of Abraham and subsequently of his descendants, the Jews, was determined by no factor more compelling than divine love. Biblical tradition firmly identifies the beginning of Jewish history with a series of patriarchal figures or *avot*, a term meaning literally *fathers*: Abraham, Isaac and Jacob. Placing them within the undisputed context of recorded history, however, has frustrated scholars.

Yom Kippur

By the waters of Babylon

The Messiah

Jewish costumes

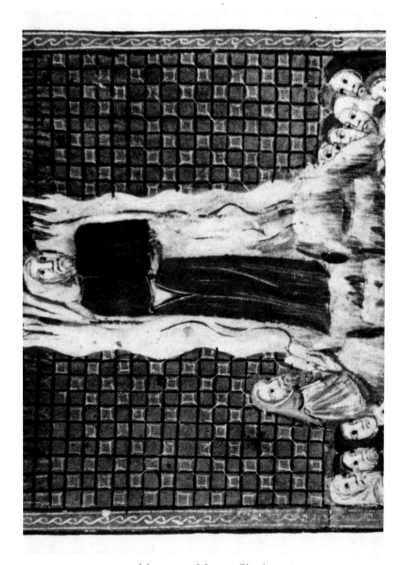

Moses on Mount Sinai

Idolatry

Burning of Jews in the Middle Ages

Jericho

שכו לכה לה שבו. חיכור   והנה אי.   ויעקד את יצחק בנו

Abraham and Isaac

The Torah in the Ark

Scribe writing the Scroll of the Law

Studying the Torah

Prayer

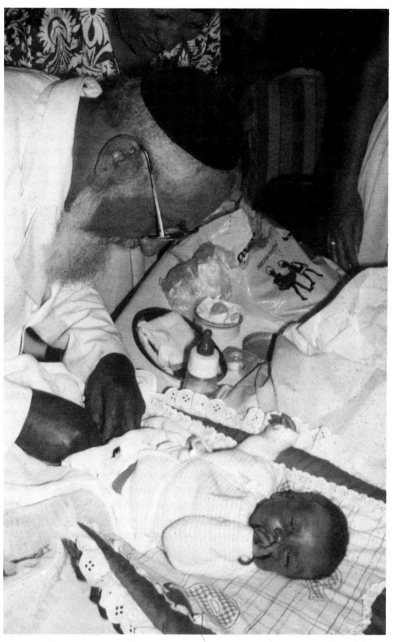

Circumcision

A Bar Mitzvah reading a portion of the Law

Blowing the ram's horn at Rosh Hashanah

The menorah

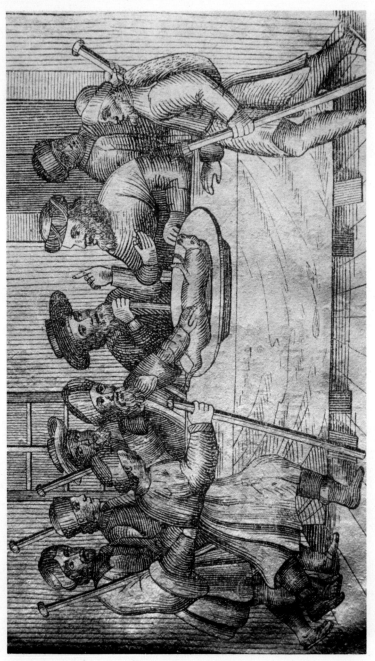

Feast of the Passover

Some are tempted to establish links between Abraham and the Amorites, a Semitic people of Western Asia who made an incursion into Israel-Palestine sometime in 1900-1800 BC, but the connection is tenuous. Though Jewish scholars do not challenge the biblical affirmation of Abraham as founding head of Judaism, they do question the accuracy of events associated with the avot, especially their relationship one with another. Some consider Isaac, Jacob, and the rest as direct descendants of a single clan head, Abraham. Others attribute to the avot the status of tribal chiefs, not necessarily related, whose popular legends gradually developed into a single narrative.

The debate about the details of Jewish origins is largely academic. The general narrative is not in dispute. Biblical tradition states that Abraham's God promised him and his descendants a permanent territory or land in the area where the Canaanites dwelt. It was under these circumstances that Abraham, along with the members of his tribe, and his flocks and herds, settled in Canaan. After his death, his son Isaac and then his grandson Jacob succeeded Abraham as leaders. Then, according to biblical tradition, famine followed cyclical drought forcing Jacob and his people to migrate once more, this time to Egypt.

Tradition relates that everything went well in Egypt for several centuries until the advent of an Egyptian Pharaoh whose passion for building large cities and monumental temples prompted him to draft his subjects into forced labour and slavery. Among them were the Israelites, progeny of Jacob's descendants. Once established, their bondage persisted without relief until some time in the thirteenth century BC when one of them, called Moses, found himself in the corridors of power and in a position to give substance to a revelation vouchsafed to him by the God of the avot. The result was the successful 'Exodus' of the Israelites from Egypt and their subsequent experience at Mount Sinai in the desert.

The biblical record of these events leaves little doubt that the religion that Moses advocated was unequivocally monotheistic. The precise nature of pre-Mosaic religion, however, is not at all clear. Were the patriarchs polytheists or monotheists? Certain scholars accept the biblical tradition which represents the many names of gods as different titles for the one God. Others argue that the number and variety of names suggest a pantheon of some sort: *El Shaddai* (God Almighty), *El Elyon* (God Most High), *El Olam* (God Everlasting), and *El Roi* (God Seeing). Besides these fairly frequent references, the Bible records other designations that identify God or gods: *El* of Abraham, *Pahad* (Kinsman) of Isaac, *Abir* (Champion) of Jacob, *Gad* (possibly Fortune), *Dan* (Judge), *Asher* (perhaps a masculine counterpart of Asherah), and Elim or Elohim (plural of El). What is the implication of so many distinctive names? Was the nature of patriarchal faith polytheistic or monotheistic? Did the avots strike a bargain with one god or several?

The belief that the patriarchs were monotheistic is difficult to accept (cf. Joshua 24:1-15). A more credible speculation is that the god of Abraham, Isaac, and Jacob was a tribal god with whom they entered into a covenant and that this god became their sole worshipping focus. This is not to say that the patriarchs rejected other gods. The evidence suggests the contrary (Genesis 31:34-35; and Joshua 24:23).

So Jacob said to his household and to all who were with him, 'Put away the foreign gods that are among you . . .'

Genesis 35:2

There would be no reason to make such a remark to a people that followed only one God.

Reference to Laban and Rachel suggests similar evidence for the same conclusion: patriarchal faith was polytheistic. Although Laban and Rachel may have adopted YHWH as their God (Genesis 30:20,28), they also worshipped other gods. The fact that Laban kept household gods attests to some kind of commitment to them and to the importance he associated with them when they suddenly disappeared.

Now Rachel had taken the household gods . . . and sat upon them. Laban felt all about the tent, but did not find them. And she said to her father, 'Let not my Lord be angry that I cannot rise before you for the way of women is upon me.'

Genesis 31:34-35

The evidence that patriarchal people recognized other gods seems conclusive.

Despite their imperfections then, the Patriarchs are depicted in the Bible as objects of God's blessing and of His protective care. In return, He demands loyalty, obedience, and the observance of certain practices. These practices included circumcision and sacrifice and prayers offered beside stone pillars or trees or altars constructed for the occasion. In return, God promises land and fecundity. There is no reference in the patriarchal covenant to a 'jealous' God, or to specific proscription of idolatry. These were terms or conditions deferred to a later period when the covenant was revised and ascribed to Moses.

Moses

The Lord made His ways known to Moses,
His acts to the people of Israel.

Psalm 103:7

The life of Moses is usually regarded as the cornerstone of Jewish religion. It began in bondage, a context familiar to even modern Jews. Tradition states that after centuries of living in Egypt, the Jews had grown so populous that they were viewed as a threat by the Egyptian government of the day. In a measure calculated to reduce the population and discourage further increase, the Egyptian Pharaoh ordered the systematic slaughter of all male babies born to Jewish families. It was during this period in about the thirteenth century BC that Moses was born and suckled in secret at home for three months. Then, in a tradition hallowed by convention before and since (Sargon in Mesopotamia and Romulus in Greek legend) the baby Moses was placed in a waterproof basket in the rushes along the Nile river. Soon, he was discovered by Pharaoh's daughter, who reared him in her palace as her own adopted son.

Grown to manhood, Moses was witness to a scene that became a turning point in his life: an Egyptian overseer beating a Jewish bondsman. Moved by a sudden outburst of anger, Moses struck and killed the Egyptian on the spot. Fearing that rumours of the murder would catch up with him, Moses fled eastwards and found refuge with a Midianite priest named Jethro. Later, he married Zepporah, the daughter of Jethro, and had two sons.

A second turning point occurred while Moses was herding Jethro's flock of sheep near Mount Horeb. There he experienced the presence of a divine being emanating from a burning bush. The encounter not only changed his life, but altered the destiny of his people in Egypt. He was to bring them out of the land of their enslavement into the land of the Canaanites, where their ancestors had lived. Reluctant to accept such a responsible mission, Moses was persuaded by this divine presence, or God, that he was endowed with the power necessary to persuade Pharaoh to let the Jewish people go.

As it happened, the ruling Pharaoh was singularly unimpressed by Moses' credentials. He remained obdurate through nine terrible plagues threatened, imposed, and relieved each time in return for an undertaking to free the Jews. In all this, Moses acted as God's agent, persisting until Pharaoh broke his word for the ninth time. The tenth and last plague was the clincher. It struck and killed all the first-born sons of the Egyptians, including the Pharaoh's. Only Jewish children were spared, and to this day it is remembered as the 'night of the Passover' or the Passover feast. Finally Pharaoh conceded defeat. He set his Jewish slaves free.

Tradition records how Moses led the Jews miraculously through the waters (of the Red or Reed Sea) and across the desert beyond to the foot of Mount Horeb (sometimes referred to as Mount Sinai). Though the exact location of this mountain has never been established beyond question, the events that took place there are a matter of record. There, with Moses acting as intermediary, a confrontation between God and the Jews resulted in a solemn pact, commonly known as the Covenant. Tradition relates how Moses left the people at the foot of the mountain while he went up to communicate with God. Several days later he returned with two stone tablets, delivered to him by God, inscribed with the 'commandments' of God.

Two texts related to these commandments are recorded in the

Bible. One is the familiar formulation of an ethical code known as the Ten Commandments (Exodus 20). The other is largely ritualistic (Exodus 39). Scholars are divided in their opinions of which is the earlier text. Some think the second text antecedes the first text but that neither properly represent the original pact made between God and Moses. The dispute is quite academic. Later tradition has obscured so much of the original forms that the precise terms of the Mosaic Covenant are irrecoverable. One text with its origins in these ancient events is known as the Ten Commandments (Exodus 20):

1. You shall have no other gods before me.

2. You shall not make yourself a graven image, or any likeness of anything that is in heaven above, or that is in the earth beneath, or that is in the water under the earth; you shall not bow down to them or serve them; for I the Lord your God am a jealous God, visiting the iniquity of the fathers upon the children to the third and the fourth generation of those who hate me, but showing steadfast love to thousands of those who love me and keep my commandments.

3. You shall not take the name of the Lord your God in vain; for the Lord will not hold him guiltless who takes his name in vain.

4. Remember the sabbath day, to keep it holy. Six days you shall labour, and do all your work; but the seventh day is a sabbath to the Lord your God; in it you shall not do any work, you, or your son, or your daughter, your manservant, or your maidservant, or your cattle, or the sojourner who is within your gates; for in six days the Lord made heaven and earth, the sea, and all that is in them, and rested the seventh day; therefore the Lord blessed the sabbath day and hallowed it.

5. Honour your father and your mother, that your days may be long in the land which the Lord your God gives you.

6. You shall not kill.

7. You shall not commit adultery.

8. You shall not steal.

9. You shall not bear false witness against your neighbour.

10. You shall not covet your neighbour's house; you shall not covet your neighbour's wife, or his manservant, or his maidservant, or his ox or his ass, or anything that is your neighbour's.

Exodus 20:3-17

A Covenant of a specific nature between God and the people of Israel dates from this period—so does their special status as the elect people of God. At least, that is the conclusion of some scholars though there is no unanimity among them concerning the Jewish concept of 'election'. It is usually assumed that Judaism was from the first based on a 'unique and exclusive' relationship between the Jews and their God YHWH, but scholarly interpretations of the relationship have resulted in radically differing conclusions. Suffice it to say that three of these interpretations dominate scholarly opinion:

i) the term 'chosen' people is a relatively late religious expression, since early Jewish religion was nationalistic and YHWH was the symbol of national unity;

ii) the conviction that YHWH 'chose' the Jews originated in a religious community dating from the time of Moses—a sort of community that had not previously existed;

iii) the concept that God 'chose' the Jews is the product of two traditions, patriarchal and Mosaic, merged or edited by biblical scribes and scholars during the seventh and sixth century BC.

Another tradition that originated with Moses was to enshrine the two stone tablets inscribed with the terms of the Covenant. They lay within a box or chest carried in a portable shrine called the Tabernacle of God. It became a focus of worship for Jews in their nomadic, desert interlude and a holy place of seclusion where Moses was able to commune with God.

The development of religious traditions like the Covenant,

the special status of the Jewish people as God's elect, and the Tabernacle of God, may be seen as a measure of Moses' success in blending a number of disparate or variant beliefs and practices into a conceptualized form of religion: a national tutelary deity called YHWH. Moses was not as successful in persuading his people to reject their old beliefs and practices. They grumbled their way across the desert and finally suited their actions to their words by raising their golden calf: 'These are your gods, O Israel, who brought you up out of the land of Egypt' (Exodus 32:4).

Worshipping images was obviously a custom firmly embedded in ancient Jewish society, and people immediately turned to them whenever it appeared that Moses' leadership was falling short of expectations. Every time events took a turn for the worse, people then, much as they do now, reverted to any stratagem that seemed to have worked for them in the past. In fact, had it not been for Moses' leadership, people would have been more likely to forsake YHWH Himself than their more familiar gods. Moses did not believe in retribution deferred. His leadership bordered on tyranny. Fear of death was cited as ample justification for the worship of YHWH (Leviticus 24:10-14). When his followers ignored him, Moses spared no pains to advertise the consequences. 'So Israel yoked himself to Baal of Peor. And Moses said to the judges of Israel, "Every one of you slay his men who have yoked themselves to Baal of Peor."' (Numbers 25:1-5).

Draconian measures seem to have served Moses well in the desert but they failed him when the Jews reached the borders of Canaan with the intention of invading it. The courage and resolution of the invaders flagged. They ignored the injunctions of God and Moses and retired to the desert for further years of nomadic existence. The occupation of Canaan was left, therefore, to Joshua, the successor of Moses, who led his forces successfully across the river Jordan into the 'promised' land of Canaan.

That, in essence, is the Mosaic epic recorded in Exodus, but scholars cannot agree on its historicity or the degree to which subsequent events accord with fact or legend. Some maintain that much of the account is a later, pious fabrication. Others argue that all events occurred precisely as they are described. Still others insist that, while much of the account is embellished by later editors, the memory of major events survives in a record that is substantially accurate. Wherever the truth may lie, even the most sceptical must admit that something happened to the Jewish people during this period that gave them a new sense of destiny.

The Judges

Whenever the Lord raised up judges for them, the Lord was with the judge, and He saved them from the hand of their enemies all the days of the judge . . . but whenever the judge died, they turned back and behaved worse than their fathers, going after other gods, serving them and bowing down to them.

Judges 2:18-19

The historical interval between Moses and Samuel, from the thirteenth to the eleventh century BC, is identified as the period of judges. These individuals enjoyed a special kind of auton- omy, inherited from Moses, as Jewish war leaders and legal magistrates wielding both temporal and spiritual authority as agents of God to govern their people and deliver them in time of oppression.

A series of military campaigns led by Moses' successor, Joshua, ended in the occupation of several major Canaanite cities spread over an area roughly corresponding to the modern state of Israel. The Canaanites were settled farmers; the invading Jews were pastoral nomads. The religion of the Canaanites revolved around fertility cults and agricultural activities, while Mosaic Judaism involved tribal ideas and desert practices. Short of the dominance of one ideology over another, the inevitable result was syncretism, though scholars know very little of the form it took.

Archaeological discoveries, and the Book of Judges in the Bible, are the two main sources for reconstructing the course Judaism followed during the period of the judges. The Book of Judges is organized according to repeated cycles of religious advance or retrogression: the apostasy of the Jewish people, their oppression by their enemies, their appeal to God, and God's response in the form of judges of heroic proportions: Gideon, Ehud, Jephthah, Deborah and Samson.

The biblical record makes it obvious that the claim of the national Jewish god, YHWH, to exclusive worship was ineffectual. The incursion of the Jews into Canaan coincided with the adoption of Canaanite gods and practices:

So the people of Israel dwelt among the Canaanites . . . and they served their gods.

Judges 3:5-7

And the people of Israel . . . went after other gods, from among the gods of the peoples who were round about them, and bowed down to them . . .

Judges 2:11-12

At the head of the Canaanite pantheon stood the god El, representing concepts such as King, Father and Bull. Next was the young god Baal (meaning 'Lord'), a god of fertility, who also functioned as a dragon slayer. He was also the god of vegetation who died each year with the advent of winter when the god Moth (Death) killed him, but was restored to life each spring by Anath, his sister. Two other goddesses also featured prominently in this pantheon though their attributes are a bit vague. One, Athirat (the biblical Asherah), was the consort of El. The other was Athtart (the biblical Astarte). The possibility exists that these two goddesses may have represented manifestations of the goddesses of love and war respectively.

The identification of the Canaanite god El with the Jewish God YHWH occurred most probably during this period of which Judges forms the record. The Bible contains no polemic against El. Indeed, El is identified interchangeably with YHWH, though it is impossible to determine when exactly this identification took root. All that can be said with certainty is that it was well established before the Book of Judges was written. The text shows no evidence that there was any hostility between adherents of El and YHWH whereas adherents of Baal and YHWH become in the course of the biblical narrative irreconcilable foes, especially during the period of the prophets.

Hand in hand with the evolution of a Judaic theocracy went the elaboration of ritual and worship. The focus of worship remained fixed on Moses' portable shrine, the Tabernacle of God, identified among followers of the judges as the ark: the ark of God, the ark of YHWH, the ark of the covenant, or the ark of the testimony.

Right from the beginning, from its inception as a handy portable shrine for desert nomads, magical properties were ascribed to the ark, first as the receptacle of God's law and then as a sanctuary in which Moses might commune with God. It became God's throne, a vehicle or repository for His very presence, a battle standard or war palladium to carry even in the van of a counter-attack. Some passages of Scripture make no distinction between YHWH and the ark as if, indeed, the ark were God made manifest.

And whenever the ark set out, Moses said: 'Arise, O Lord, and let Your enemies be scattered; and let them that hate You flee before You.' And when it rested, he said: 'Return, O Lord, to the ten thousand thousands of Israel.'

Numbers 10:35-36

Evidence for the belief in the magical properties of the ark as an embodiment of God survives in the account of the Israelites crossing the Jordan river (Joshua 3-4), and in the story of the capture of Jericho (Joshua 6-7). The record documented in I Samuel 4-7 clearly indicates that the ark was not only regarded as a war palladium, but as a magical portable object, the possession of which might bring either good luck or misfortune. For instance, the defeat of the Jews by the Philistines was attributed to the absence of the ark (I Samuel 4:1-3). Then, when the ark was brought back from Shiloh, the general assumption was that a second attempt against the enemy made amidst joy and shouting around the ark (I Samuel 4:4-9) would bring the Philistines to their knees. It did not. Instead the Philistines prevailed once again. This time they captured the ark and carried it in triumph to their own temple of Dagon in

Ashdod (I Samuel 4:10; 5:1-2). Predictably, their glee was short-lived. Although normally the possession of the ark meant good luck, even for non-Jews (II Samuel 6:11), on this occasion it brought only disaster, or so the Philistines seem to have believed. They returned the ark as soon as they could (I Samuel 5:3-7:2).

After a lapse of some twenty years, King David decided to instal the new ark in his new capital, Jerusalem. He had it transported from the house of Abinadab, its custodian, in a joyous, religious, musical procession. Abinadab's sons, Ahio and Uzzah, escorted the new cart on which the ark was carried. When Uzzah inadvertently extended his hand to steady the ark (II Samuel 6:6-7), sudden death struck him down within minutes. David attributed Uzzah's accidental death to YHWH's displeasure in having the ark moved (II Samuel 6:8-9). Judging that discretion was the better part of valour, David cut short the parade and had the ark accommodated at the house of Obed-edom the Gittite, where it remained for three months.

In the interval, Obed-edom prospered to such a degree (II Samuel 6:10-12) that David felt encouraged to complete the transfer of the ark to Jerusalem. Like a bomb disposal crew handling an explosive device, the bearers of the ark first walked six paces in the direction of Jerusalem. When nothing happened David accepted the absence of immediate retribution as a sign of divine assent. The transfer of the ark was resumed, and it was brought to Jerusalem amidst general rejoicing, the sound of horns, sacrifices, and even with a royal dance led by the King himself robed in a priestly garment. Ultimately, the ark found a permanent home in the inner sanctuary of the Temple in Jerusalem (I Kings 8), where it remained until the fall of the Jewish kingdom in 586 BC.

Besides veneration of the ark as God's repository, sacrifices were offered at particular 'sacred' sites which the Jews simply took over from the Canaanites. Biblical scholars have been able to identify several such as Bethel, Shiloh, Gilgal, Mizpah, Dan, and Ophrah. What is difficult to understand, however, is why the Jews adopted the Canaanite custom of offering human sacrifices, a practice that featured as part of Jewish ritual during the period of the judges and was occasionally repeated later on. The story of the sacrifice of the only daughter of Jephthah in fulfilment of an oath he had made is recorded without the slightest hint of critical comment (Judges 11).

Another innovation the Jews of this period probably borrowed from the Canaanites was the pilgrimage, or in Hebrew, *hag*. These pilgrimages to sacred sites consisted of celebrations during which women danced (Judges 21:19-21). Three annual pilgrimage festivals, *hags*, are listed in Exodus 23:14-17, namely, the *hag* of unleavened bread, the *hag* of weeks, and the *hag* of ingathering.

Finally, one further religious practice foreign to earlier Hebrew traditions began during the period of the judges: the holy war. The Hebrew term used in the Bible is *herem*. It was initiated by the sanctification or ritual purification of all warriors in the Jewish forces (Joshua 3:5; I Samuel 21:5; II Samuel 11:11), intercession with God to secure divine endorsement (Judges 4:7,14; 7:9,15; 20:23,27,35; I Samuel 7:9), and the courage to fight bravely in His name (Judges 7:3; Joshua 8:1; 10:8). During battle, confusion and panic among opposing forces was attributed to God (Judges 4:15; 7:22; I Samuel 14:15). The successful conclusion of war marks the climax of *herem*: the consecration or dedication of all booty to God through its total destruction.

Thus, during the period of the judges, Jewish religious traditions more often blended than conflicted with Canaanite religious traditions. Religious unity and conformity, however, evolved gradually. A strongly defined Jewish religious ethos is not apparent until the introduction of the monarchy, the conquest of Jerusalem, and the rise of the prophets.

The Prophets

If a prophet arises among you, or a dreamer of dreams, and gives you a sign or a wonder, and the sign or wonder which he tells you comes to pass, and if he says, 'Let us go after other gods,' which you have not known, 'and let us serve them,' you shall not listen to the words of that prophet or to that dreamer of dreams . . . but that prophet or that dreamer of dreams shall be put to death, because he has taught rebellion against the Lord your God . . .

Deuteronomy 13:1-5

The cautionary prescription from Deuteronomy signals the period that followed the judges—a period marked by a proliferation of prophets. Of course, there had been prophets before. Abraham is identified as a prophet (Genesis 20:7) in his role as intercessor between God and His people. Moses, too, (Deuteronomy 18:15; 34:10) is considered a prophet, though his place in Judaic tradition is more closely related to the role of leader—a man who speaks on behalf of God in a very special sense. There were also prophetesses such as Miriam, Moses' sister (Exodus 15:20), and Deborah (Judges 4:4). But the earliest references to an established prophetic order appear during the time of Samuel and Saul in the middle of the eleventh century BC. Endowed with a vision sometimes called 'second sight', the prophets were thought of as 'seers'. Some of them were priests but they did not have to be members of the priesthood. Their distinguishing characteristic was their extra-sensory perception. Some were charlatans. Others were recognized as leaders of integrity. The most famous of these was also a priest: Samuel (I Samuel 9:5-9).

At the height of the prophetic period, bands of ecstatic prophets apparently moved about the country and played various musical instruments (I Samuel 10:5-6). Some prophetic bands lived together in semi-monastic fashion, having their meals in common, in a community somewhat like a modern commune. Their number varied from one hundred (I Kings 18:33) to as many as four hundred (I Kings 22:6) to a group, each very probably organized under a leader, like Elisha (II Kings 4:38; 6:1). Though they may have supported themselves to some extent, by and large they seem to have been dependent on the gifts of others (I Kings 14:3; II Kings 5:15; 8:9).

The Jewish kings both consulted and retained at their royal courts many prophets who were qualified to interpret oracles and use divinatory methods to deliver important messages. For instance, King Ahab and Jehosophat summoned four hundred prophets before attempting a military venture (I Kings 22).

The prophets who appeared between the eleventh and eighth centuries BC are usually regarded as the 'former' or 'pre-literary' prophets. This simply means that their sayings or oracles did not survive in print if they were ever recorded. These were men who were primarily interested in the immediate effects of their words and deeds rather than in lasting recognition.

While many prophets were members of organized bands, some were totally independent thinkers often opposed to the establishment and the existing regime. Nathan, for instance, was the prophet who had the courage to challenge King David, first for having an affair with someone else's wife and later for arranging the murder of her husband when she became pregnant (II Samuel 12:1-15). Ahijah was another declared prophet and a 'separatist' at heart. Not only was he connected with a revolution, but he instigated and supported the division of Israel's kingdom into two after Solomon's death (I Kings 11:26-40). Similarly, Elisha inspired the army commander Jehu to revolt against Ahab his king and claim the throne (II Kings 9).

These pre-literary prophets defied simple definition. Some were members of organized groups, while others were strong individualists. Some were experts in delivering oracles on important occasions, while others distinguished themselves by the courage with which they delivered moral judgement even on their own kings. Some were associated in one way or another with the royal courts, while others openly revolted against the ruling king. Many were ecstatic, while a few opposed ecstasy.

Not all prophets were respected by virtue of their calling. Many were objects of suspicion and contempt and accused of being false prophets. Micaiah ben Imlah deserves to be remembered as the first prophet who boldly challenged the unanimous prediction of the four hundred false prophets (I Kings 22). Their oracle to King Ahab predicted safety and victory if the king undertook the military campaign against Ramoth-Gilead. Micaiah advised against it unless the king were prepared to accept death and defeat which, as events proved, were the consequences of the king's choice. Similarly, the dramatic contest of Elijah with the false prophets of Baal on Mount Carmel culminated in the killing of hundreds of them (I Kings 18:19-40). The fallibility of many only served to enhance the prescience of the few. The impact of the best of those pre-literary prophets paved the way for the dynamic independence and moral concern of those that followed in the prophetic tradition.

The main achievement of later prophets was to mould and shape the religious and moral fabric of the Jewish people. They were chiefly responsible for the progress, development and character of Judaism. Through a period of two centuries, (eighth to sixth century BC) they gradually replaced the idea of a tribal, jealous, and national God with the idea of a universal God and examined the social systems, institutions, and practices of their time in relation to values and standards which they interpreted as God-given.

The first of these prophets was Amos, a herdsman, who suddenly appeared one day in the market-place at Beth-El to predict God's judgement on surrounding nations and the impending doom of Israel (Amos 1 and 2). Amos was not moralizing or preaching but merely calling the shots the way he saw or prophesied them. It was not his concern whether or not the Jewish people were faithful to the covenant and the Torah, nor whether they were idolatrous. What angered him were the injustices he saw around him in the course of day-to-day living. His God was a righteous God who expected his chosen people to reflect the divine image of justice and righteousness in their daily activities.

A younger contemporary of Amos was the prophet Hosea, a man of very different temperament. Like Amos, his message was a message of judgement tempered by a new insight about God. Israel seemed to Hosea much like his own unfaithful wife Gomer, who had deserted him in preference to foreign lovers. Just as he himself had to buy her back and finally dragged her home, so did Hosea expect God to bring back the wayward, unfaithful Jews. Hosea believed that, in spite of their infidelity to the covenant, God still loved the Jews.

Isaiah, next in the line of prophetic visionaries, was married, had at least two children and acted as an advisor in the royal court at Jerusalem. Like Amos, Isaiah was courageously outspoken and more concerned about social behaviour than religious observances. He was less impressed by piety than he was by kindness, selflessness, and common courtesy. He despised the hypocrisy of piety for its own sake. There was no sense, he said, in performing any religious ceremonies or observing feasts or offering prayers unless they were accompanied by measures to relieve social injustice and to mitigate the effects of oppression and cruelty (Isaiah 1:11-17). But Isaiah's stern words went unheeded. Haunted by the vision of divine holiness (Isaiah 6:3), Isaiah clearly envisioned God as the Lord not only of the Jews but of all nations. He anticipated that God's judgement would soon come like a flame to consume and purify. Isaiah did not have the slightest doubt that the armies of invading empires would serve as God's instruments in executing judgement over the Jews.

Micah, following the tradition established by his predecessors, spoke out against religious formalism and ritualism. He too was less concerned about forms of worship than social behaviour. He stressed that ethical and moral obligations— principles related to human character and the conduct of daily life—were more important than ceremonial religiosity (Micah 6:8).

If Isaiah altered the narrow, nationalistic concept of God, Jeremiah finally shattered it. The popularity of prophets, never high, hit a nadir with the advent of Jeremiah. He more than any other prophet ran counter to the dominant public sentiment of the day. Naturally, he was opposed and persecuted. The doctrine that caused him so much grief was his insistence that God was supremely an ethical God and the Lord of the whole world. Hence, he argued, nothing short of a change of heart would be acceptable to God. He furthermore stressed the relationship between mere theory and application. He defined true piety as the personal relationship of an individual with God. He envisioned God as wanting to write a new covenant, not through a corporate agent like Moses on tablets of stone, but through personal contact on the hearts of individuals (Jeremiah 31:31-34).

Consciously or unconsciously, these prophets gradually shaped and moulded the character of Judaism in their day and, through their writings, the character of Christianity also. The five centuries during which they were most active coincided with the rise and tragic end of the Jewish kingdom. The establishment of a monarchy gave rise to a nobility—and consequently to a nation—highly influenced by Canaanite elements. The result was an inevitable mixture of polytheistic religious practices. King Solomon, for one, greatly hastened the process, as the biblical record attests:

I [YHWH] am about to tear the kingdom from the hand of Solomon . . . because he has forsaken me, and worshipped Ashtoreth the goddess of the Sidonians, Chemosh the god of Moab, and Milcom the god of the Ammonites . . .

> I Kings 11:31-33

The kings that succeeded Solomon to govern his divided kingdom accepted an even greater variety of worship and occult practices. In the north, Jeroboam introduced the worship of two golden calves and the rites appropriate to them (I Kings 12:26-33; II Kings 17:21-22). His people quickly followed suit as did other Jewish kings of the northern kingdom (II Kings 14:14-24; 15:9,18,24,27; 18:4), including Jehu (II Kings 10:29) and Omri (I Kings 16:25-26). Apostasy and the eagerness with which the Jews and their leaders embraced the religious practices of their neighbours are only too evident in the biblical record:

The people of Israel . . . feared other gods and walked in the customs of the nations whom the Lord drove out before the people of Israel, and in the customs which the kings of Israel had introduced . . . They went after false idols and they followed the nations that were round about them . . . and made for themselves molten images of two calves; and they made an Asherah, and worshipped all the host of heaven, and served Baal. And they burned their sons and their daughters as offerings, and used divination and sorcery . . .

> II Kings 17:7-18

The kings and the people of the southern kingdom were no different. Male cult prostitution (I Kings 15:12), human sacrifice

(II Kings 16:3), idol worship (I Kings 15:12) and various occult practices (I Kings 22:43; II Kings 12:3; 14:4; 15:4; 15:35; 16:4) became part of Jewish religious tradition. There is no better evidence of this development than in the assessment made of the reign of Manasseh, under whose jurisdiction his people worshipped idols, offered human sacrifices, and dabbled in the occult (II Kings 21:1-7).

As the demand for such esoteric mysteries grew so did the variety of exponents and mediators: sorcerers, soothsayers, mediums, necromancers, wizards, charmers, augurers, diviners, dream-experts, seers, and prophets. The prestige that these practitioners enjoyed within Jewish society was very high, to judge by the statements of at least two prophets, Isaiah (3:2-3; 8:19) and Jeremiah (27:9), who may be forgiven even the suspicion of envy. Their ratings ranked low by comparison.

What exercised critics like Isaiah was that practices which he regarded as perversions and superstitions were not restricted to unlettered people who knew no better. Kings were their role models (I Kings 18:19). Saul himself consulted mediums, wizards, cleromancers and prophets (I Samuel 14:36-46; 28:3-19). When David succeeded Saul as king he inherited his predecessor's court experts in magical practices and divinatory arts. He often consulted them, especially in times of national emergency (II Samuel 5:17-25). King Solomon, in his turn, not only inherited these court functionaries of the occult but appointed a fresh host of qualified experts who performed various magical practices and divinatory arts associated with their respective deities: Ashtoreth, Milcom, Molech and Chemosh. Similarly, both King Ahab and King Manasseh made use of soothsayers, augurers, sorcerers, medium-experts and wizards (I Kings 20:30-34; 22:1-28; II Kings 21:6).

The failure of attempts at reform by both King Hezekiah and King Josiah indicate how deeply rooted was the belief in the efficacy of magical practices and divinatory arts (II Kings 18:4; 23:4-24; II Chronicles 29:3-31:20; 34:1-7). Since plagues, diseases, and all sorts of disasters were attributed to demons and evil spirits (Psalm 78:49; 91:6; Isaiah 13:21; 30:6; 34:8-15), many people wore protective amulets to avoid them and almost everyone applied any remedy to placate them (Deuteronomy 32:17).

Not everyone did, however. The clamour of dissenting voices culminated in an intense power struggle between those who accepted occult practices in the name of God (YHWH) and those who applied them in the name of other deities. The former denounced the latter as 'false' through and through— false practitioners passing on false messages from false deities (Deuteronomy 32:16,17; Jeremiah 14:14; 27:9-10). Though both factions had shared a mutual antipathy for each other from the first, their enmity grew to the point where it dominated a political struggle for power on a national scale.

Adherents of YHWH condemned all occult practices that excluded YHWH as evil or abominable (Deuteronomy 18:9), as improper media of intercourse, as a prostitution of worship and as ritual fornication (Exodus 34:15-17; Leviticus 17:7; Isaiah 1:21; Jeremiah 2:20). These imprecations, delivered by the prophets of YHWH, made such an impact that they continued to influence Jewish society long after the event. The deep concern of these prophets with the social systems, religious institutions, and ritual practices of their time fated them to become architects responsible for the character and development of the Jewish religion. Their models and values established precedents and initiated patterns of behaviour and thought that have survived with little change to the present day.

Exile

And the Lord said: 'Because they have forsaken My law which I set before them, and have not obeyed My voice, or walked in accord with it, but have gone after the perverseness of their own heart, and after the Baals which their fathers taught them . . . I will feed this people with wormwood, and give them poisonous water to drink. I will scatter them among the nations whom neither they nor their fathers have known, and I will send the sword after them, until I have consumed them.'

Jeremiah 9:13-16

Normally, exile marks an interlude in the history of individuals, nations, and people. However, for countless generations of

Jews scattered all over the world, exile, *galuth*, represented a way of life and centuries of unfulfilled hope. It was a period that spanned over two and a half thousand years: from the Babylonian captivity in 586 BC to the establishment of the State of Israel in 1948. Exile subjected the Jewish people to the floodtide of world, rather than regional, events. It shaped the evolution of Judaism like floodtides shape the course of a river. Many scholars, in fact, identify the beginning of this dispersion as the event that distinguishes biblical religion from the rise of Judaism.

Separated from their homeland, their central Temple and place of worship, the Jews were forced to accept change in their religious and social institutions and practices. Synagogues replaced the national, spiritual centre in Jerusalem. Rabbis or scholars and teachers replaced prophets in interpreting how the Law should be applied to satisfy the conscience of the Jewish people. Rabbis also assumed in exile, the priestly role of leading worship in the synagogue. Their dual role destined them to act as intermediaries between Jews and their God and between Jews and their rulers.

At times Jews enjoyed jurisdiction over their own affairs; at other times they were denied such privileges and became subject to the state in which they lived. Alternating phases of relative freedom and rigid control accelerated the process of dispersion and the development of complex and closed communities of Jews each reflecting the unique circumstances in which they flourished or merely survived. One response to this fragmentation was the advent of different religious groups and sects representing different ways of coping with new circumstances. Another response was the collection and codification of scattered Jewish traditions.

This process continued for several centuries until all the collections attained the status of Scripture—the Bible. Meanwhile, the conception and development of an Oral Law enabled the Jews to reconcile conflicts arising between loyalty to traditions and adjustments demanded by the imperatives of survival.

It is not practical nor very useful in a book of this scope to examine every aspect of Jewish religious development during this long exilic span. What may be of some use is to identify a number of important developments in Judaism, especially those of far-reaching consequences.

One consequence was a preoccupation with the search for a meaning to explain the exile and another with speculation about its probable duration and the redemption of the Jewish homeland. In other words, Jewish thinkers throughout the centuries of exile were obsessed with two central questions: Why did the exile happen? How long was it going to last? Had God utterly forsaken His chosen people or was life on foreign soil to be of short duration?

Judaism had to come to terms with both issues and to reconcile responses to changing circumstances. The rationale in the early stages of exile differed from later interpretations. Among these were: the suggestion that the exile was a direct consequence of the sin committed by the 'chosen and holy' people of God of breaking the covenant; divine challenge, not sin, had caused the Jewish dispersion; God willed dispersion so that the Jewish people might actively participate in the restoration of a good society; dispersion and persecution were divine tests of faith, and so on. The search for a rational explanation of the exile was more than a preoccupation among Jewish thinkers. It became an obsession.

The conquest of the Middle East (336-323 BC) by Alexander the Great also influenced the subsequent development of Judaism. Under the impact of Alexander's successors, Greek culture, or Hellenism, became the adopted lifestyle of a large segment of the Jewish people. Jewish education, sports, theatres, and libraries, all attained a high level of Greek culture. This process of Hellenization went so far that in time many Jews, even pious ones no longer understood Hebrew. Consequently, a Greek translation of the Torah, known as the Septuagint, came to serve Hellenized Jews.

When King Antiochus III (247-187 BC) of Syria occupied Palestine in 198 BC, he determined to complete the process of Hellenization among non-conformists including stubborn Jews who resisted it. Then, in 168 BC, Antiochus IV (175-164 BC) declared Judaism illegal. As a result, he prohibited Jews, on pain of death, from keeping the Sabbath, from practising the rite of circumcision, and from owning copies of the Torah. Instead, he forced Jews to place the statue of Zeus in their national temple in Jerusalem and to worship the deity by offering pigs.

Horror and indignation among traditional Jews led to an open rebellion against the king. Mattathias, an aged Jewish priest, called on all Jews to return to the 'way of their fathers'. His five sons and a large number of supporters took up arms, occupied most of Jerusalem, and restored Jewish traditional religious practices—a triumph which is annually celebrated as the Feast of Hannukah.

In spite of this success, Hellenistic influences continued to pervade Judaic institutions especially its literature. Among others, the books of Ruth, Esther, Jonah, Job, and Ecclesiastes are thought to have made their appearance at this time. But the greatest and the most famous achievement of Hellenized Jewish literature is represented by the voluminous writings of Philo. Philo (*c*. 25 BC to *c*. AD 40), a native Alexandrian Jew, set himself the task of reconciling Jewish theology with Greek philosophy, particularly that of Plato. Three elements of Philo's thoughts are quite significant:

i) he interpreted the Torah symbolically, in the same way that Greek thinkers interpreted Homer's poems, the *Iliad* and the *Odyssey*;
ii) he formulated the concept of the divine Logos, the Word of divine Reason, identified also as 'the second God', and sometimes as 'the son of God' (a concept with far more compelling application later to Christianity than to Judaism);
iii) he determined the future character of philosophy, especially of Jewish, Christian and Muslim medieval philosophy, since he made philosophy the handmaiden of revelation.

Another important literary contribution by a Jewish author who betrays Hellenistic influences is embodied in the massive works of the historian Flavius Josephus (AD 37-100?). Josephus, or more appropriately, Joseph ben Matthias, was a native

Palestinian Jew of royal and priestly descent. His writings are basically defences of Judaism. His twenty-volume history of the Jews, entitled *Jewish Antiquities*, is considered a deliberate parallel of the work of the Greek Dionysius of Helicarnassus, *Roman Antiquities*. Similarly his *Jewish War* represents a Jewish counterpart to Thucydides' *History of the Peloponnesian War*.

This period is also distinguished by the appearance of various Jewish groups and parties. Members of the wealthy, aristocratic, and somewhat liberal Jewish group were known as the Sadducees. Their interest in disseminating Greek culture made them active Hellenizers. By contrast, another group of pious Jews known as Pharisees represented those whose main passion was the Jewish religion. They had no interest in Greek culture, much less in politics. They paid great attention to oral tradition, harnessed Messianic concepts to their hopes and aspirations, preached resurrection, and struggled against the fetters that bind people to human concerns rather than to God's.

Three other groups came into existence during the Roman domination of Palestine (63 BC to AD 640). The Herodians comprised one group which supported the Roman administration. Another group, the Zealots, opposed the Roman government because in their view submission to the Romans meant forsaking God. Recourse to the sword, they believed, might also hasten the Messiah's coming. The third group, called the Essenes, lived in a monastic commune, practised non-violence and awaited the end of the world at which time they believed they, as the 'sons of light', would triumph over the 'sons of darkness'. It is to this group that the famous Dead Sea Scrolls found near Qumran are attributed.

In AD 66, towards the end of Emperor Nero's reign, discontent of the Jews against the Romans broke into open rebellion. Despite the heroic resistance of the rebels, Rome finally triumphed. Amidst indescribable savagery and slaughter, Jerusalem was razed and the Temple set on fire. A last band of insurgents survived for three years in the mountain fortress of Masada. They held the Romans off until the prospect of starvation drove them to suicide.

One final attempt to liberate Palestine from Roman rule

followed in AD 132. It was led by Bar Kokhba, supported by Akiba, the greatest rabbi of the time. The uprising lasted for three years before the Romans dealt the blow which finally dispossessed the Jews. It represented a territorial loss they were not to recover till the establishment of the modern State of Israel in 1948.

The destruction of the national Temple in Jerusalem and the end of all hope for national independence now forced the Jews to turn their dynamism to the development and consolidation of their religious life. Rabbinic ideology and practice provided a unifying preoccupation among Jewish communities scattered throughout the Middle East and Europe. As most Jews withdrew into their tight, closed communities, one Jewish sectarian group grew, developed, and spread. Its members called themselves Christians.

Christianity was more positively disposed towards Hellenism than was rabbinic Judaism, thanks particularly to the leadership of Paul, a thoroughly Hellenized Jew. However, the percentage of Jews converted to Christianity was extremely small, as can be evidenced from the frequent references of Christian writers to the stubbornness of the Jews. The tenuous link that held early Christians within the orbit of Jewish religious and cultural traditions snapped under the strain created by four sources of enmity:

i)   the refusal of Christians to struggle against the Romans in Jerusalem in AD 70;
ii) the failure of Christians to support the Messianic leaders Lukuas-Andreas and Bar Kokhba in their revolts against the Romans in AD 115–117 and AD 132–135 respectively;
iii) a prayer against heretics among the Eighteen Benedictions introduced by Rabbi Gamaliel II Ben Simeon around AD 100;
iv) the tensions and animosities created by the teachings of Paul, particularly his teachings on God, the covenant, the Chosen People, and inherited sin.

Soon Christians greatly outnumbered Jews and Christianity became a political, as well as a spiritual, force. The result was catastrophic for Judaism. Christian states repressed Judaism; Christian theologians provided the rationale for their actions, and the Christian masses, for whom Christ died, salved their consciences by indicting the Jews for committing the crime of deicide.

Ostracized and defamed, Judaism thrust Christianity out of its orbit to demonstrate that it could prevail against the world, and that faith in God was proof against the hatred of its enemies and a firm bulwark to sustain human strength in spite of all adversity. Consequently, Jews came to cling with even greater tenacity to ancient traditions, particularly to the conviction that the Messiah was yet to come. The evidence seemed to them conclusive. As long as persecution and oppression were commonplace aspects of their everyday lives it was unthinkable to assume that the Messiah had come. Besides their expectation of the Messiah, what sustained them even more through their most trying years were their intellectual and religious activities, and the rabbinical record of what the Jews did and thought.

This record became, over the course of centuries, an enormous body of tradition. Starting from the simple Mosaic Law, it grew, by dint of repeated elaboration and interpretation, into innumerable collections of commentaries and codes. Today, these huge tomes of rabbinic law are known as Mishnah, Gemarah, Talmud, and Midrash. More will be said about these books in Chapter Four.

For a while, Jewish life and thought survived in pockets around the Mediterranean wherever leaders gathered adherents about them. But then, in the seventh century, a new Arabian faith, Islam, swept out of the desert to make an impact on Judaism as profound as it made on the rest of the known world.

After the death of their founder and prophet Mohammed, Muslim believers emerged from the deserts of Arabia to conquer the world. Invested with an irresistible power, these followers of Islam overran the once magnificent Persian and Roman empires, and in a very short time extended their faith eastward through India into China, and westward through North Africa into Spain. But though they were almost fanatical about their own convictions, Muslim rulers were tolerant of the beliefs of others. Instead of compelling their subjects to adopt Islam, Muslim conquerors were content to accept homage and heavy tribute.

Although Mohammed expelled and persecuted the Jews in Arabia, the policy of his successors, known as Caliphs, was liberal by comparison. Under Islamic rule, Jewish life went on unmolested for centuries. In fact, in the Islamic capital of Baghdad, Jews rose to positions of distinction and influence. Jewish secular authority was vested in an official known as the *Exilarch*, while spiritual authority resided in the *Gaon* (Eminence; plural *Geonim*), who was also the head (somewhat like a President) of the Jewish Academy in Baghdad.

Two important Jewish Academies existed in Babylon (modern Iraq) and the Geonim exercised their authority by virtue of their pre-eminence as teachers and expounders of the Talmud. It was the task of the Geonim to develop and determine principles regarding all matters—religious, civil, social and domestic. They attracted Jewish students from far and near, compiled legal codes and occupied themselves with fixing the order of divine worship.

One major achievement of the Jewish Academies was the 'standardization' of the Hebrew biblical text. A group of scholars known as Masoretes ('those who hand down') became specialists in assigning to the Hebrew biblical text vowel points, accents, symbols representing pronunciation, and interconnection of words, and in noting all the existing variants and peculiarities. The Masoretic texts of Babylon differed from those of Palestine only in their systems of vocalization and application of consonants.

Amidst all this unprecedented peace and freedom under Islamic rule the Jews could not leave well enough alone. A current of Jewish opposition developed against the supremacy of the Talmudic interpetation of Judaism. One formidable protest came in Syria in the eighth century from a Jew called Serene who created a focus for disaffection—anything but serenity. He identified himself as the long-awaited Messiah, divinely ordained to reclaim the Holy Land from the Muslims. He abolished several Talmudic regulations including dietary (kosher) laws, holy day observances, and domestic practices. Because he canalized disaffection adroitly, Serene gained the support of thousands of Jews; but his Messianic pretensions effectively ended when the Muslim Caliph Yazed II captured and turned him over to the local Jewish civil authorities for punishment.

Again, revolts took place during this period in Isfahan and Baghdad. Obaiah Abu Isa of Isfahan denied the authority of Talmudic Judaism, claimed he was the last of the five forerunners of the Messiah, and led his followers among Iranian Jews to believe that he had come to establish God's kingdom on earth. In Baghdad Anan Ben David vigorously denied the pretensions of Talmudic Judaism and founded a new sect which later became known as the Karaites or 'leaders of Scripture'. This new movement spread quickly to Egypt, Syria and south-east Europe, threatening the Talmudic status quo as the Judaic ideal of the supreme life.

The popularity of the Karaites was short-lived, eclipsed in the tenth century by the rise of a powerful champion of Talmudic Judaism. This Jewish champion was Saadiah Ben Joseph (AD 882-942) of Egypt. He disputed the principles expounded by Anan and the Karaites, defended the Talmudic cause and earned a reputation as a formidable literary and religious critic. His fame spread throughout the Jewish diaspora, particularly after he accepted the headship, as Gaon, of the Académy of Sura in Babylon. His contribution to Jewish philosophy is acknowledged by scholars, especially his claim that divinely revealed truth in Judaism is entirely based on reason. Since his time, mainstream Judaism has emphasized its character as a religion of reason.

Meantime a new centre of Jewish leadership had developed. This new centre was in Muslim Spain, where Jews had settled as early as the Carthaginian occupation and had lived in relative peace for a thousand years until AD 589, when the Visigoth King Reccared I accepted the Christian faith. Then, for over a century the Jews, along with other 'heretics' lived constantly in the shadow of Christian persecution. Restrictions imposed aginst them had the effect of undermining their economic life, depriving them of their personal possessions, prohibiting them from practising their faith, and reducing them to the status of slaves.

The Muslim invasion of Spain in AD 711 was welcomed by the Jews, and for the next seven centuries Spanish Jews were to become the leaders of worldwide Judaism. They entered the fields of government, science, medicine, philosophy, literature, and architecture, making some outstanding contributions. Little wonder that scholars identify this flowering of Jewish intellect in Muslim Spain as the Golden Age of Judaism.

The phenomenal prosperity of Jews in Muslim Spain produced a brilliant succession of Jewish scholars and philosophers. The first to introduce this long succession of distinguished Jews was Hasdai Ibn Shaprut (AD 912-961), whose most enduring achievement was the founding and financing of a Talmudic Academy in Cordoba. Soon this Academy became world famous and Jewish scholars came from all over Europe and the east to pursue their Talmudic studies. Hasdai's work was carried forward by another versatile Jew, Samuel Ibn Nagdela (AD 993-1069), whom his people called *Ha-Nagid*, the Prince. Among his scholarly works he wrote an introduction to the Talmud, and interpretations of Scripture stressing the importance of Torah and Mitzvot ('Observances' of Jewish Law) for the Jews.

Three other Jewish philosophers of Muslim Spain rank among the elite of Iberian Judaism. One was Solomon Ibn Gabirol (AD 1021-1069), who wrote several works, but whose genius is seen in a short philosophical treatise entitled *Fons Vitae* (The Fountain of Life), in which he develops his conceptions of God and the universe emanating from Him. Another was Judah Halevi (AD 1080-1140), whose poems survive in modern Jewish liturgy, including the poem for which he is most remembered—one he composed on the Holy Land of Israel. His words, which express his undying love for his people and for the land of Israel, were a continuing source of comfort and sustained the spirit of Judaism through centuries of difficulties. A third intellectual giant among giants was Moses Maimonides (AD 1135-1204), who earned the verdict: 'from Moses till Moses there arose none like Moses!' He fused Jewish tradition with Aristotelian ethics; he condensed the beliefs of Judaism into a formal creed of Thirteen Articles (though they came under attack following his death, their relevance is debated to this day); he underscored the social significance and absolute importance of Mitzvot; and he insisted that philosophy was absolutely necessary to reinforce the faith. Medieval scholars, such as Albertus Magnus and Thomas Aquinas, owe a debt of gratitude to Maimonides for his masterly analysis of the role of revelation and reason.

These few individuals represent a sampling of the intellectual power that contributed to the greatness and splendour of Jewish life and thought in Muslim Spain. However, these glorious days were soon to end. As rulers of Christian Europe slowly dislodged the Muslims, Jewish life deteriorated correspondingly. Jews became targets of Inquisitorial torture and persecution, mass hysteria, and insensate slaughter. Finally, in 1492, King Ferdinand and Queen Isabella decreed the expulsion of all unconverted Jews from Spain. Jewish converts to Christianity, known as *marranos* ('dirty fellows'), survived for centuries despised as Jews in spite of their overt conversion but practising their Jewish faith in secret. They had a long wait. It was not till 1969 that the edict of expulsion was finally revoked officially by the Spanish government.

Meanwhile, hundreds of thousands of Jews expelled from Spain settled in Turkey, Poland, and other East-European countries. Among them was a young boy, who was destined to establish a great reputation in Judaism. Joseph Karo (1488-1575) was born in Spain, grew up in Turkey, and died as a mystic in the Holy Land. His most outstanding contribution is the *Shulhan Arukh* ('Prepared Table'), a code book that outlines in minute detail the performance of Jewish Law, or Mitzvot. With some minor modifications made by Moses Isserles (1530-1572), the *Shulhan Arukh* has remained *the* code of traditional Judaic law.

The fate and destiny of Judaism in northern and western Europe were quite different from the experience of Jews in Muslim Spain. It can best be understood against the background of a Christian medieval society with an unenviable reputation for spawning and perpetuating a period identified, with some justice, as the Dark Ages. Constant warfare, endless power struggles, frenzied religious animosity disguised as Crusades, poverty and ignorance are the main characteristics of Christian medieval society, much as they are of Christian twentieth-century cultures. Kings, emperors, popes and people co-operated in plunging Jews into shame, despondency, degradation and oppression. Vicious propaganda and false accusations no less scurrilous than the worst excesses of Nazi Germany led the public to hate, riot, and burn Jews and their possessions. Time and again Jews were expelled from their adopted homelands: England (1290), France (1306, 1322, 1394), Germany (1348), Austria (1421). Pope Paul IV (1555-1559) was the first to impose the restrictions of the ghetto upon the Jews. The first Jewish community identified as a ghetto was in Venice in 1516. By the end of the sixteenth century there was scarcely a city or a province in Europe where Jews were not herded together in ghettos.

And yet, in spite of these indignities, West-European Jews also produced some remarkable masters of Judaism. Gershom Ben Judah (AD 960-1040), Gaon of the Academy in Mainz, expounded the intricacies of the Talmud so well that he earned for himself the title, 'Light of the Exile', while his ordinances were accepted as binding by all West-European Jews. Another outstanding scholar was Rabbi Solomon Ben Isaac, familiarly known as Rashi (AD 1040-1105), who wrote commentaries on both the Bible and the Talmud which to this day are sources of reference in all Jewish Academies. Europe, too, produced the 'world's greatest speculative thinker', also a Jew, though his timing was poor. Baruch (Benedict) Spinoza (AD 1632-1677) was ostracized from his community for his opinions on God, on the imperfectibility of the Bible, and on freedom of thought in religion and philosophy. It was centuries before his views were accepted by Reform Jews and Christian theologians.

The fate of Jews settling in East-European countries following the Spanish expulsion ranged from well-being to mass murder and pogroms. At first, Jews were accorded freedom of movement and of enterprise. In Poland, for instance, they obtained the right to self-government. Rabbis were recognized by most governments as chief administrators of Jewish communities. A large number of Jews assumed power and prestige as financiers and as overseers of the estates of Christian nobles.

The status of Jews was therefore secure as long as governments were secure, but there are risks attendant on associating with power holders and brokers. The rich exploited the poor and Jewish entrepreneurs tended to serve the rich. A lunatic fringe of self-acclaimed Jewish Messiahs and mystics did little to offset the image of the affluent and acquisitive Jew.

The inevitable outcome of exploitation was the Cossack uprising of 1648 led by Bogdan Chmielnicky. Villages were uprooted; houses and castles were torn down stone by stone; the Polish gentry were hunted down and then flayed alive or sawed or burnt; Catholic priests and Jews were hanged from trees. Indiscriminate rape, pillage, murder, and mass slaughter spread everywhere, in villages and in towns. A year later Chmielnicky entered Kiev in triumph, massacring the entire community, including its Jewish population.

Jewish life under the Russian Czars was not much better. Severe social and economic restraints, legal disabilities, misery, bloody riots, massacres, and pogroms constantly afflicted Russian Jews. Judaism all across seventeenth-century Europe was at its lowest ebb. Religion had degenerated into superstition, learning into a mass of corrupted formulae, and Messianic imposters made incredible claims and attracted large Jewish followings.

Yet, the spark of Judaism was not completely extinguished. Three great individuals, each appealing to a different element, gave Judaism its required boost. These remarkable individuals were Israel Baal Shem (1700-1760), founder of Hasidism; Elijah Ben Solomon (1720-1779), who advocated some far-reaching reforms in Judaism; and Moses Mendelssohn (1729-1786), whose writings, though vigorously attacked in his time, hastened the day of enlightenment and emancipation among Jews.

Settlement in the New World gave many Jews the opportunity to escape the miseries of Europe. It is believed that in 1654 twenty-three Jews were among the first settlers in New Amsterdam (renamed New York by the British in 1664). In the fullness of time, the Founding Fathers of America, following in the true spirit of enlightenment, paved the way for social justice, equal rights, and religious freedom. Without surrendering their faith, Jews became, together with the dispossessed of the far east and west, citizens of the United States of America. In the 1800s millions of Jews left Europe, particularly eastern Europe, to settle in the United States of America. The fulfilment of the aspirations of such immigrant Jews on American soil coincides with the modern era of emancipation for all types of people—an era of new theological movements and new religious patterns in the life of Judaism.

Emancipation

To Jews as individuals we shall give everything; to Jews as a nation, nothing.

Clermont Tonnère (1751-1815)

The quotation attributed to Tonnère, Whoremaster to the Imperial Court of Napoleon, identifies with some precision the dilemma that faced world Jewry at the dawn of the Age of Enlightenment in the eighteenth century. On the one hand Jews were beneficiaries among all oppressed minorities of the emancipating influences of enlightenment. On the other hand, they were not ready for the sudden dissolution of the ghetto mentality which had served to make them a people apart. They had no alternative to the ghetto and the special status imposed on them by an indifferent world—no homeland, no fortress, no sceptred isle. As Tonnère implied, enlightenment promised no rose garden.

Starting first in the Netherlands and England, the Enlightenment reached France, where discontent gave place to violence, culminating in the Revolution of 1789. The movement then spread rapidly to Germany and other European countries. The effects of emancipation upon Jews as well as on all conditions of men and women are still felt today in all walks of modern life.

The forces of enlightenment and emancipation revolutionized, if they did not entirely shatter, the basis of Jewish life and thought. To most Jews, political emancipation meant access to the rights and privileges of full citizenship in the countries of their adoption. This liberty and freedom, though they had the effect of making every Jew part of a national team, meant loss of ethnic solidarity and religious autonomy. As long as Jews were classed as outsiders, Jewish society was segregated, governed by a classical legal tradition prescribing study of the Torah, and resigned to living among gentile nations on foreign soil pending a return to the Holy Land. The most dramatic consequences of emancipation on this society were acceptance and rapid assimilation. Traditional religious values were undermined, rabbinic status and authority were challenged, existing institutions lost adherents and members, ancient forms of worship were consigned to oblivion as outmoded, and the study of Torah and observance of Mitzvah were questioned.

The powerful current of modern secularization that bore heavily on every religion forced many Jews to abandon Judaism and the Jewish people. Other Jews rejected Judaism on the grounds that it was a useless and dead religion without denying their identity as Jews or their association with the Jewish people. They sought instead, a new meaning in being Jewish.

Judaism survived the onslaught of these modern agents of erosion because new champions stood ready to step into the breach. One of the most aggressive champions to buttress ramparts crumbling against the secular flood was the German-Jewish socialist Moses Hess (1812-1875). In his classic work, *Rome and Jerusalem*, he identified historical evidence for his confidence in the indestructibility of Jewish nationality. He argued, in fact, that the only salvation for Judaism was Jewish nationality:

It is only with a national rebirth that the religious genius of the Jews, like the giant of the legend touching Mother Earth, will be endowed with new strength and again be inspired with the prophetic spirit. No aspirant of Enlightenment (Haskala), not even a Mendelssohn, has so far succeeded in crushing the hard shell with which Rabbinism has encrusted Judaism, without at the same time destroying the national ideal in its innermost essence.[1]

The idea of an inseparable relationship between religion and nationality, that is, between Judaism and the Jewish people, was developed further by the German-Jewish neo-Kantian philosopher, Hermann Cohen (1842-1918). He held that the fulfilment of the Messianic ideal, whatever form it might take, would have the effect of maintaining the existence of the Jewish people, not necessarily the acquisition of a distinct territory, nor the creation of a separate Jewish state. He did not dismiss the proposition that Jews represented both a religious community and a secular nation, but he sharply distinguished between nationality and nationhood. The latter had reference to a political unity with a specific territory; the former to a unifying biological and historical heritage. This unifying heritage rather than a cosmic champion or event was the medium through which the Jewish people were to maintain their nationality within existing political systems as witnesses of the Messianic ideal.

One of the most significant influences on contemporary Jewish theology is Franz Rosenzweig (1886-1929). Drawing on the Hegelian philosophy that history is a constant process of unfolding, particularly the unfolding of the Absolute, Rosenzweig explained Christianity as it related to Judaism from a completely new perspective. He argued that humanity is ever moving towards God, and that Christianity was an agent or a vehicle in this historical process. In evidence, he cited John 14:6: 'No one comes to the Father, except through me.' This conviction, Rosenzweig claimed, provides the challenge for Christians who believe that no one comes to God except through Christ. But, he added, those who are already with the Father, namely the Jews, have no need of Christ, the intermediary, since their pilgrimage to God is already complete. The existence of Jews, Rosenzweig concluded, is in itself proof that humanity can come to God just as the Jews did thousands of years ago.

To this original and radical theology, Rosenzweig added yet another significant interpretation of Judaism. He pictured the cosmos as a triangle with God at the apex and humans and the world at the base. The three dynamic forces of evolution he considered to be creation, revelation and redemption. The harmonious interaction between these forces, still incomplete among the rest of humanity, is complete in Judaism. So Rosenzweig named the process and his book *Star of Redemption*.

An individual who influenced Christian theology as much as Jewish theology was Martin Buber (1878-1965). He regarded Judaism as a communal model of the universal I–Thou relationship—a relationship which identifies active dialogue between human beings as dialogue with God. In other words, person-to-person contacts associated with daily activity express an I–Thou relation with the Eternal Thou. Buber's interpretation of nationalism is an outcome of his philosophic formulation. He maintained that in order for Jews to achieve the I–Thou ideal in full measure they needed their own land, Israel, and the co-operation of all peoples and nations on the basis of equality and brotherhood. It was a vision that ignored Talmudic teaching. Mitzvot (the observance of Jewish practices) was irrelevant to the kind of society Buber advocated.

Naturally, these four thinkers were not the only Jews to document their responses to the effects on Judaism of the modern period of Emancipation. Leo Baeck (1873-1956), Abraham Heschel (1907-1972), Mordecai Kaplan (1881-1984), and many others debated the merits of various responses to the challenges created for adherents of Judaism by modernity. The result reflected different ways of adjusting old and traditional patterns to accommodate new ideas and gave rise to several new religious movements in Judaism, such as Reform, Neo-Orthodoxy and Conservatism. The lives of all religious people, including Jews, was in some measure affected by the compulsion to defend and justify beliefs and strongly held convictions against the pragmatic scepticism of modern science.

This compulsion led to the establishment of rabbinical seminaries for the training of qualified spiritual leaders. Today many of these seminaries, mainly located in Israel, Europe and the Americas, have grown into great institutions of learning and occupy a unique role in the religious and spiritual life of millions of Jews.

One of the most difficult issues for Jewish religious apologists to address in the new climate of political and intellectual emancipation was, and still is, the significance of revelation, particularly the credibility and authenticity of the Bible. Modern biblical criticism has tended to undermine the dogmatic Talmudic assumption that every word and every letter in the Bible was revealed by God to Moses on Mount Sinai, and that later tradition, oral and written, was guided by divine inspiration. It was an assumption challenged at least in part by the comparative study of religion which called into question the uniqueness of many of the ideas, ethics, and practices described in the Bible, since close parallels were found to have existed also in several ancient Near-Eastern religious traditions.

In addition to such intellectual problems, the consequences of repeated changes to political and social institutions within the space of a decade or less have created stresses and tension for all people no less than the Jews. Formerly, Jews had lived in isolation in both Christian and Muslim controlled countries. Obedience to Jewish religious and cultural observances encouraged a considerable degree of segregation from non-Jews. Non-Jews very often imposed it. With the advent of social and political emancipation, many Jews, quite understandably, questioned the justification for continued segregation. Nobody consciously chooses to play the role of social pariah except saints and criminals. The Jews were no exception. They viewed segregation as an obstacle to complete social integration.

Finally, the mobility of world populations is forcing Judaism to confront a new global challenge: the principle of religious pluralism. Dialogue with Christian, Muslim, Hindu, Buddhist and other religions has begun and progress is being made in spite of difficulties, historical as well as theological. The initiative for such interchanges was conceived by individual Christians, but was formally adopted first by Roman Catholics at the end of the Council of Vatican II, 1962-1964, and then by the World Council of Churches (composed of Protestant, Anglican and Orthodox Churches) in 1971.

Based on mutual recognition, respect and love, dialogue is seen by many, including Jews, as one of the true achievements of this age. Indeed, the Vatican II decree reveals a profound concern with Jewish beliefs and offers a great deal of hope. Nevertheless, Jewish reaction to the document ranges from approval to reservation—from disappointment to apprehension.

Apprehension is implied by some of the questions Jews raise: What is the purpose of dialogue? Is there an ulterior motive? Are Jews eventually to be converted through this subtle pressure? Others, however, consider the declaration of Vatican II as being of utmost importance in combating anti-Semitism and welcome inter-religious dialogue in order to explore and to resolve the deep-rooted differences among various religious traditions.

Genocide

At times, it is true, one's heart could break in sorrow. But often too, preferably in the evening, I cannot help thinking that Ernie Levy, dead six million times, is still alive somewhere, I don't know where . . . Yesterday, as I stood in the street trembling in despair, rooted to the spot, a drop of pity fell from above upon my face; but there was no breeze in the air, no cloud in the sky . . . there was only a presence.

A. Schwarz-Bart, *The Last of the Just*[2]

The modern historical event that dominates Jewish theology is the destruction of millions of Jews under the direction of the German leader Adolf Hitler and his cohorts during World War II. The accumulated venom of centuries of hatred against the Jews was released to accomplish genocide. It was well planned, systematically implemented and carefully recorded by Nazi bureaucracy.

The magnitude of the slaughter beggars imagination and the methodical search for effective techniques of routine extermination defies rational explanation. Jews refer to this demonic design as 'the Holocaust' (i.e., immolation by fire, total destruction). 'Auschwitz' has come to symbolize to them the several extermination camps where the plan was executed. These camps, where the infamous gas chambers stood ready to receive their victims, were terminals for trainloads of European Jews.

Those who died on the way in the cattle cars, where they

stood squeezed together without food or drink, were more fortunate than those who finally arrived at the extermination camps. These victims were herded in front of the chemical plants, made to strip and then crowded into the gas chambers. Corpses were retrieved with hooks, stacked together like piles of wood and dumped into the ovens of the crematoria, or rendered down for the manufacture of by-products like soap.

In all recorded history, only two groups of people, the Armenians and the Jews, have been victims of attempts at total annihilation on such a scale. The Jewish genocide followed on the heels of the Armenian genocide, which had occurred under the direction of the Turkish leader Mustafa Kemal Attaturk during World War I. Wholesale massacre is not unique to the human experience, but these two genocides—deliberate attempts to exterminate a whole race or nation—are unparalleled. They were not calamities suffered in consequence of resistance or insurrection but rather the result of well-devised, premeditated plans of demonic individuals. And ironically, both genocides occurred in the age of 'Enlightenment and Emancipation' following the 'barbaric' age, but perhaps only because the barbarians lacked the technology and organization for wholesale slaughter.

Genocide has shaken both Jewish and Armenian existence to the core. Both suffered irreparable loss. Worse still, the memory of degradation and loss persists as a permanent national scar.

It is true that the Jewish genocide weighed heavily upon the conscience of Western governments and Christian peoples. They have attempted to make material and moral reparation in an effort to restore the dignity of the Jewish people among the nations of the world, but their trial by fire and the sword has had spiritual as well as material implications for many Jews. A new generation of Jewish theologians is trying to come to grips with this most shattering event in the history of the 'Chosen People'. They cannot help speculating whether or not God has abrogated His covenant with the Jewish people, the very people whom He chose as His Elect.

Eminent Jewish philosophers dismiss this theology of despair as fruitless introspection. They argue that God's purpose lies beyond the limits of mere human logic and reason. They remind their people instead of their traditional role: to serve as witnesses to the living God even when His purpose, in human terms, seems incomprehensible. To many modern Jewish thinkers, the Jewish will to live and to reclaim the land of Israel bears vibrant testimony to their continued trust in the living God. In the words of Emil Fackenheim:

Why hold fast to mere Jewishness? Because Jewish survival after Auschwitz is not 'mere' but in itself and without any further reasons or theological justifications a sacred testimony to all mankind that life and love, not death and hate, shall prevail.[3]

Not all modern Jews share the philosophy of Fackenheim. The American Jewish writer and journalist Elie Wiesel points to the insurmountable contradictions in the theology of the Jewish genocide. In his opinion Judaism must believe and the Jewish people must live, but 'holocaust literature there cannot be. Auschwitz negates all literature as it negates all theories and doctrines . . . the concept of a Jewish theology of Auschwitz is blasphemous for both the non-believer and believer . . .'[4]

Jewish attempts to understand and interpret genocide theology stem from their inner perception of God, Covenant and the redemption of humanity. Yet, it is naïve to expect that the response of Jewish theologians will be identical. Their responses are still, by and large, tentative and far from unanimous. Some adopt the existentialist outlook of Martin Buber, Franz Rosenzweig and Leo Baeck. Others espouse the naturalism propounded by Mordecai Kaplan, founder of Reconstructionism. Then, there are some on whom the genocide has made such an impact that their conclusions are deeply pessimistic. One such is the American Jewish theologian, Richard Rubenstein.

In his works, *After Auschwitz* and *The Cunning of History: Mass Death and the American Future*, Rubenstein insists that the genocide proves that the traditional Talmudic belief—that the Jewish God is the God of history and that the Jewish people have been elected to promote justice and peace in the world—is in error. Auschwitz proves that humanity remains savage and cannot be improved. Throughout human history dominant groups have found ways to exterminate non-conforming segments of the masses they dominated. The Nazis employed the most efficient method with a wholly detached and highly effective bureaucracy. In the light of this genocide, Rubenstein argues, it is horrifying to imagine what instruments improved technology may place at the disposal of future despots to accomplish the liquidation of people they see as a threat to their security. Consequently, Jews ought to forsake the God of history and return to the God of nature. This is archaic 'paganism', which includes all the festivals of sacred moments throughout the seasons of the year. In his words:

The European catastrophe marks the death of the God of history . . . In the religion of nature, a historical, cyclical religion, man is once more at home with nature and its divinities, sharing their life, their limits, and their joys . . . An insightful paganism, utilizing the forms of traditional Jewish religion, is the only meaningful religious option remaining to Jews after Auschwitz and the rebirth of Israel.[5]

The atrocities perpetrated against the Jews throughout the centuries, including the genocide of the twentieth century, represent the most tragic examples of inhumanity in recorded history. In contrast, the indestructibility of the spirit, culture, and civilization of the Jewish people also presents a lasting testimony.

Return

Thus says the Lord: I have returned to Zion and will dwell in the midst of Jerusalem; and Jerusalem shall be called a city of truth . . .

Behold, I will save My people from the east country and from the west country; and I will bring them and they shall dwell in the midst of Jerusalem; and they shall be My people, and I will be their God, in truth and in righteousness.

Zechariah 8:3-8

The year 1948 marks one of the turning points in the history of the Jewish people. Nineteen hundred years of exilic life characterized by intermittent and unpredictable intervals of hatred, mass execution, expulsion, and persecution were vindicated by the establishment of the State of Israel. A field of magnetic forces drew all the scattered elements together.

The yearning for national freedom from intolerable pressures, the search for meaning and spiritual vitality, the Messianic ideal, and the Zionist Movement were mainsprings of the State of Israel.

Zionism as a movement is a new phenomenon in Jewish life. True, longing for a return to Zion is an old religious refrain, dating back to the days of Jewish exile in the sixth century BC. But the founders of modern Zionism stressed the national concentration of the Jews in a secular state, stripped of traditional Messianic ideals. Inspired by nineteenth-century European nationalism, Zionism represented an attempt to transform the Jews from rootless, nomadic wanderers in hostile lands to a nation with a territorial base or native homeland like all other nations.

Hence, even though Zionism was nurtured in the soil of religious idealism, its contemporary expression was a blend of three elements: exile, with all its pains and sufferings; nationalism, in all its modern manifestations; and a secular form of messianism which interpreted the kingdom of God in economic and social terms, something like the 'Social-Gospel' movement in Christianity. Zionism, then, was born as a political movement to create a Jewish state.

Jewish longing for a return to the ancient homeland in Palestine is not new. Ever since the destruction of their political state by the Roman legions in the first century AD, Jews had lamented the loss of their glorious Zion and prayed for its quick restoration—a prayer that so dominated their thinking that it passed into their liturgy. Each year at the Passover festival and on High Holy Days they concluded with the words symbolic of their hope: Next year in Jerusalem!

This age-old sentimental attachment to their ancient homeland came to be more symbolic than a real expectation for most Jews until the revival of anti-Semitism in the nineteenth century became widespread in Europe. While some Jews hoped that the phenomenon of anti-Semitism would soon spend itself, others seethed with excitement at the prospect of initiating a Jewish nationalist movement.

In the forefront of the most aggressive exponents of Jewish nationalism was Leo Pinsker (1821-1891) who proclaimed that the only valid responses to anti-Semitism and intolerable persecution were self-emancipation and national independence. Asher Ginzberg (1856-1927), more popularly known by his pen name, Ahad Ha-Am (One of the People), added his voice even before Pinsker's fell silent. Ginzberg elaborated on the same theme. No people could be creative culturally or spiritually unless they had their own land. He pleaded for the restoration of Palestine as a centre for Jewish life and religion. But the founder of a political movement that was to culminate in 'the creation of a Jewish, internationally recognized homeland in Palestine' was Theodor Herzl (1860-1904).

Under the leadership of Herzl, Jewish nationalism ceased to be a dream. It soon materialized as an organized world movement with political aspirations and it was one of his supporters, Nathan Birnbaum (1864-1937) who, in 1892, coined the name 'Zionism' for the movement inaugurated by Herzl. In 1895 Herzl published his ideas in *Judenstaat* (*The Jewish State*) and two years later, in 1897, the first Zionist Congress convened in Basel, Switzerland.

No sooner was the movement launched than it met strong opposition from other Jews. Some interpreted 'political' Zionism as a betrayal of political loyalty to the country to which they pledged their allegiance as full-fledged citizens. Others opposed it because they distrusted the political goals of Zionist leaders and the effect their policies would have on the religious life and practice of Jews. But many adopted Abraham Isaac Kook's (1868-1935) ambivalent view, namely that even though Zionism was infected with a secular bacterium it was, in the final analysis, 'religious at heart'.

Controversy associated with the idea of a Jewish state persisted until 1917 when, at the initiative of Chaim Weizman (1874-1952), Great Britain pledged itself, under the terms of the Balfour Declaration, to create a 'national home' for the Jews in their ancestral homeland. Thirty-one years later, on 14 May,

1948, the Zionist leader David Ben Gurion declared the establishment of the State of Israel. The vision conjured by the prophets, the longing it inspired among the Jewish masses, and Herzl's dream, were all fulfilled after over two thousand years of exile.

The majority of the founders of the State of Israel were non-religious socialists. But concessions had to be made to resident Orthodox rabbis (a different breed from their neo-Orthodox Western brethren), who had maintained the Jewish presence in Palestine for centuries, both during the rule of the Ottoman Empire and later under the British mandate. These Orthodox rabbis refused to accept any change and clung inflexibly to their local traditions. As a result immigrant Jews found themselves isolated at first because they were denied equal status with the resident Orthodox Jew. Through a series of compromises, an unusual phenomenon emerged in the State of Israel: an Orthodox rabbinate with political power in a State governed by non-religious Jews. Through its party representatives in the Knesset, Israel's governing body, this Orthodox group still exerts a significant influence in preserving the religious status quo.

The establishment of the State of Israel created yet another religious difficulty: the distrust of Muslims and Christians towards Jews and Judaism. The sources of this distrust were as much historical as they were religious and political. Suffice it to say that, while some Christians hailed the return of the Jews to their ancestral homeland and readily entrusted the care of the holy shrines in Jerusalem and elsewhere to the Jews, other Christian groups felt a sense of loss. This sense of loss was even more acute for Muslims, exacerbated, as it still is, by the problems and the tensions associated with Arab refugees. Unquestionably, these tensions are going to be factors in the future development of Judaism. Whether or not the people in the Golden Crescent at the head of the Mediterranean are prepared to eliminate stereotype misconceptions of each other remains to be seen.

Judaic Groups

There is indeed no other way to become completely Jewish . . . All recipes, whether Zionist, orthodox, or liberal, produce caricatures of men, that become more ridiculous the more closely the recipes are followed . . .

Franz Rosenzweig, On Being A Jewish Person[6]

Like the adherents of most other religions, the adherents of Judaism fall something short of complete unanimity. Some time during the Graeco-Roman period, a number of sects emerged which survived until the destruction of the Jewish Temple in Jerusalem in AD 135. In recent years a whole literature has grown up about four of these groups: the Pharisees, the Sadducees, the Essenes and the Zealots—all of them confined to the area now associated with Israel, Jordan and Lebanon. During the Middle Ages several new important groups evolved in Europe, including the Sefardim, the Ashkenazim, the Karaites, the Kabbalists and the Hasidics. These in turn gave way in modern times to several more groups, the most important ones being: Reform, Neo-Orthodox, Conservative and Reconstruction Jews.

In addition to these groups divided on doctrinal lines are numerous smaller sects within Judaism distinguished by national or cultural differences: the sects in Yemen, in Ethiopia, in India, in China and in various other parts of the world. All these groups are widely divided in terms of beliefs and practices. A sampling of some of them follows in order to illustrate the differences between the most important groups.

Sadducees and Pharisees: The two groups that dominated Judaism during the Graeco-Roman period were the Pharisees and the Sadducees. The Sadducees prided themselves on being descendants of Zadok, the priest who anointed the biblical Solomon as King of the Jews, hence their name, a corruption of Zadokites. Members of the Sadducees were wealthy, aristocratic, fanatically nationalistic, and religiously conservative. They were also distinguished by their rejection of almost everything the Pharisees held sacred: the validity of an oral Torah; the inspiration of the Prophetic Books of the Bible; the providential guidance of the universe; belief in angels, and apocalyptic convictions such as the resurrection of the dead and retribution in a life hereafter. To the Sadducees, God was essentially a tribal, national God, the God of the Jews, whereas the Pharisees recognized God as the God of all humanity. Consequently, the Sadducees developed an intense and aggressive spirit of nationalism.

The Pharisees derived their name from the Hebrew term *Perushim*, meaning the 'Separatists' or the 'Puritans'. They became gradually reconciled to the Roman occupation and the futility, short of divine intervention, of forcing the Romans to go home. As a result, they withdrew from politics, after several unsuccessful revolts, and were content to devote themselves to the study of Torah. This gave rise to two Sanhedrins, supreme national governing councils: one political and the other religious. The twenty-three members of the political and civil Sanhedrin were comprised primarily of Sadducees. Political issues, particularly relations with the Roman State and foreign affairs, were the concern of the Sadducees. The seventy members of the religious Sanhedrin, which was presided over by the High Priest, came largely from among the Pharisees. All religious and moral matters were adjudicated by the religious Sanhedrin.

Though their temporal powers were limited, it was the Pharisees, not the Sadducees, who exerted the most basic and lasting impact on the evolution of Judaism. While the Sadducees and all other sects contemporary with them declined and vanished after the destruction of the Temple, the heritage of the Pharisees endured. Jews have revered the Pharisees throughout history, especially since the rabbis idealized them and saw themselves as heirs of Pharisaical tradition epitomized by Shammai and Hillel who were influential some twenty-five years or so before Christ. They were rivals of contrasting temperaments but it is Hillel who is remembered as the living embodiment of the golden rule: do not unto others that which is hateful to you.

Essenes: In contrast to the national-religious ideologies of the Sadducees and the Pharisees, the Essenes held apocalyptic beliefs—that the world was coming to an end and that life should be a preparation for it. Little is known of the Essenes, except that they lived in isolated, secluded communities in the neighbourhood of the Dead Sea. From documents known as the Dead Sea Scrolls discovered in 1947 at Qumran, near the Dead Sea, it seems that the Essenes adhered strictly to the letter of biblical law and that their observances were accordingly marked by extreme rigorism. They practised a rigid asceticism which excluded marriage and normal human intercourse and attached fanatical importance to daily ritual purification. They shared their possessions and, in complete silence, ate their meals together. We only know this much because the Essenes were indefatigable writers. They wrote on scrolls; they wrote hymns, apocalyptic materials, commentaries on portions of the Bible, and a Manual of Discipline for members.

One characteristic of Essene belief is interesting because it is reflected in later Judaic and Christian theology. The Essenes believed in dualism—the conflict between two opposing spirits in the universe: a 'good' spirit and a contrasting 'evil' spirit symbolized by light and darkness, or truth and error. The dualism of the Essenes presupposed that both these spirits are under the supreme rule of God who eventually awards victory to the good spirit after its lengthy cosmic battle against the forces of evil. The Essenes taught that human beings, who are completely evil, can be redeemed by being admitted into the Essene community and by adhering to the rigid discipline dictated by the sect. Two 'anointed' Messiahs—a priest and a king—were to apear at the end of time to bring about God's triumph.

Modern scholars have difficulty in fully evaluating the role and function of the Essenes and the influence they may have exerted on Judaic and Christian theology. Some interpret the dualistic concept espoused by the Essenes as the product of Zoroastrian influences. Some have tried to establish a link between the Essenes and the teaching of John the Baptist. Still others have suggested a relationship between early Christian mystics, the Gnostics, and the Essenes. Whatever the final consensus is, one thing is certain: the Essenes were a Jewish monastic community that was in existence before and during the time of Christ. Since their creed proscribed procreation, the survival of their communities depended on a steady influx of disaffected members from other Jewish groups.

Zealots: The Zealots were a priestly order founded some time in the first decade after the birth of Christ. They were eschatologically oriented which means that they were preoccupied with last things: death, judgement, heaven, and hell. They had much in common with the Essenes, but the Zealots substituted passion for introspection, the sword for the quill, and aggression for withdrawal. While the Essenes were prepared to wait stoically for the world to end, the Zealots never appeared loath to accelerate the process when circumstances seemed to invite their active intervention.

The Zealots refused to acknowledge the Roman Government or to pay tribute to it on the grounds that God alone was their Master. Their watchword was: 'No God but YHWH, no tax but to the Temple, no friend but the Zealot.' Dedicated to keeping the Jewish Temple and its cult pure from all foreign defilement, they advocated the overthrow of the Roman legions and resorted to guerrilla tactics to this end. Finally, fired by national and religious pride, a group of Zealots captured the clifftop fortress of Masada from the Roman garrison, put them to the sword, and held the fortress for almost three years after the fall of Jerusalem in AD 70. The imperial legions, however, placed them under siege. When starvation reduced the beleagured survivors to impotence, all the men, women and children—about 967 of them—committed suicide rather than fall into the hands of the Romans.

Sefardim (Sephardim): The medieval world was divided into two main branches of Judaism: Sefardic and Ashkenazic. One group of Jewish people, who followed the route of Roman legions into Italy, Germany, France, Britain, and East European countries, established great learning centres in Germany, Poland, and Russia. They came to be identified as the achievement of Ashkenazic Jews. Their descendants constitute the majority of east and west European Jews. Another group of Jewish people followed the advance of Islam in the seventh century and established great cultural and intellectual centres in North Africa and Spain. The name they adopted, Sefardim, means the people from Spain. It was their influence that dictated the choice of their Hebrew dialect as the official language of the State of Israel.

Sefardic developments, especially in Muslim Spain, generated a fever of literary creativity in Jewish cultural and religious life. Just as the Muslim savants traced the source of Islamic power to the vitality of the Arabic language and the Qur'an (the Muslim Scripture), so also did Jewish scholars attribute their insights to their philological mastery of their own heritage: the Hebrew Bible. What distinguished the Sefardic scholars from previous Jewish intellectuals was their critical and rational examination and assessment of hallowed texts and traditional doctrines uninhibited by taboos and rigid dogma. This unprecedented ferment of religious creativity was the justification for identifying the period as 'the Golden Age' of Jewish literature.

The salient trends of Sefardic Judaism yielded fresh insights into Hebrew morphology (the study of language forms) and biblical prophecy. This in turn stimulated comparative philological and exegetical research (the study of scriptural literature and exposition) resulting in biblical grammar that has survived unchallenged to this day. Liturgical and secular poetry achieved a level of distinction which has seldom been matched since. Among these enduring achievements perhaps the most significant contributed by the Sefardic scholars was the redefinition of religious faith in the light of Greek and Arab philosophical theories. Henceforth, philosophic inquiry became a common attribute of Rabbinic Judaism.

Ashkenazim: The term Ashkenazim like the term Sefardim is a collective noun, not an adjective, identifying the people of a particular geographical region—in this case, Europe.

The destiny of this branch of Judaism can be fully understood against the background of medieval Christian society. Developing independently and along quite different lines from the Sefardim, Ashkenazim regarded their own heritage from a perspective shaped exclusively by rabbinic interpretations. The interaction of Jew and Christian, unlike the interaction between

Jew and Muslim, provoked discord instead of harmony, the hardening of intellectual arteries rather than the free, full flow of ideas. The bloody upheavals of the First Crusade (1096-1099) unleashed a tide of hatred and violence against Jewish communities and the imposition of restraints on their freedom which forced the leaders of the Ashkenazic group to fall back on their own resources and their deeply ingrained traditions.

Thus, isolated from the mainstream of society, bobbing little enclaves drowned in an ocean of surging Christians, Ashkenazim immersed themselves in study of the Torah and Mitzvot. Occasionally Ashkenazic rabbis gathered in regional synods to enact legislation on problems for which there was no adequate precedent in the Bible or the Talmud. Their decisions were binding in the community, at home, in the market place and in the synagogue. Amongst the most enduring measures were the circumvention of laws against usury and against the traffic of wines with non-Jews; the adoption of severe disciplinary measures against men who abandoned their wives or divorced them arbitrarily; and the excommunication of those who informed or appealed to non-Jewish authorities in judgements involving Jews. It was a record of sorts but nothing to compare with the intellectual flowering characteristic of Sefardic Spain.

By the middle of the twelfth century, Ashkenazic leaders had evolved indigenous cultural and religious traits. These ranged from popular pietism to esoteric interpretations of divine nature and glory. For the Jewish masses, liturgical poetry, biblical tales, lives of scholars and saints comprised a body of teaching calculated to reaffirm God's choice of the Jews and His plan of Messianic redemption.

Karaites: The Karaite movement was initiated at about the middle of the eighth century by an unsuccessful and therefore embittered candidate for the Exilarchate, the political leadership of the Babylonian Jewish community. His name was Anan Ben David and he set the entire Jewish world on its ear and threatened it with complete disintegration. He successfully organized an anti-rabbinic movement, named it Karaites, meaning literally 'Readers of Scripture', because he renounced the Talmud as a spurious invention of the rabbis and insisted on exclusive adherence to Scripture (Old Testament).

The inevitable effect of rejecting Talmudic law, rules, and regulations in favour of ad hoc interpretations of Scripture was an invitation to disaster. The result was an anarchy of conflicting religious observances, even a division among Karaite communities on the ordering of the religious calendar.

Karaite Judaism differed from rabbinic Judaism not so much in matters of theology as in matters of religious practice. Keeping to the strict letter of the Scripture, Karaite literalism burdened life with rigorous restraints and restrictions. For instance, Karaite laws governing fasting, food, clothing, and ritual cleanliness were more severe than those advocated in the Talmud. In civil and criminal law, the Karaites insisted on the literal application of the Scriptural injunction 'eye for eye, tooth for tooth, hand for hand, foot for foot, burn for burn, wound for wound' (Exodus 21:24) whereas Talmudic interpretation substituted cash for restitution in kind. The Karaites also proscribed human intervention in the healing process on the grounds that it violated the will of God, for He had said: 'For I am the Lord, your healer' (Exodus 15:26).

The most extreme example of revisions to traditional rules was in the application of the Sabbath law. The Scriptural injunction, 'You shall kindle no fire in all your habitations on the Sabbath day' (Exodus 35:3), was accepted at face value. Accordingly, the use of light and fire was prohibited on the Sabbath, with the result that Karaites spent Friday nights in total darkness and Saturdays, especially during the winter, shivering in the cold. In addition to this restriction, Karaites were forbidden on the Sabbath to leave their houses or to attempt even the least exacting household task such as washing, wearing anything more than a shirt, or carrying anything from one room to another.

The attraction of Karaism was derived from its appeal to individuals to interpret Scripture in the light of their own consciences, understanding, and judgement. But its chief attraction was also the source of its greatest weakness. Instead of developing a uniform and consistent form of life and worship, Karaism was splintered by internal dissention into fragmented groups. Even though it established itself in the Middle East and spread from one Jewish enclave to another as far as Europe and Asia, it was nevertheless destined to failure. Mounting pressure from traditional Jewish groups proved devastating to Karaism. It survives today only in small, isolated communities in Turkey and in the Russian Crimea.

Kabbalah: The Hebrew term *Kabbalah* means 'tradition' and derives from the root word *Kabel*, meaning 'to receive'. In Jewish mysticism Kabbalah means 'oral tradition received through special transmission', that is to say, the transmission of secret doctrines to a few selected disciples. Kabbalah is also often used as a general term for mysticism.

Mysticism has always been associated with Judaic tradition. Several biblical prophets, such as Isaiah and Ezekiel, had mystical experiences. Some Talmudic rabbis, who warned the uninitiated of the dangers and risks of mysticism, were themselves mystics. During the Middle Ages, Jewish mystics were influenced by Christian and Muslim ideas. In modern times a renewed interest has been kindled among many Jews, thanks to two influential individuals: Gershom Scholem (1897-) and Martin Buber (1878-1965).

There is no room in a book of this scope to say much more about the place of mysticism in Jewish thought except with reference to two Jewish schools of mysticism that have survived to the present day: the Kabbalah and Hasidism.

The origin of Kabbalism is obscure. It is believed that in the course of its long history, Kabbalism adopted elements outside the Judaic tradition from different schools of thought including Gnosticism, Neo-Platonism, Zoroastrianism and Sufism (an Islamic brand of mysticism). At least two seminal Kabbalistic works—the *Sefer Yetzirah* (Book of Formation) and the *Shiur Komah* (Measure of Height)—stem from Babylonia, dating back to a period between the sixth and ninth centuries. From Babylonia, Kabbalism spread to Europe—into Italy, Spain, and Germany—wherever Jews had settled in large numbers. By the thirteenth century there were several Kabbalistic titles in circulation, including classic works, such as *Masechet Atzilut* (A treatise on Emanation), *Sefer Habahir* (The Luminous Book) and *Sefer Hatemunah* (Book of the Image).

The book that made the greatest impact, however, and the one which came to be regarded as the 'holiest' of all Kabbalistic writings, was the *Zohar* (Splendour). The Zohar came to be regarded, and is still regarded, as the very epitome of Jewish mysticism. It was written some time in the thirteenth century by Moses de Léon, a Spanish Jewish mystic. Soon the Zohar became *the* textbook of Jewish mystics. Today, its influence on Judaism rates only second to the Talmud.

The central themes of the Zohar are the nature of God; the mysteries of His divine names; His manifestation to the world; the soul, nature, and destiny of the individual; the principles of good and evil; heaven and hell; the order of the angels; the role and function of the Torah; redemption and the Messianic ideal.

With the advent of the Zohar, Kabbalism ceased to be the secret doctrine of a few privileged disciples. It spread like wildfire among the Jewish masses. Almost everybody studied the Zohar. Even Christian medieval scholars were attracted to it. Prominent among them were John Reuchlin, Pico della Mirandola, and Raymond Lully.

Leading rabbinic authorities were often less enthused because some of them doubted that mysticism could survive the enthusiasm of a popular movement without being corrupted by supposition. They argued in vain that mysticism was the proper concern of scholars. To Kabbalists, every word, letter, and vowel in the Old Testament of the Bible represented profound mysteries.

In spite of these informed misgivings, the movement spread and, by the sixteenth century, several major centres were established, with Poland and Palestine leading the rest of the world. Among the foremost Kabbalists of this period were Moses Cordovero (1522-1570), Isaac Luria (1533-1572) and Chayim Vital (1543-1620). Luria greatly influenced the subsequent development of Kabbalism. The popularity of Hasidism (also written as Chasidism), a mystical movement of Eastern Europe in the eighteenth and nineteenth centuries, was the direct result of Lurianic Kabbalah.

Hasidism: The founder of the modern mystical movement known as Hasidism was Israel Baal Shem Tob Besht (1700-1760), a Ukrainian Jew whose purpose was to bring comfort and hope to compatriots sunk in degeneracy and despair after the Cossack uprising of 1648. Baal Shem Tob ('Good Divine Name', as he is commonly addressed) was a simple man who had a deep love and concern for the uneducated Jewish masses, commonly described as *Am-haaretz*, people of the soil.

Like the soil, everyone treads upon the Jew, but God had in this very soil put the power to bring forth all kinds of plants and fruits wherewith to sustain all His creatures. In the soil are also to be found all such treasures as gold, silver, diamonds and all other precious and important metals and minerals. So too are the Jewish folk: they are full of the finest and most precious qualities that man can possess, even the most ordinary among them.[7]

Baal Shem Tob was revered as a saint, a mystic, a miracle worker, and a healer. His own charismatic personality, combined with the organizational skill of his disciples, attracted a large following from among uneducated Jewish working people as well as the academic community of the Polish Ukraine. People flocked to listen to Baal Shem Tob, who touched a responsive chord among Jews seeking spiritual solace. Many roused themselves into ecstasy, their bodies swayed and danced in worship, and their spiritual ardour produced luminous personalities.

Hasidism advocated inner peace, contentment, meekness and modesty, without suppressing in any way the natural spontaneous impulses of the individual. Instead of promising a Messianic deliverance in the distant future, it lifted the gloom and misery of the depressed and impoverished masses here and now. Mysticism, according to Hasidism, was no longer to be regarded as an esoteric doctrine reserved for the chosen few or as a system of asceticism, but as a vital, singing faith of the people.

Dov Baer of Meseritz (1710-1772) one of the foremost disciples of Baal Shem Tob, possessed a talent for organization and a powerful gift for oration. He sent out missionaries, who

won the masses of the Polish Ukraine to the Hasidic movement. But he is best remembered for introducing the concept of
the *Zaddik*, a role model of the perfectly righteous man like a
Jewish version of a Hindu Guru, a teacher who could help
develop the spiritual faculties of adherents and secure earthly
and heavenly favours for them. This concept was further
developed by other disciples until it grew into the Zaddik cult.

What distinguished the Zaddik from the rabbi was charisma
rather than intellect. The Zaddik was thought to possess
supernatural insights, psychic forces, ecstatic visions, and
miraculous powers. Some of the more gifted Zaddikim (plural
of Zaddik) established dynasties, perpetuating their leadership
by passing it on from father to son. Whereas the Jewish masses
honoured and respected their rabbi, they loved their Zaddik
with a degree of attachment and faith that entirely monopolized
their allegiance. In Jewish communities converted to Hasidism
and distinguished by the leadership of a local Zaddik, Jews
followed him with a fervour and ecstatic joy unmatched by
their responses to anyone else.

Inevitably, the rabbis lost in influence what the Zaddikim
gained—and they did not like it. The emotional response of
their people to the Zaddikim outraged the puritanical sensibili-
ties of the rabbis, whose angry reaction led to bitter conflict and
senseless persecution.

What particularly infuriated *Mithnaggedin*, as opponents of
the Hasidic movement came to be known, was that the Zaddik
cult had elevated the Zaddik from teacher to tetrarch. He was
no longer just teaching the rules. He was making them. By
virtue of his personality, the Zaddik came to be understood as a
source of inspiration as authoritative as the Bible itself. This
dangerous precedent was compounded by another: the fragmentation of Jewish communities breaking up under the
influence of rival Zaddikim. Rabbinic Judaism reacted to the
prospect of the Jewish entity splitting into tribal sects. It could
not tolerate the possibility.

Despite the opposition, Hasidism made great progress. It is
estimated that during the nineteenth century its adherents
represented nearly half of all the Jews around the world. Only

the rise of the *Haskalah* (the Jewish Enlightenment) could effectively challenge the power of Hasidism. Although its momentum faltered under the impact of hostility generated by apostles of the Haskalah, Hasidism continued as a living force in Russia (until the Bolshevist Revolution of 1917) and in Poland, Hungary, and Romania (until World War II. Today, it survives in attenuated form in Israel, America, and several European countries.

Though Hasidism was at times interpreted as a threat, no one can deny its positive spiritual values. Jewish life and culture have been enriched by the glowing faith, the optimistic outlook, the exuberant folklore and folksong expressed in the lives of adherents of Hasidism.

Reform Judaism: All modern movements in Judaism represent responses of Jews of Western Europe to the liberalizing influences of the eighteenth-century Emancipation. In 1787 the United States of America adopted a Constitution based on the principles of equality and of liberty of conscience. Four years later, in 1791, the French National Assembly established the principle of religious toleration and enfranchised all the Jews in France. Soon, one country after another followed suit, bestowing rights of citizenship on Jewish subjects.

This newly acquired status of the Jews after centuries of exclusion created choice where there had been little or none. A large number of Jews chose to abandon their faith without repudiating their cultural heritage. Others accepted total assimilation, by renouncing both their religious and cultural traditions. Still others accepted the best of both worlds by identifying themselves with their neighbours in social, political, and cultural affairs while retaining their unique religious identity. This last choice came to be known as Reform Judaism and its primary justification was to win back for Judaism those who no longer found their traditional beliefs and customs relevant to everyday life.

David Friedländer (1756-1834), a German Jew, is considered the originator of Reform Judaism. The basic principles he proposed have survived, with minor changes, to this day. His purpose in introducing reforms was to offer an alternative to an irrevocable break with tradition—an alternative that represented a positive medium of transition from isolation to full assimilation with local citizens. For instance, he proposed the substitution of German for Hebrew as the language of worship, and the omission from all prayers of references to Jewish national sentiments. But religious tradition was firmly entrenched. Though Friedländer appealed to many dissidents, none dared to put his proposals into action until 1810.

It remained for Israel Jacobson (1768-1828) to found and to build, at his own expense, the first Jewish Reform Temple in Seesen, Brunswick. The name even proclaimed a break with tradition since the term Temple had always been associated with one place of worship only: the Temple in Jerusalem. The term used in the context of a neighbourhood place of worship implied the present rather than an appeal to the past or the future. 'Reform Temple' had a contemporary ring. In form, if not in substance, Jacobson modelled his building and the services performed within on the German Lutheran Church— the church of the majority. His purpose was not to emulate Christians, but to conform to patterns familiar to nineteenth-century Germans so that the Jewish community blended into the larger community instead of contrasting with it. Eight years later, in 1818, another Reform Temple was established in Hamburg after the pattern in Seesen. Reformers in Western society continued to divest Judaism of 'incompatible' customs in order to conform to the cultural and intellectual standards of contemporary society.

Although Reform Judaism was initiated in Europe, it did not achieve any great success until the movement was exported by German Jewish emigrants in the 1840s to the United States of America. Coalescing with earlier American Jewish reform trends, Reform congregations were established in almost every city. In 1873 the Union of American Hebrew Congregations was formed and two years later, in 1875, the Hebrew Union College was established.

Reform Judaism identified itself with the rational tradition in Judaism. Its main task today is no longer to accommodate medieval Judaism to modern society but rather to reaffirm Judaism as a viable religion in a secular and nationalistic world. Accordingly, its dominant teachings are the universal and the ethical principles of Judaism without ignoring the particularistic and the ceremonial. The vernacular in worship, a revised liturgy, instrumental and vocal music, family pews, confirmation of girls as well as boys are all characteristic of Reform congregations. Members of Reform congregations adhere to the universal prophetic view that their Messianic task is to co-operate with all mankind in establishing on this earth universal brotherhood, justice, truth, and peace. The ultimate goal of Reform Judaism is the establishment of the Kingdom of God on earth.

Neo-Orthodox Judaism: The bulk of the Jewish people in Western and Central Europe resisted change. They were hardly affected by the efforts of Reform Jews, who distinguished them from their own ranks by identifying them as Orthodox Jews. Indeed, the strength of Orthodox Judaism and its implacable traditionalism survived intact. Jews of Orthodox persuasion regarded Hebrew as a sacred language, the Hebrew Bible as an ultimate authority, the law of Moses as a divine revelation, the admonitions of the prophets and the sentiments of the Psalmist as the only appropriate sources of liturgy, the study of the Bible as a religious obligation, and the fulfilment of their Messianic hope as the historic destiny of the Jewish people. For thousands of years, Orthodox Judaism held unwaveringly to its course as delineated by Moses, the prophets, and the rabbis.

The denial of the authority of the Bible and the Talmud, and the repudiation of age-old traditional practices in favour of the conformity to modern influences, advocated by Reform Judaism, provoked spirited opposition from traditionalists. The most bitter denunciations of Reform Judaism came from Moses Sofar (1763-1839), who was instrumental in preventing the new heresies from spreading any further than they did in Europe. The most effective champion of the traditionalists however was Samson Raphael Hirsch (1808-1888) because he offered an alternative to radical change: a modern and militant form of orthodoxy identified as Neo-Orthodoxy. Under his leadership, this group grew in influence both in Europe and in the United States of America. In fact, Hirsch's form of Neo-Orthodoxy became the intellectual model of all Orthodoxy, particularly because it posited a theoretical division between religion and culture: Jews could become Western in manners and culture and still retain their traditional religion.

Today, Neo-Orthodox Judaism interprets biblical and Talmudic regulations as rigidly as possible. Hebrew is the official language of prayer and worship. Males and females cover their heads once they enter the synagogue and sit in separate areas. Only kosher food (food that is ritually sanctioned) is permissible and the observance of the Sabbath is strictly prescribed.

Conservative Judaism: Conservative Judaism is regarded by many Jews as a cultural and religious movement, or school of thought, not a party or sect. It had its origin in Germany during the middle of the nineteenth century under the aegis of several exponents, such as Isaac Bernays (1792-1849) and Zechariah Frankel (1801-1875). Later, under the energetic leadership of such men as Sabato Morais (1823-1901) and Solomon Schechter (1847-1915), the Conservative movement grew numerically and influentially to become a major force in the social, intellectual, and religious life of Jews, particularly American Jews.

Conservative Judaism occupies a position midway between Reform and Neo-Orthodoxy. On the one hand, it has adopted a number of external forms of worship from Reform Judaism, and on the other, it has accepted from Neo-Orthodoxy the entire structure of rabbinic tradition with certain modifications. Unlike Neo-Orthodoxy but like Reform, Conservative Judaism rejects the doctrine of resurrection though it accepts belief in immortality.

But adherents of Conservative Judaism have no set pattern of principles or dogmas; only a general agreement on objectives. This allows for considerable latitude in matters of practice and belief among its constituent members.

Conservative Judaism has three objectives: the perpetuation of Jewish tradition, the cultivation of Jewish scholarship and the fostering of a Jewish commonwealth in the ancestral homeland. The first objective is exemplified in the recognition of the authority of Jewish religious law as it developed from the Bible through the Talmudic and later rabbinic periods to modern times. This religious law is subject to change and development, but any modification must conform to the essential character of the law. For instance, though Hebrew occupies a place of paramount importance in synagogue services and in Jewish school curricula, prayers may be recited in the vernacular.

A marked characteristic of the second objective is the emphasis placed on the application of modern scientific methods of research to the discovery of new knowledge about Jewish life and religion, past and present. Consequently, the ranks of Conservative Judaism, have yielded a number of scholars who have rescued Jewish history and religion from manuscripts relegated to the oblivion of libraries and of private collections around the world.

The third objective, fulfilment of the hope for a return to ancestral territory, is indispensable in the view of Conservative Jews to a full and rich development of Jewish heritage. Yet that hope in no way weakens the patriotic allegiance which all Jews feel for the countries of their adoption. Thus, all three objectives represent what Zachariah Frankel called the 'positive historical Judaism'. What Frankel meant was that Judaism for Conservative Jews is the historical expression of the Jewish experience, not merely a theology of ethics.

Reconstructionism: Reconstructionism is a twentieth-century American Jewish attempt to come to grips with emancipation and secularization. Its founder was Mordecai Menahem Kaplan (1881-1984), whose philosophic ideas were influenced by Emile Durkheim, William James and John Dewey. Beginning in the 1930s as an organized institutional movement, Reconstructionism has not made the numerical gains among Jews that its originators had hoped for, though it has developed. into a full-fledged Jewish group with its own congregations and rabbinical college.

Kaplan's first premise requires that Jews recognize that they have been secularized and are living in a secular environment. It is useless, he argues, to oppose the process of secularization, for history is irreversible. Consequently, one must discover holy meanings in a secular world. Kaplan therefore offers an alternative interpretation, or meaning, for each of the five central themes of Judaism: God; the Bible (Torah); the Jews (Israel); the Land of Israel; and Observances (mitzvot).

Kaplan abandons the traditional Jewish idea of a personal God. For him, God is a transnatural force or power in the universe, not a supernatural being. As such, it (i.e., God) is part of the natural order and operates as the source or wellspring of the forces in nature, consistently and with absolute regularity. Consequently it is absurd, Kaplan claims, to think of the possibility of 'miraculous interventions', since that is inconsistent with the scientific view of the uniformity of nature.

Kaplan's view on the Bible (Torah) is again to dismiss the notion that it is mystical or supernatural. For him, the Bible is a record of the struggles of the Jews to educate their own conscience. In his words, the Bible is 'an expression of human nature at its best, the most articulate striving of man to achieve his salvation or self-fulfilment, and an expression of his most conscious recognition that only through righteousness can he achieve it.'[8] Thus, the Bible is never complete, since every Jewish generation adds to it as the collective experience of the Jewish people. Kaplan also dismisses all mythological elements in the Bible and all conclusions based on uncritical, literal interpretations.

Kaplan's interpretation of the role or destiny of the Jewish people (Israel), is thought-provoking, if not radical. For him, the Jews are a people like any other people, not a 'chosen' people. They are endowed with insights, as others are. Their contribution to the world is to promote ethics in human society. In fact, Kaplan argues that their role is to be the salvation of society, here and now, not in a hereafter. In this sense, Kaplan believes, Judaism is an 'evolving religious civilization', not simply a religion. This religious civilization expresses itself in language, literature, art, music, and even in cuisine.

To Kaplan, the recent establishment of the State of Israel

represents the biblical Land of Israel. Its people, he claims, can collectively promote the ideal of an ethical nationhood. It is, therefore, imperative to have a State, because the insights of the State of Israel can influence the Jews in the diaspora, and vice versa.

Religious observances (mitzvot), must also meet the needs of and conform to limitations set by life in a modern society. In Kaplan's words, Judaism 'has to *select* from the Judaism of the past those beliefs and practices, which either in their original or in a reinterpreted form, are compatible with what we now recognize to be authentic.'[9] For instance, Kaplan recognizes as authentic some Sabbath observances: the right to rest from work and the opportunity for recreation. Kaplan sees it as the duty of every Jew to fight for the universal human right to this sanctum (holy symbol). Another observance from the Judaism of the past that Kaplan endorses is prayer—the power that calls forth ultimate values, that releases self-transcendence, and that humanizes all peoples in the world.

Kaplan's social philosophy has gained more attention and support than his ideas for reinterpreting Judaism. What attracts many Jews is his proposal for a centralized Jewish organization without abandoning democratic diversity. Membership in such an organization would be open to all groups who desire to promote Jewish life and consciousness, in whatever form and content they understand. The constituent groups within this organization would be entitled to full autonomy, except for allocation of budget and administration of property.

Many Jews consider Kaplan to be an original thinker who brought about a 'galilean revolution'. His most radical thesis, that Judaism exists for the Jews, not the Jews for Judaism, flies directly in the face of Jewish traditional belief. Of course, it is still too early to know whether or not Kaplan's ideas will be developed to form an important movement in twenty-first century Judaism.

HOLY LAND

Whoever lives in the Land of Israel is considered to be a believer in
  God . . .
Whoever lives in the Land of Israel lives a sinless life . . .
Whoever is buried in the Land of Israel is considered as though he
  were buried beneath the Altar . . .
Whoever walks a distance of four cubits in the Land of Israel is assured
  a place in the World to come.
Living in the Land of Israel equals in import the performance of all the
  commandments of the Torah.

Sifre, R'eh

Palestine: Land of the Canaanites

Should the people of the world tell the Jewish people, 'You are
robbers, because you took the land of the seven nations of Canaan by
force,' they could reply, 'All the earth belongs to the Holy One,
praised be He. He created it and gave it to whom He pleased. When
He willed, He gave it to them, and when He willed He took it from
them and gave it to us.'

Rashi's Comment Genesis 1:1

THE name commonly used in the Old Testament for the
historic region between west Jordan and the south-eastern end
of the Mediterranean Sea is Canaan (Numbers 13:29). This is
where the Canaanites lived and this is the 'Promised Land' the
land of 'milk and honey' to which the Jews aspired (Genesis
12:5-7). But, the area is also known as Palestine, which is
derived from *Pelishtim* (I Samuel 4:1), a tribe of 'Sea Peoples'
from the Aegean Islands who invaded the territory in the
twelfth century BC from the Mediterranean Sea on their way to
conquer and settle in Egypt. The Greek historian Herodotus

was the first in the fifth century BC to call the region 'that part of Syria called Palestine'. Since then, the term Palestine has displaced the biblical one, Canaan.

No area in the world has played a more important role in human affairs, or has been as often and as bitterly contested as Palestine. Three religious traditions—Judaism, Christianity and Islam—make claims on Palestine as a Holy Land, and on the city of Jerusalem as a Holy City. During the long centuries of dispersion, pious Jews consistently prayed for reunion 'next year in Jerusalem'. As they have for centuries, they still make pilgrimages whenever possible and contribute financially to support the Jewish community in the Promised Land.

To Christians, Palestine is a Holy Land because it is the place where the Incarnation, the Divine-human drama, took place. During the Middle Ages, it represented both battlefield and booty for the Crusaders of Christian European powers waging Holy Wars, the Crusades, to reclaim the Holy City of Jerusalem in order to secure the Holy Sites against the 'infidel Muslims'.

To Muslims, Palestine is a Holy Land because it is the birthplace of the Jewish Patriarchs, the Jewish prophets, and Jesus, whom they acknowledge as prophets (or messengers) of God. According to tradition, the prophet Mohammed made a nocturnal journey from Mecca to Jerusalem during which he met with the earlier prophets, including Jesus, ascending to heaven to be instructed by God before returning that same night to Mecca. Today the Dome of the Rock, completed by Caliph Abd-el-Malik in AD 691, identifies the site of Mohammed's prophetic meeting and ascension. It rises on the foundations of the Temple of Solomon which preceded Palestine's first Dome.

During most of its history, the boundaries of Palestine have fluctuated according to the fortunes of the people that ruled the territory. Because it straddled a corridor of power, trade, and conquest it formed a perpetual arena for violent conflict between nomadic tribes, agricultural city-states, empires, and colonial powers. It is still a killing ground for tribal factions perpetuating ancient rivalries and feuds, except that its strategic importance now rests on oil rather than trade. Conflict between Arab and Jew simply exacerbates tensions that are global rather than regional. The Holy Land's potential for unholy war has changed little through the centuries except for the size of the explosion and the length of the fuse that triggers it. The reasons for its volatile politics have been five thousand years in the making.

Excavations in Palestine have produced evidence of flint stones dating from the Palaeolithic period (any time before 12,000 BC) and of settlements from the Mesolithic period (about 10,000 BC). The oldest remains of village life unearthed at Jericho date from about 5000 BC. Other ancient towns such as Beth-shean, Megiddo, Byblos and Ugarit have been identified in the same way—by digging, not by written records. The earliest recorded history of Palestine (which comes from Egyptian sources), supplemented by archaeological discoveries, dates from about 3000 BC. From then on, the region was subject to successive waves of invasion and occupation by migrating Semitic tribes.

But even before these random invasions began, the country oscillated between two great civilizations: the Egyptian and the Babylonian. During the reign of the Egyptian King Snefru (2614-2591 BC) Egyptian expeditions made successive forays to expropriate cedarwood, possibly from Lebanon. By 2600 BC King Lugalzaggisi of Babylonia, and his renowned successor King Sargon, ruled a large part of the region. Egypt controlled key cities, such as Lachish and Megiddo, but even then Egyptian and Babylonian occupation was intermittent. Throughout the second millenium BC, nomadic tribes, such as the Amorites, the Arameans, the Hittites, the Hurrians, the Hyksos, and later the Canaanites and the Philistines, kept interrupting the even tenor of garrison life in Egyptian and Babylonian outposts.

The Canaanites were a Semitic offshoot which spread into the area of Palestine some time during the second millenium BC. However, the Canaanites were never able to form a homogeneous civilization, but remained divided into a number of independent kingdoms with specific local traditions. They were followed by other invading groups among whom were the Hurrians, the Hittites, and the Hyksos. The Egyptians reoccupied ancient Palestine around the fifteenth century BC only to be challenged again a century later by the Hittites and by nomadic tribes from Babylonia. (Some scholars speculate that among these Babylonian migrants came the ancestors of the Jews.) Egypt survived these onslaughts only to be faced by a fresh challenge between 1200 and 1000 BC: the Philistines.

The Philistines, who are considered to have come from the Aegean Islands (or according to another account, from Crete), occupied the south coast of Palestine. They captured Canaanite cities and established a strong confederation of five city-states: Gaza, Ashdod, Ashkelon, Gath, and Ekron. They built two temples dedicated to the deity Dagon, another to the goddess Ashtoreth and another to the deity Baalzebub.

The Philistines were constantly at war with surrounding tribes, especially with the Jews (known then as Israelites). Though their name has survived as a synonym for whatever is gross or uncultured, little is known about them beyond the dramatic tales recorded in the Bible of epic battles between the Philistines and the Jews. Typical of such episodes are the stories of Shamgar single-handedly killing six hundred Philistines (Judges 3:31), Samson pulling down the Temple of Dagon over Philistine ears (Judges 16:23-31), fresh-faced David overcoming the Philistine champion Goliath (I Samuel 17:31-58), and King Saul falling on his sword at Mount Gilboa to avoid capture (I Samuel 31:1-6).

The Philistine invasion and colonization of Palestine around the eleventh century BC coincided with the Jewish invasion and settlement of the same territory. Their timing could not have been much worse. It was little wonder, then, that their struggle to establish an independent Jewish kingdom was so hard fought. Only their vision of the Promised Land drove the Jews on to conquer and settle in Palestine.

Palestine: The 'Promised' Land

I will give to you, and to your descendants after you, the land of your sojournings, all the land of Canaan, for an everlasting possession . . .
Genesis 17:8

There is hardly a major passage in the first five books of the

Bible (the Five Books of Moses) which omits reference to the promise God made to Abraham and his descendants: possession of the Land of Canaan. Biblical authors were apparently quite aware that the land was inhabited by other people. Their justification for claiming ownership is based on two principles: that the tribes in possession had forfeited their rights by defiling their heritage with their sins (Joshua 22:19); and that the Jews could claim ultimate ownership because 'the Lord God had promised it unto them' (Joshua 23:5). Here is how biblical authors interpreted the record of Israel's acquisition of the Promised Land.

The Patriarchs—Abraham, Isaac, and Jacob—are identified in the Bible as the founders (or forefathers) of the Jewish people. It is believed that around 1800 BC Abraham, who is thought to have come from the city of Ur in ancient Mesopotamia (modern Iraq), migrated first northwards to Haran, in northern Mesopotamia (modern Syria and Turkey), and then southwards to Palestine, passing through Syria. After an interlude in Egypt, he returned to Palestine, the 'Promised Land'.

Biblical stories of Abraham are characterized by two closely associated themes: God's double promise of 'land' and 'descendants'. Thus, Abraham set out with a wife who was barren to take possession of a land that was not his. In Palestine, he moved among the Canaanites (Genesis 12:6), and entered into negotiations with the Hittites (Genesis 23). On his journey southwards to Egypt he met the Amorites, the Hurrians and the Elamites (Genesis 14-15) but without any immediate prospect of the fulfilment of God's double promise of seed and land.

Abraham then returned to Palestine to spend the rest of his life there. Once again the God who had summoned him and now led him assured him of a male heir and of land as an inheritance. It was at this point that Sarah, Abraham's wife who was barren, took matters into her own hands. She suggested that Abraham have an offspring by her maid Hagar. Hagar conceived and a son, named Ishmael, was born. But growing hostility between the two women finally prompted Hagar to steal away into the desert taking her son with her. Arabs consider themselves to be the descendants of Ishmael, the son of Abraham.

Finally, when both Abraham and Sarah reached old age, Sarah conceived and gave birth to a son, whom they named Isaac. The splendid faith that father and son had in each other and that they both placed in God during their crucial test before a homemade altar is beautifully described in biblical tradition. Then, before his death, Abraham bought a burial plot in Macphelah (Genesis 23), where both he and his wife were buried. Thus, the double promise of seed and land seems to have been honoured in a legal sense at least.

However, Isaac, the son of Abraham and the fruit of divine intervention was reminded by God to wait patiently in the Promised Land, so that he and his descendants could take possession (Genesis 26:3-4). Following his father's wish, Isaac married Rebekah, not a native Canaanite, but the daughter of his father's relatives from Haran (Genesis 24). The couple lived in Canaan for twenty years before Rebekah gave birth to twins: Esau and Jacob. Isaac's two sons represented further evidence of the fulfilment of God's promise.

Jacob, the younger of the twins, en route to Haran after tricking his brother Esau out of his birthright, had a dream about the double divine promise of seed and land (Genesis 28:10-15). In Haran, Jacob married Leah and Rachel, the daughters of his uncle Laban, in return for fourteen years of service. In time, twelve children were born to him—six from Leah, two from Rachel, and two each from two maids, Zilpah and Bilhah, procured for him by his wives (Genesis 35:22-26).

Then Jacob returned to Palestine in order to claim his inheritance. He bought a piece of property in the city of Shechem and built an altar to his God (Genesis 33:18-20). The rest of the Jacob narrative in the Bible focuses on three aspects of his life: the change of his name from Jacob to Israel (Genesis 32:27-29; 35:9-13); the places and people associated with him during his life; and the close relationships he enjoyed with his family, especially with Joseph, the eldest of Rachel's two sons. Some time after Jacob's return to Palestine, his favourite wife, Rachel, died and was buried in Bethlehem (Genesis 35:16-20). Jacob died later in Egypt where Joseph and his brothers had taken him to live but was buried by his sons, according to his wishes, in the family sepulchre in Macphelah, Palestine (Genesis 50:13).

The descendants of Jacob (or Israel) lived in Egypt for almost four hundred years and increased both in numbers and in influence (Exodus 1:1-7). The stories of the hardships endured by the Jews at the hands of the Egyptians, the role of Moses chosen by God to lead the Jews out of Egypt, and the long years spent in the wilderness before the occupation of the Promised Land, are detailed in an earlier chapter. Suffice it to say that centuries had passed before Moses was reminded of the divine promise:

Go and gather the elders of Israel together, and say to them: 'The Lord, the God of your fathers, the God of Abraham, of Isaac, and of Jacob, has appeared to me, saying, I have observed you and what has been done to you in Egypt; and I promise that I will bring you out of the affliction of Egypt, to the land of the Canaanites, the Hittites, the Amorites, the Perizzites, the Hivites, and the Jebusites; a land flowing with milk and honey . . .'

Exodus 3:16-17

The Exodus from Egypt in the thirteenth century BC marks the beginning of the fulfilment of God's undertaking of a Promised Land, but traditional records make it difficult to distinguish fact from myth. Events associated with the Exodus and the subsequent arrival of the Jews at Mount Sinai under the leadership of Moses are full of contradictions and discrepancies, but at least two events occurred for certain: a nomadic interval spanning years spent in the wilderness before the Jews settled in Palestine, and the death of Moses before he was able to lead the Jewish occupation of the Promised Land.

The conquest of Palestine began under the leadership of Joshua, the successor of Moses. The biblical record is set down in the books of Joshua 1-11 and Judges 1:1-2:5. And yet, a precise historical accounting of these events lies beyond the reach of modern biblical scholarship. Why is this so? For three reasons: the omission of important historical details, the emphasis on the religious or mystical significance of events, and the frequent discrepancies. In consequence, interpretation of the biblical record rests on scholarly speculation rather than hard evidence. There are four plausible alternative conclusions.

First, the Jewish conquest of Palestine was accomplished through a decisive, united, military assault under Joshua's leadership, culminating in victory and the partition of conquered lands among the 'twelve' Jewish tribes.[1] Second, family groups that later comprised the twelve-tribe Jewish confederation penetrated Palestine peaceably and gradually occupied the territory.[2] Third, the Jews penetrated Palestine at different times and from different directions so that occupation and conquest alternated between gradual and peaceful infiltration and bloody military conflict.[3] Fourth, Jews who had settled in Palestine among the Canaanites, perhaps as early as Abraham's time, had joined forces with marauding desert nomads, Jewish survivors of the great exodus from Egypt, and succeeded in taking over portions of the land.[4]

The biblical record lends little credence to the theory of a swift and conclusive conquest and occupation. The overall narrative suggests that the conquest of Palestine by the Jews was a slow, complex process involving both bloodshed and relative calm. The record of events between the time of Joshua and David, a period spanning some two centuries or more, illustrates how a series of seemingly endless problems inhibited the Jews from effective action. They were never able to form a group strong enough to establish firm control. The resentment of resident Moabites, Ammonites, Hittites, and Canaanites—not to mention the antagonism of Philistines and other warlike groups—would have tested the mettle of even a well-organized confederation. What seems astonishing is that the Jews managed to maintain a foothold in their Promised Land for so long.

This loose tribal organization of Jews in Palestine was finally unified by the impressive accomplishments of three kings: Saul (c. 1020-1000 BC), David (c. 1000-961 BC), and Solomon (c. 961-922 BC). This united Jewish monarchy survived for· a hundred years. In fact, the conquest of virtually all of Palestine did not become a reality until David's reign. King David captured Jerusalem and expanded his territory to control everything from Syria to the Arabian desert, and from the

Mediterranean to the borders of Mesopotamia.

However, the Jewish kingdom did not last very long. A little over a century after its establishment it split into two. The northern part, which was called 'Israel' and represented the larger of the two was destroyed by the Assyrians in the eighth century BC. The southern part, called 'Judah', survived for a while but eventually it, too, succumbed to the Babylonians (also known as 'Chaldeans') in the sixth century BC. The events that precipitated this debacle are important because they support the tradition that God lost patience with His Chosen people.

In 722 BC, the Assyrians invaded and captured Samaria, the capital of the Northern kingdom of Israel, took King Hoshea as prisoner, deported the Israelites to the remotest eastern parts of the Assyrian Empire and resettled the territory with foreign colonists. This displacement of populations it seems, was so complete that eventually the identity of the 'Israelites' was lost beyond recall. The ancient kingdom of Israel passed out of history and off the map after two centuries of independent, but turbulent, survival. The kingdom of Judah by comparison enjoyed a reprieve or the respite associated with execution deferred, though it was not a respite completely free from foreign interventions and political intrigue. The crisis, however, started a little over a century later when the Assyrian Empire came to a sudden end in 609 BC and the two prevailing rival powers, Babylon and Egypt, struggled for the control of western Asia. Instead of pursuing a policy of non-intervention, Judah decided to side with Babylon. This was a miscalculation which eventually resulted in the absolute disaster and tragic downfall of Judah.

Egypt dealt the first crushing blow to Judah in 608 BC, when the latter attempted to bar the advance of the Egyptian forces against the Babylonians. Its forces shattered and cowed, Judah had no recourse but to reverse its policy and to side with Egypt. Three years later, when the Egyptians themselves were defeated by the Babylonians, Judah had to submit to the Babylonians. Before long, however, Judah, at the instigation of Egypt, rebelled against Babylon. The consequences were catastrophic.

In March 597 BC, the Babylonians, led by their King Nebuchadnezzar, captured and plundered Jerusalem. Judah's king, his mother, his palace retinue and many of the inhabitants were taken captive and exiled. Nebuchadnezzar then appointed Zedekiah, under an oath of allegiance, as his puppet king of Judah. But the Jewish population of Judah refused to submit to their new overlord, seized every opportunity to stir up trouble and soon rebelled once again.

The Babylonian reprisal was so severe this time that it proved almost fatal. Nebuchadnezzar and his military force beseiged Jerusalem for almost two years. The defenders of the beleagured city suffered all the horrors of a prolonged siege. In its final stages, people died in such numbers that their corpses decayed where they lay in streets and cellars. When Babylonian troops finally breached the defences in August 587 BC the end came abruptly. The Temple, the palace, and most of the homes were burned; the city walls were totally destroyed; Jerusalem was razed to the ground; the princes, the priests and the elders were tortured and put to death. King Zedekiah was blinded and exiled to Babylon along with most of the inhabitants.

Judah was now reduced to the status of a colony, and Gedaliah, the former mayor of the palace, was appointed its governor. Five years later, in 582 BC, a few disillusioned and discontented survivors of the Davidic dynasty assassinated Gedaliah at a community banquet. Fearing the consequences of this open defiance, those who could fled to Egypt, while the rest faced inevitable deportation by the Babylonians. Thus was the fate of Judah sealed—a mass of ruins and debris.

For seven hundred years, the Jews had struggled to subdue and to control Palestine, the Promised Land, only to be forced out by the ambition of mighty warring powers. Twenty-five hundred years were to pass before they were able to re-establish a Jewish state on a portion of the site of ancient Palestine.

Palestine: Under 'Foreign' Rule

O Lord our God, who brought Thy people out of the land of Egypt with a mighty hand . . . let Thy anger and Thy wrath turn away from Thy city Jerusalem, Thy Holy Hill . . .. Jerusalem and Thy people have become a byword among all who are round about us . . .

Daniel 9:15-16

The destruction of Jerusalem and the forced expulsion of the
Jews from the Promised Land at the hands of the Babylonians in
587 BC represented something more than military defeat. The
Jews interpreted their loss as abandonment, retribution, the
execution of justice. There were Jews who believed that God
would intervene in history in a strikingly new way to effect
their imminent return to their homeland, but many were
convinced that their exilic period was going to be a long one.
All of them, however, found themselves in times of rapid
political change.

The Babylonian state followed a steady course of decline.
Meanwhile, a new power was emerging in Persia (Iran). After
defeating and uniting various tribes, a new Persian leader,
Cyrus (549-529 BC), led his army victoriously into Asia Minor.
Then, in 539 BC, he conquered Babylon and ultimately
established the Achaemenian Empire.

The imperial policy of the Persian Empire (of the Achaeme-
nids) under its founder Cyrus was remarkably enlightened.
Cyrus broke the tradition of victor as despoiler and avenger.
Instead of invoking fire, the sword, the mass deportation of
whole populations, and the rigorous suppression of all nationalistic aspirations among subjugated vassals, he conceded to the
vanquished a high degree of cultural and political autonomy,
including religious freedom. In keeping with this policy of
conciliation Cyrus gave all displaced Jews the option, in 538 BC,
to return to their homeland. It is estimated that some 40,000
Jews made their way back to Jerusalem, but were soon
disillusioned and disheartened by the desolation they found on
their return. Their first attempt to rebuild the Temple proved
beyond their resources. It was not until much later that at the
urging of two prophets, Haggai and Zechariah, they resumed
the task and completed it in 516 BC. Thus, seventy years after its
destruction, a second temple rose on the ruins of the old.

The small Jewish community in Palestine enjoyed relative
calm for the next two hundred years, like other Jewish
communities scattered all over the Near and Middle East. Even
in Palestine, the Jewish minority was surrounded by resettled
strangers, but they survived unmolested until another martial
star suddenly flamed in the east.

Alexander the Great, King of Macedon, burst into the Near East in 334 BC. In four years he completed the conquest of the entire Near East, except Arabia. Then, in 327 BC, he advanced eastwards to India and penetrated as far as the Indus river. But, in 323 BC, on the eve of an expedition to conquer Arabia, he fell ill and died at the age of thirty-three.

After Alexander's untimely death, his Macedonian generals contended for his empire. There followed a series of struggles and civil wars resulting in the division of the Near East into three kingdoms: the Ptolemaic, the Seleucid, and the Antigonid. The Antigonids assumed a tenuous hold on Alexander's European possessions. The Ptolemaics retained Egypt, Cyprus, and part of the eastern Mediterranean coast including Palestine. And the Seleucids acquired the rest of the Near East except Asia Minor, where several independent Hellenistic states were founded and developed during the following centuries.

Palestine became a killing ground once more. Only the protagonists had changed: Ptolemaics thrusting from the south and Seleucids from the north. Ptolemaic armies prevailed in Palestine at first, followed over a century later (in 198 BC) by Seleucid rulers. In the course of the fighting which ensued, Jerusalem again suffered the consequences of repeated siege. When it was finally annexed by the Seleucids, special privileges were granted to the Jews to repair the damage to the city and the temple.

This concession, however, had its unfortunate repercussions. The growing influence of Hellenistic culture produced a division among the Jews. The reckless haste with which the Seleucid ruler Antiochus IV Epiphanes attempted to Hellenize the Jews, provoked a popular revolt in 167 BC under the leadership of the Hasmoneans (or Maccabees). The Seleucid armies were driven out of Palestine and a small but independent kingdom was re-established under the Hasmonean rulers.

The Hasmonean dynasty lasted for a century before it, too, collapsed owing to family quarrels and sectarian conflicts. Rome, already looming as the next world power, intervened. Pompei and his armies occupied Palestine in 63 BC and the Hasmonean state became a Roman protectorate. In 40 BC,

Herod the Great (known as the 'Puppet king'), deposed the last of the Hasmonean princes, and proclaimed himself 'king' of Palestine answerable only to the Roman Senate. Shortly after the beginning of the Christian era (AD 7), Palestine was placed under the rule of Roman procurators.

Direct Roman administration resulted in repeated Jewish revolts. The first Roman-Jewish conflict occurred in AD 66-73 culminating in the destruction of the city of Jerusalem, including the Jewish Temple. Another rebellion occurred in AD 115-117 and again in AD 132-135 resulting in the expulsion of Jews from Jerusalem. The city was subsequently reconstructed as a Roman city and renamed Aelia Capitolina.

When the Roman Empire split, its eastern section became the Byzantine Empire, inaugurated by Constantine the Great in May 330, and Palestine came, perforce, under Byzantine suzerainty. But conflict and war were endemic, the region was gravely weakened, and incapable of a unified defence. In 611, Palestine was invaded by the Persians, and in 614 Jerusalem was sacked. Although Emperor Heraclius reclaimed his Byzantine territories, including Palestine, he failed to anticipate the rise of a new world power—the Arabs.

Arabic-speaking peoples had always played a substantial role in the history of the Near East from very early times. Biblical records indicate that King Solomon had diplomatic (and possibly commercial) contact with the Queen of Sheba—Sheba being Saba, an old South Arabian kingdom. Arabs inhabited the territories east of the Jordan River, the Dead Sea, and the eastern desert of Syria long before the Assyrians came in contact with them in the ninth century BC. The ruins of Petra and Palmyra (both located in modern Jordan) bear witness to a high degree of settled urban Arab life long before the Greeks and the Romans ruled the Near East.

In the seventh century a new religion, proclaimed to the Arabs by the prophet Mohammed, transformed the course of history in the Near East. United under the name of Islam, the various tribes of the Arabian peninsula generated a potential that finally struck with the speed and force of lightning in all directions. Syria and northern Palestine were conquered in 636,

and a year later Jerusalem surrendered to the superior force of
the Arabs. The Arab conquerors left the Jewish and Christian
population and their holy sites unmolested. Soon, the
Umayyad Dynasty (661-750) established its centre in Damascus, Syria. Palestine experienced a century of tranquillity and
prosperity. During this period Caliph Abd-el-Malik (685-705)
built on the site of the Jewish Temple the magnificent Dome of
the Rock with its adjacent Aqsa mosque.

But Palestine's privileged status came to an abrupt end when
the new Abbasid Dynasty (750-1258) transferred the seat of
government from Damascus to Baghdad, Iraq. Palestine now
became a subordinate province and suffered from misrule and
frequent civil wars. Then, in 1072, the Seljuk Turks came from
Central Asia and invaded Palestine. As new converts to Islam,
the Seljuk Turks saw no reason for making concessions to the
infidel and treated the Christian population in Palestine accordingly. They considered themselves the inheritors of the ancient
Roman territories. This claim was the last straw. It provoked
the European Crusades.

The sermon preached by Pope Urban II at Clermont, France,
in 1095 epitomizes the reaction of European Christendom:

Distressing news has come to us (as has often happened) from the
region of Jerusalem and from the city of Constantinople; news that the
Seljuk Turks, an alien people, a race completely foreign to God . . .
has invaded Christian territory and has devastated this territory with
pillage, fire, and the sword . . . They have completely destroyed some
of God's churches and they have converted others to the uses of their
own cult. They ruin the altars with filth and defilement . . .

Who is to revenge all this, who is to repair this damage, if you do
not do it? . . . You should be especially aroused by the fact that the
Holy Sepulchre of the Lord our Saviour is in the hands of these
unclean people, who shamefully mistreat and sacreligiously defile the
Holy Places with their filth. Oh, most valiant knights! Descendants of
unconquered ancestors! Remember the courage of your forefathers
and do not dishonour them! . . . Begin the journey to the Holy
Sepulcher; conquer that land which the wicked have seized, the land
which was given by God to the children of Israel . . . the land which
the Redeemer of mankind illuminated by his coming, adorned by his

life, consecrated by his passion, redeemed by his death, and sealed by his burial. This royal city, situated in the middle of the world, is now held captive by his enemies and is made a servant, by those who know not God, for the ceremonies of the heathen.[5]

The forces of the First Crusade arrived Syria in 1097. Two years later, in 1099, the Holy City of Jerusalem was captured. Pillage, arson, and slaughter followed, matching and sometimes surpassing in savagery the depradations of the Seljuks. Members of the small Jewish community were herded into the synagogues, which were then torched, while thousands of Muslims were butchered in the Holy area of the Dome of the Rock. In celebration, the crusaders along with the resident Christian population gathered for their Christian ceremonies in the Holy Sepulchre Church.

The Latin Christian kingdom of Palestine, including Jerusalem, survived precariously until 1187 when the Egyptian Muslim Salah-el-Din, better known as Saladin, regained Palestine and occupied Jerusalem. Succeeding Latin Crusades to the Holy Land of Palestine were nearly all total failures, with two exceptions. Emperor Frederick II held Jerusalem from 1229 to 1244, and Louis IX, held Acre and other seaports from 1250 to 1291.

For the next two centuries (1291-1516), Palestine became a province of the Mamluk Dynasty of Egypt, even though Mongols and Tartars from Central Asia overran and invaded the territory. Finally, Sultan Selim I (1512-1520) of the Ottoman Turks defeated the Mamluks in 1516 and added Palestine to the Ottoman Empire. His son, Suleiman I the Magnificent (1520-1566), extended the Ottoman domain to include Hungary, Yugoslavia and North Africa. He also rebuilt the walls that still stand today around the 'Old City' of Jerusalem.

The impressive and powerful Ottoman Empire lasted for four centuries, till the end of World War I. Its collapse was a consequence of increasing internal rivalry during the eighteenth and nineteenth centuries coinciding with the growing power of European imperialism and a rising tide of nationalism. The

French revolutionary army of Napoleon Bonaparte invaded the Ottoman provinces of Egypt, Syria and Palestine in 1798-99. Though the occupation was short-lived, it presaged the shape of things to come. The Russian Empire posed a constant threat and finally, at the end of World War I, Western European powers delivered the final blow to the tottering Ottoman dynasty, already weakened by the revolt of local Arab nationalists who themselves were exploited by rival powers both regional and European. Those powers, particularly the British, the French, the Italians and the Russians, negotiated among themselves the partition of the Ottoman Empire and with the leaders of the Zionist movement the creation of a Jewish state on the site of Palestine, their ancient homeland. In a sense, it was back to square one: the fragmentation of the Middle East and the resumption of ancient feuds after centuries of hegemony and comparative peace.

Two pistol shots fired at the Archduke Francis Ferdinand of Austria-Hungary on 28 June 1914, in Sarajevo, signalled the start of World War I. An armistice signed between Germany and the Allies, on 11 November 1918, ended the war. During this momentus interval of four years when the Central Powers (Austria-Hungary, Germany and the Ottoman Empire) were at war with the Allies (Belgium, France, Great Britain, Russia, Serbia, with other countries joining later), Palestine went through many complicated changes.

Ottoman Turk and German armies occupied Palestine, including the neighbouring territories, until 1917. Jews and Arabs collaborated with the Allies to rid themselves of the Ottoman Turks, but with totally different aspirations: Jews expected to repossess their ancient land and to govern it autonomously; the Arabs, too, wanted freedom from foreign domination and the return of all their lands. The Allies preoccupied first with winning the war and then with dividing the spoils made several conflicting statements regarding Palestine.

First, the Hussein-McMahon letters exchanged during 1915-16 promised British assistance in the establishment of Arab independent territories but without exactly specifying the limits implied by the term Palestine. Later, the Arabs and the British hotly disputed the intention of the pledge, since the Arabs defined the territory identified as Palestine far more liberally than the British, who maintained that the agreement related only to a slice of Palestine on the west bank of the Jordan.

Second, the so-called Sykes-Picot Agreement, concluded secretly in 1916 between Great Britain and France, provided for the division of the 'Fertile Crescent' (the present territories of Syria, Lebanon, Jordan, Israel, and Iraq) between the two of them. Palestine, however, was to be internationally administered, though Britain would control Haifa and Acre. Unfortunately for the two accomplices the provisions of this secret pact were leaked by the Bolsheviks. The revelation did little to promote mutual trust.

Third, when the French and British armies under General Edmund Allenby, with the support of both Jews and Arabs, were preparing to invade Palestine, the British government issued in November 1917 the Balfour Declaration pledging 'the establishment in Palestine of a national home for the Jewish people', provided the civil and religious rights of non-Jews were in no way affected. Unfortunately, the conflicting territorial claims of the various groups in the country were not clarified. Arab nationalists were deeply offended since their original assumption had been that they were to reclaim all the Arab lands, including Palestine.

On 10 December 1917, the British, under General Allenby, entered Jerusalem. Three years later, in 1920, Great Britain was assigned the mandate under the terms of the San Remo Conference of the Allied Council to administer the government of Palestine. Despite Arab riots and protests, the mandate was approved by the Council of the League of Nations in 1922 and legalized by the Treaty of Lausanne in 1923.

The period between 1923 and 1948 is marked by a great tragedy: two peoples—Arabs and Jews—each claiming legitimacy locked in bitter conflict over the same terrain. Prior to World War II, much of the violence occurring in Palestine originated with the Arabs: the Wailing Wall outbreak in 1929, the organized rebellion of 1936, and widespread terrorism in

1938 represent examples of such incidents. Then, on the eve of World War II, Britain issued a new statement of policy concerning Palestine. It represented plans for 'the establishment within ten years of an independent (binational) Palestine State.'

The proposal was repudiated by both Arabs and Jews and put in limbo at the outbreak of World War II. A temporary political truce placed a moratorium on further Arab-Jewish negotiations.

During World War II, Jewish organizations in Europe and in the United States intensified their efforts to achieve recognition of the demand for a Jewish commonwealth in Palestine. In Palestine, Jewish terrorist groups, such as the Irgun Zvai Leumi and the Stern Gang, put an end to the political truce in the region by initiating their own campaign of violence. Officially, many Jewish political leaders were quick to denounce terror-ism, though they may have turned a blind eye to the Haganah, a secret Jewish army, organized to protect Jews from Arab attack, to smuggle Jews (especially those who had escaped the Nazi holocaust) into Palestine, and to steal arms and ammunition from the British. In fact, both Jews and Arabs took advantage of the situation to privately and secretly arm themselves.

The Palestine problem became even more complicated after the war ended in 1945. United States President Harry S. Truman appealed to the British Government to admit 100,000 Jewish refugees and displaced persons from Europe into Palestine. The British response was not untypical: a proposal for the formation of an Anglo-American Committee of Inquiry. The surrounding Arab States immediately formed the Arab League, comprised of Syria, Lebanon, Jordan, Saudi Arabia, Yemen, Iraq and Egypt. Then in 1946, the Anglo-American Committee of Inquiry recommended that Palestine be neither partitioned nor granted independence, but remain under the British mandate until hostilities ceased, and that 100,000 European Jews be admitted immediately to Palestine.

The Committee's recommendations outraged Arabs and Jews alike resulting in further outbreaks of violence. Anti-British guerrilla warfare initiated by a Jewish group forced the British to refer the Palestine problem to the United Nations. The decision of the General Assembly of the United Nations in

November 1947 in favour of the partition of Palestine into separate, independent, Jewish and Arab States, with a special international jurisdiction reserved for Jerusalem, created immediate disturbances in Palestine. For a while total chaos reigned in the region with much bloodshed on both Jewish and Arab sides. Since both sides refused to recognize—let alone comply with—the terms of the General Assembly's recommendations, the British declared that they would formally terminate their mandate and withdraw from Palestine by 15 May 1948.

By early 1948, Jews and Arabs were locked in fierce guerrilla warfare. The Haganah soon gained the initiative with the capture and control of several small towns, including Haifa and Jaffa. The embittered Arabs saw themselves as victims condemned to forfeit their lands in reparation for the indescribable crimes inflicted for hundreds of years by Europeans on Jews. Demonstrations in Damascus, Syria, in Beirut, Lebanon, in Baghdad, Iraq, and in Cairo, Egypt, finally provoked leaders of neighbouring Arab states to take concerted action against Palestinian Jews. But by this time the Jews were highly organized, single-minded, well led, and in a position to defy any effort that opposed the establishment of a Jewish State. And the British, the last of the 'foreign' rulers, were ready to abandon the Holy Land.

Palestine: The State of Israel

And the Lord your God will bring you into the land which your fathers possessed, and you shall possess it . . .

Deuteronomy 30:3-5

Keep your voice from weeping and your eyes from tears . . . for you shall come back from the land of the enemy . . . and your children shall come back to their own country.

Jeremiah 31:16-17

On 14 May 1948, the British left Palestine. The Jews, under the leadership of David Ben Gurion, proclaimed the establishment of the State of Israel and the armies of the Arab League countries invaded the Holy Land. The decades since represent survival—the survival of Israel, of refugees, of festering animosity. Four landmarks plot the rutted course of the region's recent history: the full-scale Arab-Israeli wars of 1948, 1956, 1967, and 1973. The intervening years were uneasy truces punctuated by guerrilla and terrorist attacks.

Though the conflict is well documented, few analysts and commentators are able to agree on very much except on dates, events, and Israeli survival measured in terms of territorial gains. The first round of the Arab-Israeli war erupted on 14 May 1948 for a period that lasted for nine months alternating between war and truce. The 1949 settlement extended Israel's boundaries a little beyond the limits specified in the United Nations' plans of partition. Egypt kept the Gaza Strip and part of the Negev area, Jordan annexed most of the areas of the Jordan River (sites of ancient Samaria and Judea), while Jerusalem remained bisected between Israel and Jordan.

On 26 July 1956, Egypt seized control of the Suez Canal, which was then under international control. Great Britain, France and other Western nations protested the seizure. Then, on 29 October 1956, Israeli troops invaded Egypt by quickly overrunning the Sinai Peninsula and the Gaza Strip. Two days later, on 31 October, British and French troops attacked Egypt in an effort to restore international control of the Suez Canal. Russia threatened to intervene on the side of Egypt. The United States urged the withdrawal of Britain and its allies. By March 1957 Britain, France and Israel agreed to comply with the request presented by the United Nations to withdraw from Egypt. Israel ceded the ground it had occupied.

The third major Arab-Israeli clash occurred on 5 June 1967. Egypt and its Arab allies had demanded and obtained in May the withdrawal of the United Nations Emergency Force (UNEF) stationed at the Gaza Strip and the Sinai Peninsula. Israel took the initiative, and in a lightning 'preventive attack' destroyed the entire combined Arab forces. During the course of this 'Six-Day War', Israel reoccupied territory it had ceded in the past and advanced into new Arab land. It included not only the entire Sinai Peninsula and the Gaza Strip from Egypt, but the Golan Heights above the Sea of Galilee from Syria, and the entire West Bank of the Jordan River, including the Old City of Jerusalem from Jordan.

The fourth round of the Arab-Israeli war, known as the Yom Kippur War, erupted on 6 October 1973. The fighting broke out with dramatic suddenness on the holiest day of the Jewish year. The attack came simultaneously on two fronts: from the Golan Heights, assaulted by the Syrians, and from the Sinai Peninsula, by the Egyptians. They struck into territories occupied by Israel since 1967. When a cease-fire proposed by the United Nations' Security Council ended the fighting on 22 October the results were inconclusive. All three participants— Egypt, Syria and Israel—had gained and lost territory.

Hopes for an ultimate resolution of Arab-Israeli conflict over the entire territory seem quite dim. Peace talks and peace treaties are compromised by terrorist acts, guerrilla warfare and violence which still continue to erupt between Arabs and Israelis. Among the several major issues of controversy is the 'occupied' city of Jerusalem. In May 1980, the Israeli parliament passed a law declaring Jerusalem to be Israel's capital. Many Jews and non-Jews around the world deplored this decision, though nothing was done to change the resolution. Tension and turmoil in the region continue to mount, reflecting local as well as global conflict between the two superpowers, the USA, and the USSR.

Palestine is no more. The State of Israel has supplanted it. To appease the guilt they felt for the crimes committed against Jews, European leaders acceded to the Jewish demand for a national homeland in Palestine. The result has been devastating. The 'Holy Land' has become a byword for terrorist acts, guerrilla warfare, bloody assault, embittered feuding and despair. And now, the Western powers coolly blame both the Arabs and the Israelis—the Arabs for refusing to accept Israel's existence on the soil of Palestine; the Israelis for refusing to withdraw from occupied Arab lands. What does the future hold for the 'Holy Land'? The superpowers have always settled the issue in the past, Assyrians succeeding Philistines, and Babylonians, Egyptians, Persians, Greeks and Turks taking over in their turn. It is not a very cheerful prospect.

HOLY BOOK

You taught Your people the Torah and commandments; You instructed them in its statutes and its judgements. O our God, when we lie down as when we are awake, we shall always think and speak of Your ordinances, and rejoice in the Torah and its commandments. It is Your Torah that sustains us throughout life; on its teachings will we meditate day and night.

Jewish Daily Prayer Book

Torah

The words of the Torah are compared to a life-giving medicine. . . . Thus the Holy One, praised be He, said to the Israelites, 'I created within you the impulse to evil, but I created the Torah as a medicine. So long as you occupy yourselves with the Torah, the impulse to evil will not dominate you. But if you do not occupy yourselves with the Torah, you will be delivered into the power of the impulse to evil.'

Sifre Deuteronomy 45

ALMOST all of the religions of the world have amassed collections of writings which the faithful accept as definitive statements of ultimate standards of faith and practice, and therefore, constitute a Holy Book or Holy Bible, from *biblos*, the Greek word for 'book'. Christianity, however, is the only major living religion that reveres and includes the entire Holy Book of Judaism with its own, by placing it on an exact level with the distinctive books of Christian believers. The one distinction Christians make is to identify the Holy Book of Judaism as the Old Testament representing the 'Old Covenant' made by God with His elected people through Moses. Christians then added to the Old Testament the New Testament, a collection of sacred writings representing the 'New

Covenant' made by God with His 'newly' elected people through Jesus Christ.

The terms Old Testament and New Testament are quite irrelevant to Judaism. There is just one Holy Book, the contents of which are identical to those of the Old Testament in Christian Scriptures, except that they are arranged and numbered differently. Unlike the topical arrangement of the thirty-nine books in the Christian Old Testament, the Jewish Holy Bible contains twenty-four books and is divided into three parts:

1. *The Law (Torah)*, which consists of five books: Genesis; Exodus; Leviticus; Numbers; Deuteronomy.

2. *The Prophets (Nevi'im)*, which consists of eight books: Joshua; Judges; I and II Samuel; I and II Kings; Isaiah; Jeremiah; Ezekiel; and the twelve minor prophets (Hosea, Joel, Amos, Obadiah, Jonah, Micah, Nahum, Habakkuk, Zephaniah, Haggai, Zechariah, and Malachi).

3. *The Writings (Ketuvi'im)*, which consists of eleven books: Psalms; Proverbs; Job; Song of Solomon; Ruth; Lamentations; Ecclesiastes; Esther; Ezra-Nehemiah; I and II Chronicles; Daniel.

Several important questions have to be dealt with before turning to examine the contents of the Holy Book. How was the Jewish Bible formed? How did the notion arise that God 'wrote' or 'dictated' one or more books for the guidance of His people? What do the terms 'inspiration' and 'revelation' mean to Judaism?

Judaism, like all other ancient religions in the Middle East, taught that a god could reveal himself and make known his will to certain select human beings. This manifestation of the godhead might be a visible image or entity (cf. Exodus 33:11), a vision (I Kings 22:19), or a dream (Genesis 28:12-13). In addition, a god could inspire certain individuals to speak as people possessed by the spirit of that deity. Such individuals came to be known as prophets, and their oracles and prophecies were put into writing.

Long before the rise of Christianity, the Jews began to collect and preserve these written works. Among them were the early national stories of Adam, of the Patriarchs, of Moses and of the Judges; the writings of several prophets, such as Amos, Hosea, Isaiah and Micah; accounts of the Kings, such as Saul, David, and Solomon; and ancient poems and laws. It is not likely that the scribes or scholars, prophets and kings who kept these records had any inkling that they were inscribing Holy Writ. Their records form part of a collection of writings (since identified as sacred) at least partly because they survived. Many did not. They were destroyed or misplaced—lost to posterity.

Biblical scholars usually distinguish three stages in the process through which the selections comprising the Jewish Bible came to be regarded as the Holy Book. The first stage they identify with authorship and the creative task of writing. The second stage is associated with the editorial function: assembling materials, arranging them in sequence, clarifying and developing consistency. And the third stage marks the selection process and the inclusion—the canonization—of specific items within the final collection.

Stage one, authorship of parts of the Holy Book, took place from about 1100 BC to 100 BC. During this span of 1000 years the Jews, starting as a group of tribes in the desert, invaded Palestine, established a short-lived empire, and eventually were swamped by successive waves of conquerors. Thus, the literary heritage of this 1000-year period reflects these political vicissitudes, Jewish national aspirations, and the development of Jewish religious thought and practices.

Out of this vast body of national Jewish literature produced during this period, certain works were selected, presumably because they contributed to Jewish national survival and to regulating religion and morals. The editors or adjudicators responsible for making choices and canonizing the collection reserved for the Jewish Bible were absolutely convinced that their selections represented divine inspiration and/or divine revelation.

The most significant of these selections is the Torah, the authorship of which is traditionally ascribed to Moses. Scholars trace some of the basic ideas in the Torah to Moses, but the five books it comprises today accrued over a period of six to seven hundred years. They had attained the status of Scripture as early as 400 BC. Most of the Torah is an account of Israelite history from the exodus from Egypt, under the leadership of Moses, to the eve of the triumphant entry into the land of the Canaanites. Prefaced to this account are two others: the first describes events associated with the origin of the universe and of mankind (Genesis 1-11), followed by the stories and sagas of the Patriarchs (Genesis 12-50). Scattered among them are various legal, social and religious instructions or codes.

Successive biblical scholars have devoted lifetimes of study to identify the authors of the Torah, their dates, and the sequence and extent of subsequent revisions. While there are numerous minor disagreements concerning these details, the majority of critics are agreed that the Torah has been subjected to at least four editorial revisions. The first edition is believed to have been written and assembled in the southern kingdom of Judah in around the tenth or ninth century BC. This original is called the 'J' document, because one consistent characteristic of this version is that the Jewish God is identified as Jehovah (or YHWH) and is represented with human, anthropomorphic attributes. The second edition is attributed to the northern kingdom of Israel in around the eighth century BC. This version is identified as the 'E' document, because the Jewish God is now addressed as Elohim, who makes himself known not face-to-face as he does in the J document, but through visions and dreams. The third edition is believed to have been created in Judah once more in about the seventh century BC. This work is known as the 'D' document, because its main emphasis is on Mosaic law, called Deuteronomy. The fourth and final editorial revision is believed to be the work of priests in the sixth century BC during the Babylonian exile. Because it was the work of priests, the work is referred to as the 'P' document. By 400 BC, the five books of the Torah as it appears today had attained the status of Scripture.

The Torah, then, was the first section of the Holy Book to be accorded status as Scripture. In the meantime, a number of important works and oracles, believed to have been written by inspired men called prophets, gradually won special recognition in Jewish society. While the works of the prophets did not attain the same authority as the Torah, they nevertheless came to be regarded as important prophetic collections and by 200 BC attained the status of Scripture. Similarly, the collection of materials called the Writings gradually found favour, though not equal to the Torah, and was finally recognized as Scripture around the second century AD.

The intervention of Alexander the Great in Near Eastern affairs (334-323 BC) and the subsequent influence of Hellenistic culture so dominated parts of his dominion, especially Egypt, that even pious Jews there lost their understanding of Hebrew. This necessitated the translation of the Torah into Greek. The name applied to the Greek version of the Torah is *Septuagint*, a Latin word for 'seventy' and commonly abbreviated as 'LXX'. Tradition asserts that the number represents the seventy scholars responsible for the translation, who themselves symbolized the 'seventy elders who accompanied Moses up the mountain and saw the God of Israel' (Exodus 24:9) before God gave the tables of the Torah to Moses.

Tradition also contributes an interesting prologue to the events at Mount Sinai. According to this tradition, when the Torah was completed God offered it to several other nations before He offered it to the Jews. The Moabites felt that the commandments imposed too many restrictions, in consequence of which they declined. The Ammonites responded in a similar vein. Only the Jews accepted the Torah without reservations, prompting the Jews to coin two phrases to mark their commitment—one referring to God 'Giver of Torah', and the other to their own acceptance of God's gift 'burden of the Torah', a burden willingly and even joyfully assumed since it regulates and governs their lives according to God's will.

The word 'Torah' steadily acquired an expanding connotation in Judaism. The basic meaning of the word seems to have been 'casting' lots (Deuteronomy 33:8-11), or 'pointing the way' through oracular divination. Hence, in the early biblical period of Judaism, traditional interpretations of what God required of humans was provided through the medium of oracles. Later, during the monarchic period, Torah represented the basic 'instruction' provided to the Jews by God, particularly in legal matters. During the exilic period, the meaning of Torah took a more concrete form. Instead of meaning divine instruction, it now referred specifically to a single divinely-revealed 'law', namely the Five Books of Moses comprising the first and most important division of the Jewish Bible. During the rabbinic age, Torah, in its most narrow prescribed sense, still meant the 'Law' of Moses (i.e., the Five Books of Moses); but in its broader sense, Torah also embraced the entire body of divinely revealed law, namely the entire Jewish Bible.

The Torah, in its narrow sense, is the most revered and sacred object of Jewish ritual. Wrapped around two wooden poles (or rollers) ornamented in silver, the Torah is a hand-written parchment scroll of the Five Books of Moses. The text of the Torah must be letter perfect, since any two scribal errors proscribe its use in worship. The entire scroll is covered with an embroidered cloth encased in a silver breast-plate. Worshippers stand in reverence when the Torah is taken out of the Ark and carried to the reading desk or in procession within the synagogue. During the procession of the Torah, pious Jews place their prayer shawls on the parchment (since no human hand may touch the sacred scroll) and then kiss the fringes of their shawls that have brushed the scroll.

Starting with the book of Genesis, a portion of the Torah is read aloud every Sabbath during worship, until the entire Torah is read within the span of the annual Jewish calendar. Among devout Jews, Torah *is* Jewish life, without which life has neither meaning nor value. Torah prescribes the pattern of behaviour for every level of individual and communal living. To provide both stability and flexibility, leaders of Jewish communities took pains to live in accordance with the divine will as expressed and embodied in the Torah, in its widest sense.

Viewed from this perspective, Torah cannot be defined simply as Law, but as the entire content of Judaism—its Holy Book, its oral traditions, its religious affirmations, its historical recollections, and its ethical and ceremonial obligations. In a word, Torah embraces the whole of human experience, prescribing, enlightening, encouraging, warning, exhorting, solacing.

Since the end of the eighteenth century, however, this traditional dominance of the Torah has been seriously challenged both in principle and in detail by modern biblical criticism derived from the products of the improved techniques and technology of research. Biblical scholars, responding to new evidence, called for the critical analysis of the texts in the Bible and for historical evidence to verify the events documented in the biblical record. A comparison of biblical events against established historical benchmarks soon revealed discrepancies, inconsistencies, and contradictions among the ideas expressed, the unhistoricity of many events, the unreliability of the authorship or source attributed to several texts, and so on. There were three characteristic responses to this evidence.

One reaction was to repudiate the conclusions of biblical scholars. Orthodox Judaism, in fact, ignores them—teaching that the Torah is as meaningful and as reliable today as it has been at any time since its origin. Hayyim Nahman Bialik (1873-1934), one of the greatest modern Jewish poets, states:

The Torah is the tool of the Creator; with it and for it He created the universe. The Torah is older than creation. It is the highest idea and the living soul of the world. Without it the world could not exist and would have no right to exist.[1]

Reform Judaism typifies a contrasting reaction in that its adherents do not feel bound to observe the Torah either in principle or in detail, since they see the commandments within the Torah as the product of codifying or formalizing tradition over the course of centuries. To consider these commandments as the literal dictates of God delivered in person seemed unacceptable to Reform Jews. Here is how Kaufmann Kohler (1843-1926) states it:

As soon as the modern Jew, however, undertook to free himself from the tutelage of blind acceptance of authority and inquired after the purpose of all the restrictions of the Law laid upon him, ancient loyalty to the same collapsed and the pillars of Judaism seemed to be shaken. Then the leaders of Reform, imbued with the prophetic spirit, felt it to be their imperative duty to search out the fundamental ideas of the priestly law of holiness and, accordingly, they learned how to separate the kernel from the shell. In opposition to the orthodox tendency to worship the letter, they insisted on the fact that Israel's separation from the world—which it is ultimately to win for the divine truth—cannot itself be its end and aim, and that blind obedience to the Law does not constitute true piety.[2]

A third reaction was that of Conservative Judaism. It took, as it were, the middle road between blind acceptance and wary scepticism of the Torah. It regarded some parts of the Torah as obsolete and therefore to be safely ignored, while other parts it accepted as relevant, to be retained and observed. Solomon Schechter (1847-1915), the chief proponent of Conservative Judaism, justifies his viewpoint as follows:

It is an illusion to speak of the burden which a scrupulous care to observe six hundred and thirteen commandments must have laid upon the Jew. Even a superficial analysis will discover that in the time of Christ many of these commandments were already obsolete . . . while others concerned only certain classes . . . or the representatives of the community, or even only one or two individuals among the whole population . . . Others, again, provided for contingencies which could occur only to a few . . . whilst many . . . could scarcely have been considered as a practical prohibition by the pre-Christian Jew. . . . Thus it will be found by a careful enumeration that barely a hundred laws remain which really concerned the life of the bulk of the people. If we remember that even these include such laws as belief in the unity of God, the necessity of loving and fearing Him, and of sanctifying His name, of loving one's neighbour and the stranger . . . it will hardly be said that the ceremonial side of the people's religion was not well balanced by a fair amount of spiritual and social elements. Besides, it would seem that the line between the ceremonial and the spiritual is too often only arbitrarily drawn. With many commandments it is rather a matter of opinion whether they should be relegated to the one category or the other . . .[3]

Thus, though a narrow definition of the term Torah refers only to the Five Books of Moses, Talmudic rabbis applied it to a wide body of teaching. This rabbinic, inclusive application of the term unquestioningly dominated Jewish thought till the modern era and still applies among traditionalists. To this group, Torah represents not only a written Law but also an oral Law transmitted from generation to generation, and finally codified as Talmud and Midrash.

Oral Torah: Talmud and Midrash

The Talmud is the sole spring from which Judaism has flowed, the ground upon which Judaism rests, and the soul of life which shapes and sustains Judaism.

Samson Raphael Hirsch (1808-1888)

By the time the Bible had been completed and assembled, great changes had taken place within Judaism. These changes gave rise to oral interpretations and traditions concerning many of the written laws, and, though Judaism affirmed the binding character of the Torah, it also sanctioned and endorsed oral traditions which came to be known as *Talmud* and *Midrash*.

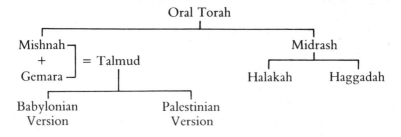

Next to the Bible, the Talmud and the Midrash are revered as the most sacred Jewish books. School children use them as textbooks; rabbis, particularly the Conservative and the Orthodox, study them as sources of precept and teaching. The Talmud is, in effect, a compendium of law and lore—the Jewish 'Encyclopaedia'. As such, it makes more sense to readers who are well read in the Torah than to those who are not, in the same way that Milton's *Paradise Lost* makes more sense to those well versed in classical mythology than to those who are not.

But the Talmud is more than just a series of legal treatises. Scholarly commentary is illustrated and elaborated by biographical sketches, humorous anecdotes, parables and epigrams that also provide an intimate glimpse into ancient Jewish life. And yet, among pious Jews, the Talmud represents a guide for day-to-day living as relevant today as it was two thousand years ago. Moral insights, spiritual values and profound truths enunciated in Talmudic text represent a large portion of it and have universal application for those who care to read it.

The same is also true of Midrash, which is a collection of rabbinical commentaries on the Bible. Ancient Jewish scholars illuminated or associated each verse in the Bible with some moral thought, often in the form of a parable or of an appropriate life situation. Reference to these commentaries from Midrash is as common in literary works as it is in formal worship and many of its aphorisms have become part of common Jewish speech.

The Talmud and Midrash are often thought of as 'oral' Torah, in contrast to the 'written' or 'revealed' Torah. Jewish tradition maintains that from the very moment that Moses accepted the written Torah on Mount Sinai there existed an oral Torah that was handed on according to tradition from generation to generation. It is more probable that oral traditions developed over centuries rather than days, weeks or decades. This accretion of debate, discussion, differences of opinion, and commentaries evolved in the search for deeper meaning in the written Torah. All such interpretations were transmitted orally from one generation to another until the volume of accumulated tradition taxed the capacity of each succeeding generation to sustain it. It is more than likely that some of it was lost before it was finally written down. In time, additional commentaries and interpretations emerged as a source of reference for these codified traditions—commentaries on commentaries. The result was a mass of accumulated traditional material all codified in legal form. The process gives substance to the conclusion that the Talmud and the Midrash developed over hundreds of years. Historical evidence, scarce as it is, confirms it.

Midrash: The earliest method of teaching and transmitting the oral Torah was in the form of an exposition, or exegesis, of the Bible. The name given to this didactic form was *Midrash*, a term derived from the Hebrew root meaning 'to search', 'to investigate' and hence, 'to expound'. Expositions dealing with legal aspects of the Bible were identified as *Midrash Halakah*, meaning literally 'walking' in the way of the law (Exodus 18:20). Expositions associated with homiletical or moralizing, devotional, and non-legal discourse were classified as *Midrash Haggadah*, meaning 'narration'.

The first identifiable exponent of the expository style associated with Midrash was Ezra in 444 BC, though there is evidence that it may have been employed earlier by others. Successive generations of teachers after Ezra, called *Soferim* ('scribes' or 'bookmen'), also resorted to sermons and lectures typical of Midrashic texts. They delivered their expositions in synagogues, in Jewish academies, and possibly in private dwellings, on public or private occasions, but especially and more significantly on Sabbaths and festivals.

When were these oral expositions committed to writing? Evidence for the existence of Haggadic Midrash books is documented by the third century AD. Books of Halakic Midrash seem to date from a century earlier. But it is exceedingly difficult to ascertain the precise date of the earliest compositions, since the original texts of most important works no longer survive. The best that modern scholarship can ascertain is that Midrashic exposition ceased soon after the sixth century AD. The centuries that followed are characterized by sorting and assembling the copious Midrashic material. This mass of accumulated material is characterized by glosses and adaptations (and gaps or apparent omissions) arranged in separate collections according to age, provenance or origin and the character of the different books of the Bible. Consequently there is no agreement among scholars as to when and where the Midrash— the oral Torah—was first recorded in writing.

The Halakic Midrash includes legal commentaries on parts of the Books of Exodus, Leviticus, Numbers and Deuteronomy. The Haggadic Midrash is devoted to non-legal expositions on all the Five Books of Moses, as well as on Ruth, Esther, Ecclesiastes, Lamentations and Song of Songs. Besides these general biblical commentaries there are other Midrashic materials with specific functions: The *Yalkut Shimenoi*, a kind of concordance or thesaurus on the Bible; the *Peshiktha Rabbathi*, a compendium of discourses appropriate to festivals and Sabbaths; and *Tanna debe Eliyyahu*, an ethical humanistic guide to conduct.

The motive that prompted the commentaries compiled as Midrashic texts was the desire to interpret the obscurities and discrepancies of the written Torah. A few examples will illustrate the conundrums that perplexed Midrashic teachers, whose function was to probe, to investigate and to interpret, not to legislate.

One of the most fundamental teachings of Judaism is the affirmation of the One God. Yet the statement in Genesis 1:26 reads: 'Let us make man in our image, after our likeness'. Why is the plural possessive pronoun used, if God is One?

Again, the verse in Deuteronomy 24:1 states: 'When a man takes a wife and marries her, if then she finds no favour in his eyes because he has found some indecency in her, and he writes her a bill of divorce and sends her out of his house.' What is the precise meaning of 'some indecency' to suggest grounds for divorce?

Or again, the prohibition against work on the Sabbath is strongly worded in Exodus 35:2: 'Six days shall work be done, but on the seventh day you shall have a holy Sabbath of solemn rest to the Lord; whoever does any work on it shall be put to death.' What type of work constitutes a violation serious enough to require capital punishment?

These examples, of course, do not exhaust the types of biblical ambiguities that demand supplementary interpretation and elucidation. By offering credible explanations of biblical texts, Midrashic teachers were able to justify the written Torah confirming its authority in order to command the continuing respect and loyalty of the people.

Talmud: Mishnah and Gemara: While the Midrashic method of

exposition was extremely effective in identifying and interpreting the perplexities, obscurities, and discrepancies of biblical texts, another oral method was introduced to teach and transmit Torah. This method was appropriately designated *Mishnah*, from a Hebrew root meaning 'to repeat', since only the repetition of oral teaching was calculated to communicate and inculcate concepts and data especially to auditors who could not read.

Unlike the technique of Midrashic teachers, who relied on a running commentary on biblical verses, Mishnahic teachers developed a distinct interpretation of law and lore, independent of biblical texts, and yet based upon the Torah. In other words, Mishnahic teachers sanctioned certain precepts or directives whose authority was not vested directly in the written Torah but on experience. Such precepts and directives were recognized and accepted because they worked.

By the end of the first century BC the Mishnahic teaching by precept superseded the didactic harangues characteristic of the Midrashic method. The popularity of the Mishnahic method, however, did not discount the Midrashic form. On the contrary, for a long time both the Midrashic and the Mishnahic methods existed side by side as means of teaching oral Torah. In order to distinguish them from Soferim, the Midrashic teachers, those who specialized in teaching the Mishnahic method, were known as *Tannaim*, from a variant Hebrew term meaning 'those who hand down orally'.

The same problem that had taxed the resources of the Soferim now came to plague the Tannaim. Mishnahic teachings accumulated to such a point that they defied human capacity to retain and communicate them all, let alone serve as a reliable guide for the socio-political conditions of the times. In addition, there developed quite naturally, differences of opinion and conflicting interpretations, which only served to aggravate the dissension which is an endemic condition of priests and lawyers at the very best of times, under the most favourable circumstances, in the best regulated societies, with the simplest issues.

At last, the task of committing Mishnahic teachings to paper or parchment began. Outstanding differences of opinion were tested against the biblical record, or some recognized tradition, or even logical reasoning. A majority vote decided every problem and dispute. Next came the task of assembling and preserving all of these resolved oral traditions and teachings.

Although there is some proof that a codified body of Mishnahic lore existed as early as AD 50, the substantive collection and systematization of the Mishnahic teachings dates from the work of Rabbi Akiba (c. 50-135). To him is attributed the arrangement of oral teachings according to main topics and sub-topics. Refinements to this initial classification by topics continued under Rabbi Akiba's disciples, foremost of whom was Rabbi Meir (c. 110-175). Meanwhile, other teachers scattered across the ancient world were also busy compiling similar material from regional and local sources, and by AD 200 several such compilations were being circulated and utilized by Jewish schools.

At this time a pressing need was felt for the organization of a recognized corpus of legal norms that would represent the views of the rabbis on every aspect of life. The person who assembled, edited and compiled the Mishnahic oral Torah into a coherent text was Rabbi Judah Ha-Nasi (the Prince, c. 135-213). His work soon gained wide acceptance and became known as 'The Mishna' though it did little to inhibit contemporary authorities from compiling and using their own rival collections, preserving those teachings which Rabbi Judah had, for one reason or another, excluded from his own anthology.

The Mishnah soon transcended the dubious authority of all rival collections and attained a quasi-canonical status. Jewish schools, both in Palestine and Babylon, came to regard the Mishnah as the authoritative canon of Oral Torah. It became the basis of instruction, study, and further investigation by Jewish scholars known as *Amoraim* (speakers, teachers, interpreters). The Mishnah, then, became the standard work of reference until a companion book of collections, known as *Gemara*, was compiled.

The Hebrew term *Gemara* is derived either from an Aramaic root meaning 'to repeat', or from a Hebrew root meaning 'to complete'. In so far as the discussions embodied in the Gemara are in the form of running commentaries, they serve as a supplement or completion of the Mishnah. Otherwise, the Gemara contains material that has little to do with the Mishnah, such as lore, history, homilies, maxims, and so on.

In many respects Gemara was identical to Mishnah except that it included selections omitted or rejected by other compilers, it cleared up obscure passages in the Mishnah, and it reconciled contradictory oral traditions championed or espoused by different schools. The Mishnah and the Gemara together constitute the *Talmud* (Study, Teaching).

Talmud: Palestinian and Babylonian Versions: The biblical scholar's task of establishing who wrote what, when, and where is further complicated by the simultaneous existence of two versions of the Talmud, each originating in two distinct Jewish centres of learning: the academies of Palestine and Babylon. The Palestinian Talmud (often referred to also as 'Yerushalmi') is written in a west-Aramaic dialect, lacks unity and coherence, and is incomplete. It is also about one third the size of the Babylonian version. So far, no satisfactory explanation has been offered to account for these two textual variants. Tradition ascribes the redaction of the Palestinian Talmud to Rabbi Johanan Ben Nappaha (died 279), a disciple of Rabbi Judah Ha-Nasi. The fact is, however, that a considerable portion of the contents of the Palestinian Talmud is of later date, from the third to the fifth century AD. For these reasons, Jewish scholars have generally given less credence to the Palestinian Talmud than they have to the Babylonian Talmud.

All subsequent codifications of the law rest on the Babylonian Talmud, which is written in east-Aramaic dialect. The accumulation of traditions orally transmitted through the centuries assumed such massive proportions that the task of documenting them became a self-evident need. It was finally undertaken by Rab Ashi (died 427), who for over fifty years applied himself to collect, sift, and classify the vast store of traditions which governed the lives and thoughts of Babylonian Jewish teachers and disciples alike.

Some sixty years later, Rabina Bar Huna (known as Rabina

II) redacted Ashi's material. Final polishing or finishing touches to Rabina's edition were added in the sixth century by the *Saboraim*, a group of 'explicators'. On the completion of the work of those scholars, revisions to the Talmud may be said to have come to an end.

The Babylonian Talmud is divided into six *Sedarim*, or Six Orders. Each Order is further sub-divided into *Massechot*, or Tractates, for a total of sixty-three. In addition, the contents of each Tractate are grouped into chapters and paragraphs. The Six Orders and the topics each includes follow:

1. *Zeraim* (Seeds): agricultural laws, such as tillage, cultivation, and the sowing of gardens, orchards or fields, and the products of harvest. An introductory tractate deals with prayers and worship.

2. *Moed* (Appointed Seasons): laws of Sabbath, festivals, holy days, fasts, and rules for ordering the Jewish calendar.

3. *Nashim* (Women): laws of marriage and divorce, including relations between males and females.

4. *Nezikin* (Damages): civil and criminal laws, as well as ethical standards which should govern human behaviour in social, domestic or political life.

5. *Kodashim* (Holy Things): laws appertaining to the Jewish Temple, sacrifices, officiating priests and *hullin* (dietary laws).

6. *Tohorot* (Purifications): laws of ritual purity and impurity, for people and things.

The study of the Talmud, like the study of the Bible, has always been regarded as a form of worship. Intimate knowledge and close association with Talmudic teaching contributed tremendously to the national survival and religious preservation of the Jews. In times of trial and tribulation, the Talmud offered the Jews solace, peace, and an indestructible bulwark against despair. It also proved a bulwark against external pressures towards cultural assimilation with host countries. The Talmud united Jews in a bond of kinship stronger than national solidarity. It does so today even though the Talmudic world is separated by centuries from modern avenues of thought. The gap has had little effect on many of the modern religious and ethical norms of Judaism which derive directly from the Talmud.

But devotion to the Talmud and the values it implied brought some disastrous consequences. During the Middle Ages, Christian Church leaders and Jewish converts to Christianity attacked the Talmud on the grounds that it contained heresies and anti-Christian statements. Public burnings of the Talmud were, therefore, not uncommon. Even in modern times, anti-Semites have claimed that the Talmud sanctions all sorts of crimes against non-Jews, such as rape, robbery and murder.

All such allegations are based, first on ignorance, and second on the tendentious selection of texts. Modern scholarship, regardless of its origin among Jews or non-Jews, has discredited claims that the Talmud advocates violence against non-Jews, or that it even disparages Christianity.

A measure of the Talmud's universality, its relevance, and its authority is its survival as a daily source of inspiration and guidance. It represents the combined genius of gifted individuals, deeply rooted in the history and tradition of their people. These gifted spokesmen were neither political leaders nor legislators nor administrators. They regarded themselves simply as teachers. Though, as teachers, they may have performed functions that were judicial, administrative, and political in character and scope, their main concern was to preserve, to transmit and to instruct on matters that centered upon human behaviour, in its legal, social, ethical and universal application.

Apocalyptic Literature and the Apocrypha

Write all that you have seen in a book, and put it in a secret place, and teach them to the wise among your people, whose hearts you know can receive and keep these secrets.

II Esdras 12:37-38

A large selection of non-canonical materials enjoyed great popularity and was widely circulated among the Jews during the Graeco-Roman period. Written in Hebrew, Aramaic, and Greek, sometime between 200 BC and AD 100, this mass of Jewish literature included legendary histories, collections of psalms, wisdom works, esoteric doctrines, and apocalyptic pronouncements. The word 'apocalyptic' derives from a Greek root meaning 'to uncover'. Hence, apocalyptic literature deals with visions heretofore unknown, describing events or things to come.

Formal canonization of these non-canonical materials, or even a list of approved texts, was not an issue at first. In fact, they were rather disparagingly identified as 'writings which do not defile the hands'. But the tragic events of the Jewish revolt, culminating in the fall of Jerusalem in AD 70, and the rapid growth of 'Christian' literature, which threatened to invade Jewish books with Christian interpolations, forced the rabbis to take drastic action at the Council of Jamnia in AD 90. They set up a canon of approved texts. All extracanonical works were considered 'outside books' and strongly condemned. Henceforth, pious Jews were called to repudiate such 'outside books' in preference to the Torah.

Consequently, many of these 'outside books' dropped out of circulation and existence if they were not systematically destroyed. Fortunately, for one reason or another, some of these manuscripts survived the vicissitudes of time. They are identified as follows according to a classification devised by C. T. Fritsch[4] since there is no special order recognized by tradition for these 'outside books'.

Palestinian 'Outside Books'
(originally written in Hebrew or Aramaic)

Testaments of the Twelve Patriarchs
Psalms of Solomon
Lives of the Prophets
Jubilees
Testament of Job
Enoch

Martyrdom of Isaiah
Paralipomena of Jeremiah
Life of Adam and Eve (incorrectly called Apocalypse of
    Moses by the editor of the Greek text)
Assumption of Moses
Apocalypse of Baruch

Alexandrian 'Outside' Books
(originally writen in Greek)

Aristeas
Sibylline Oracles (a group of fifteen books)
III Maccabees
IV Maccabees
Slavonic Book of Enoch (or II Enoch, or Books of the Secrets
    of Enoch)
Greek Apocalypse of Baruch (or III Baruch)

Many of the above listed 'outside books' contain esoteric and
apocalyptic teachings. Apocalyptic teachings are probably not
unique to Judaism. They are believed to have originated in
Zoroastrianism (a Persian religion) and to have been adopted by
Judaism during the exilic and post-exilic period (after the sixth
century BC). The basic premise of apocalyptic thought is
essentially dualistic. It presupposes two cosmic, opposing
forces of Good and Evil in constant conflict. Hence it is a cosmic
dualism, not the metaphysical dualism of spirit and matter. The
entire universe (the earth, the heavens, the underworld, and all
its denizens—mortal or immortal) is subject to the eternal
confrontation between the powers of Good and Evil.

The another characteristic of apocalyptic thought is its preoccupation with eschatology which involves a belief in two
distinct ages: the present, which is temporal and irretrievably
evil under the dominion of the Evil power; and the future,
which is perfect, eternal and destined to be ruled by the
righteous and blessed power of Good.

The protagonists of apocalyptic literature, therefore, are God
and Satan, angels and demons, and its settings are heaven and
hell. These settings in turn give rise to eschatological conjec-

ture—with events that surround the 'end' of time. Associated with these events are the symbolic signs, the cataclysmic features, the cosmic wars, the new messianic age, the resurrection of the dead, and the final judgement of all humans.

This extra-canonical apocalyptic literature was as popular among early Christians as it was among the Jews. Throughout history, the concepts contained in apocalyptic literature continued to occupy both Jewish and Christian thought. It greatly influenced New Testament writers but made an even more profound impact on Jewish beliefs, a conclusion attested to by the numerous concepts selected and incorporated in the Midrash retained in popular traditional Jewish belief, and finally adopted as basic principles of Judaism.

Some of the more favoured 'outside' books came to be regarded as containing secret or 'hidden' teachings. Gradually these books found their way into the Septuagint among Greek-speaking Jewish people. When the Christians adopted the Septuagint, they saw no reason to disparage or to ban these books. On the contrary, along with the Greek-speaking Jews, they treated them as inspired Scripture. Eventually, the collection came to be known as the *Apocrypha*.

The word *apocrypha* is a Greek term—an adjective meaning 'hidden', which is applied to books kept from the public because of their esoteric nature. The content of these books was at first highly regarded. It was only much later, sometime after the first century AD, that the word 'apocrypha' came to mean 'spurious' or 'heretical'. The fourteen books, or parts of books, collected in one volume, known as the Apocrypha, were all written between 200 BC and AD 100. With one or two exceptions, these books were included in the Septuagint.

Although the Jewish council of Jamnia, held in AD 90, did not recognize these collections as canonical, they had by then acquired a degree of holiness and were widely read among Jews for inspirational purposes. In addition, since they had been translated from Hebrew or Aramaic into Greek and included in the Septuagint for Greek-speaking Jews, the rabbis could hardly insist on their total proscription but instead asked that they be excluded from public worship. In consequence, these *Genuzim* (a Hebrew term for 'apocrypha') were restricted to individual as opposed to public worship. Hence a distinction was made between texts of fixed canon designed for public worship, and non-canonical works designed for private edification.

Gradually, however, these non-canonical books lost their authority and therefore their popularity among the Jews. Only one book, namely Ecclesiasticus, survived among Jews till the twelfth century AD because Talmudic Judaism had no room for non-canonical writings which were considered dangerous, as the following quotation indicates: 'Whoever brings together in his house more than twenty-four books [i.e., the canonical books of the Hebrew Bible] brings confusion' (Midrash Qoheleth 12.12).

The survival of Apocryphal texts to this date is due entirely to the early Christians, who found the books included in the Septuagint so interesting and so edifying that they copied them often and translated them into other languages.

Nevertheless, not even Christians unanimously endorsed this collection. Two opposing views emerged: one justified the apocryphal books as canonical on the grounds that they were included in the Septuagint; the other branded them as uncanonical because they were excluded from the Hebrew Bible. These two divergent views were never resolved, so that the difference of opinion continues to this day among Catholics and Protestants, the former accepting, while the latter reject, the canonicity of the books called the Apocrypha.

1. I Esdras
This is a chronicle of the exile to Babylon and the return to Jerusalem, largely identical with the narrative in Ezra and Nehemiah. The date may be second century BC.

2. II Esdras
The writer reflects in this book on the continuing problems of human life and God's justice. It was written after the death of Nero (AD 68). Chapters 1, 2, 15 and 16 are Christian additions, while other parts may also reflect Christian teaching.

3. *Tobit*

This book is a didactic romance concerning Tobit, a devout Jew of the dispersion whose good deeds and faithfulness result in supernatural deliverance from affliction for himself and his family. Its date is probably early second century BC.

4. *Judith*

This is another romance based on the story of the virtuous heroine who saved her people by decapitating the enemy General, whose lust she had aroused. It is contemporary with Tobit.

5. *The Additions to the Book of Esther*

Six separate fragments, added to correct the canonical book of Esther, comprise this text. A likely date is the early first century BC.

6. *The Wisdom of Solomon*

This represents the first Jewish book specifically to promise individual retribution after death. The book is a composite, with the break at Chapter 11. The first part is a translation from Hebrew; the second a Greek continuation by the translator of the first. Its date may be the first century BC.

7. *Ecclesiasticus, or The Wisdom of Jeshua ben Sirach*

Ecclesiasticus is the longest and most attractive book in the Apocrypha. It is concerned with religious truth, with emphasis on worldly wisdom that comes from experience. It dates from about 180 BC.

8. *The Book of Baruch*

Among Apocryphal texts, this book represents the closest approach to the style and spirit of Jewish prophecy. The themes are: confession of sin, encouragement in the pursuit of wisdom, and comfort for the afflicted. Appended is the *Letter of Jeremiah*, an admonition against idolatry. Its date may be the first century BC.

9. *The Story of Susanna*

Susanna rejects the solicitations of two lustful elders who surprise her at her bath; is accused by them of adultery, but is vindicated by Daniel, as she is being led to execution. Its date is the middle of the second century BC.

10. *The Prayer of Azariah and The Song of the Three Young Men*

The prayer of Azariah (the Hebrew name of Abednego), is distinguished by a formal hymn purportedly recited by the three prospective martyrs in the fiery furnace. It was written in about the second century BC.

11. *Bel and the Dragon*

This text ridicules the worship first of Bel and then of a sacred serpent. Its date is the second century BC.

12. *The Prayer of Manasseh*

This purports to be the prayer attributed to Manasseh in II Chronicles 33:18 while he was captive in Babylonia. Written probably in the first century BC.

13. *I Maccabees*

This is a concise and competent account of the course of events during the years 167-134 BC, probably by an eye-witness and a devoted partisan of the Maccabees. Though it was written in Hebrew it exhibits the characteristics of Hellenistic historiography.

14. *II Maccabees*

This book represents a parallel account, covering the years 175-160 BC. Its author describes it as an abridgement of a five-volume work by Jason of Cyrene. It seems to be an eyewitness account, but the tone is more emotional, rhetori-cal, and propagandistic than I Maccabees.

At first extra-canonical works played an important role in the life of Judaism, but their authority gradually diminished. Throughout the Middle Ages and up to modern times, these works were for the most part, neglected both by Jews and Christians. Christians regarded them as peripheral and unim-portant for biblical studies. Jews found them to be repetitious and of little educational value or relevance to the Torah. However, in recent years, and particularly since the discovery of new evidence, there has been an upsurge in interest among Jewish and Christian scholars. Tracing the social and intellectual climate, the religious premises, and the literary forms of the intertestamental period (the period between the end of the 'Old' and the beginning of the 'New' Testaments), modern scholars find a rich source of reference in the Apocrypha.

HOLY OBSERVANCES

Even unregulated actions, such as eating and drinking, walking and sitting, standing, intercourse, talk, and all the needs of the body, every one of them should be directed to the service of the creator, or as a means leading to service unto Him.

Sulhan Arukh Orah Hayim 231:1

Prayer

O Lord, our God, hear our cry!
Have compassion upon us and pity us;
Accept our prayer with loving favour . . .
For You mercifully heed Your people's supplication.
Praised are You, O Lord, who is attentive to prayer.

Amidah—The Eighteen Benedictions

PRAYER is one of the most solemn holy observances in Judaism, identified in Hebrew as *mitzvot* (singular *mitzvah*). All activities in life are encompassed in the term mitzvot. Everything, from enjoyment to suffering, is endowed with purpose and meaning, so that to act 'for the sake of God' with devotion and an aware deliberation represents mitzvot. In other words, all religious and secular activity, such as study, prayer, social justice, repossessing the Holy Land, which are pleasing to God, represents mitzvot. Thus, each mitzvah is an end in itself and its observance has an absolute value.

Pious Jews are constantly aware of the presence of God and always ready to praise and bless Him. Judaism prescribes three orders of daily prayer: morning, noon and evening. Besides these, there are prayers assigned to meals, to holy days, to the Torah, to the months of the year, and so on. These prescribed prayers are recited consistently throughout the year at stipulated times and occasions. Formal prayers are the rule, on the assumption that they express feelings and sentiments better than extemporaneous prayers. Another justification for formal prayers is that they embody the aspirations and values of a community, with all its sense of oneness. The repetition of the familiar words of formal, prescribed prayers is considered to correspond to the eternal cycle of nature—always the same, yet ever renewed. In consequence, the worshipper is led to recognize the parallel between prayer and life itself: though they are both characterized by a degree of uniformity and consistency, neither are routine activities. Both represent forms of devotion in acknowledgment of God's will, not mechanical drills.

The commandment to pray three times a day is incumbent upon every individual Jew. But there is relatively little difference between the prayer prescribed for the individual and its counterpart for public service in the synagogue. According to Judaism, prayers offered communally by a congregation are far more meaningful than those offered by an individual, though the act is considered legitimate and permissible, because it is the congregation that upholds and sustains the individual.

One unique feature of Jewish prayer is that it is performed in association with several external symbols: *tallith, tefillin, mezuzah* and skull cap. The tallith is a prayer shawl (or stole, or robe) decorated with tassels or fringes on all four corners, that is worn by Conservative and Orthodox male worshippers only during daytime prayers or services, but not at night. Reform Jews have eliminated the use of the tallith, though some Reform rabbis wear it occasionally over their gowns.

The tefillin consist of two small leather boxes (cubes, one to two inches square) containing four biblical selections (Deuteronomy 6:4-9; Deuteronomy 11:13-20; Exodus 13:11-16; Exodus 13:1-10), and are strapped to the arm (which is close to the heart) and forehead (which is close to the mind) by male worshippers only, in fulfilment of the biblical injunction (Deuteronomy 6:8). The tefillin are not worn on Sabbaths and Festivals, since such days enshrine the ideas of the tefillin.

Most Orthodox male Jews wear a skull cap at all times, not only during prayer. Conservative Jews, however, cover their heads only during acts of worship, while Reform Jews pray generally without skull caps. Extremely Orthodox Jewish women wear a wig as a mark of piety and reverence.

A mezuzah is a small scroll (three inches long), encased in wood, metal or glass, which is secured at an angle (about five feet from the floor) on doorposts of Jewish homes and offices, symbolizing God's presence. In Orthodox and Conservative homes and offices they are set on every door. Inside the case is a tiny parchment inscribed with several of the biblical selections also enclosed in the tefillin. The tefillin reminds Jews as they leave or enter a house or office that they are guided by God's presence and love.

Inscriptions on the parchment enclosed by the mezuzah and the tefillin are handwritten (like the Torah Scrolls), and include a quotation which is a prayer known as the *Shema*. The entire passage in Deuteronomy 6:4-9 is called the *Shema* because the first word it begins with is *Shema*, 'Hear'.

Hear, O Israel! The Lord our God, the Lord is One. Love the Lord your God with all your heart, and with all your soul, and with all your might. Take to heart these words which I command you this day. Teach them diligently to your children. Recite them when you are in your house, and when you are away, when you lie down and when you get up. Bind them as a sign on your hand and let them serve as frontlets between your eyes. Inscribe them on the doorposts of your homes and on your gates.

Deuteronomy 6:4-9

In one sense, the Shema is not so much a prayer as a declaration of faith which reminds Jews of the basic teachings of Judaism: the unity of God, the love of God, the obligation to learn and to teach and the ideal of holiness as embodied in specific precepts. In another sense, however, the Shema is a prayer and evokes among pious Jews what the Lord's Prayer (Matthew 6:9-13) evokes among Christians. In the morning and in the evening, the recital of the Shema represents tacit acknowledgement of the Divine Presence and of confidence and trust in God.

The order of prayer stipulates two Benedictions before the Shema, and Nineteen Benedictions (originally eighteen), known as *Amidah* (literally 'standing', the posture in which it is recited), follow. Each order of daily prayer ends with the *Alenu* (meaning 'upon us is the duty'), which confirms conviction in the Messianic hope, the universal sovereignty of God, and the establishment of His kingdom.

In addition to daily prayers, Talmudic Judaism prescribes benedictions to acknowledge God's intervention on various occasions, such as at the beginning and conclusion of meals, at the appearance of some natural phenomenon like sunrise, at the announcement of good or bad news, at the end of a successful shopping expedition for new clothes, and so on. All these benedictions express two basic Jewish feelings: dependence on God and gratitude for His wonderful creation.

Sabbath

Six days shall work be done; but the seventh day is a sabbath of solemn rest, holy to the Lord. Whoever does any work on the Sabbath day shall be put to death. Therefore the people of Israel shall keep the Sabbath, observing the Sabbath throughout their generations, as a perpetual covenant.

Exodus 31:15-16

A popular Jewish saying is: 'More than Israel kept the Sabbath, the Sabbath kept Israel.' The traditional life of a Jew builds through a succession of weekdays to a climax in the Sabbath, because the Sabbath is no mere day of rest. It is a 'holy' day—a symbolic day representing the Covenant between God and His chosen people (Exodus 31:12-17). Flouting the Sabbath or desecrating it once spelled death (Exodus 31:14; Numbers 15:32-36) and today is tantamount to the denial of God and His Sovereignty. No institution or holy ordinance in Judaism is regarded with more awe or reverence than the observance of the Sabbath. In fact, the Sabbath is *the* institution that most contributed to the survival of Judaism.

The word 'Sabbath' derives from the Hebrew word *Shabath*, meaning 'to rest' from labour. The fourth commandment of the decalogue (Deuteronomy 5:12-15) is an emphatic declaration to the effect that the Sabbath is a day of rest from all secular labour or employment, because God rested on that day from His work of creation. On this day, conforming Jews refrain from all kind of work or secular activity, such as travelling, buying a newspaper, or writing letters. The justification for the observances of the Sabbath is twofold: to rest, symbolic of God's rest from creation; and to commemorate the deliverance from Egyptian bondage.

But mere abstinence on the Sabbath is not enough. As a 'holy' day, the Sabbath is set aside for religious worship and religious instruction, including visits to the sick, the housebound and the bereaved. Though solemn, there are no strictures on the Sabbath against pleasure, joy and happiness. In fact, to proclaim the Sabbath, which starts every Friday evening at dusk, the woman of the house lights the candles, invoking God's blessing upon the household, while the man of the house recites a special benediction (*Kiddush*), preferably over the wine and bread. This is followed by a festive meal and concluded by songs and grace.

Orthodox Jews usher in the Sabbath by attending synagogue services on Friday before dinner. Some Conservative and Reform Jews attend a late evening service. For all three groups, however, Saturday is a day of synagogue worship, and families attend for worship and thanksgiving. During the service, seven people are 'called up' to follow the reader, who recites from the prescribed section of the sacred Torah, and to offer a thanksgiving for the gift of the Torah. An eighth person then reads a selection from the Prophetic Books and the service is concluded by an exhortation, or an interpretation, or a sermon on the Torah. The family then returns home for a festive meal.

The rest of the afternoon is spent either in study of the Torah or in leisure. Worshippers are called back to the synagogue where a section of the following week's portion of the Torah is read. At night, a symbolic ceremony in the home, called *Haudalah* ('separation', 'division') concludes the Sabbath. A lighted candle is extinguished in wine by the youngest member of the house, while a spice-box (often in the form of a tower) is passed around from member to member for the family to sniff, as it were, the sweetness of the Sabbath as it closes. All then greet each other with the following words: *Shabua tov*, a good week!

✶ Kosher

This is the law pertaining to beast and bird and every living creature that moves through the waters and every creature that swarms upon the earth, to make a distinction between the unclean and the clean and between the living creature that may be eaten and the living creature that may not be eaten.

Leviticus 11:46-47

Kashrut, the dietary laws, are the most pervasive holy observances in Judaism. The regulations about forbidden, *treyfah*, and permissible, *kosher*, foods may well have originated in association with taboos of antiquity. Whether or not health or hygiene determined the rules in the first place is little more than speculation, and is irrelevant to pious Jews who refuse to rationalize kosher laws. They accept them as part of a total system ordained by God, not merely as nostalgic relics of an ancient cultural tradition.

Jewish traditional writings propose two basic reasons for kashrut: to curb a person's animal appetites, and to isolate Jews in their day-to-day living as a reminder of their priestly calling. Consequently, the diet of a Jew is regulated by law. A long list of animals and products classified as 'clean' or 'unclean', 'fit' or 'unfit' appears in Leviticus 11 and in Deuteronomy 14. There is no prohibition whatsoever against vegetables, but definite rules are set regarding animals, birds, and fish.

All animals that have 'true hoofs with clefts through the hoofs and chew the cud' (Leviticus 11:3) are classed as permissible food. Included in this category then are the ox, the sheep, the hart, and the gazelle (Deuteronomy 14:4-5), but not the pig and the rabbit. The former has clefts through its hoofs but does not chew cud, while the latter chews cud but has no hoofs.

The biblical injunctions against eating certain birds, or flying insects, are difficult to apply since the species are not always identifiable from the biblical name or description. Fish that have both fins and scales are acceptable but shellfish, eel, and sturgeon are not. Birds of prey and carnivorous animals are also prohibited food.

Even permissible food, that is kosher food, must comply with certain rules and regulations. Animals that are not slaughtered strictly in accordance with Jewish dietary law are rendered inedible to Jews. One provision of the law is that slaughter is the province of a specialist, a *shochet*, trained in Jewish law. He uses a very sharp knife to cut the animal's throat, severing arteries, veins and windpipe at one stroke so that the blood drains out rapidly. After the slaughter, the shochet examines the carcass for any disease or damage to internal organs. If there is any discolouration, or if the lungs or stomach are damaged, the carcass is declared unsuitable for consumption.

Meat that passes muster is then distributed to retailers, usually Jewish butchers who remove the sinews (as per Genesis 32:33). The purchaser is responsible for washing and soaking the meat in salt to remove traces of congealed blood. After these procedures, the meat is considered kosher: fit for consumption.

Following biblical injunctions, Judaism imposes three further conditions on the consumption of meat and dairy products: they may not be eaten together, cooked together, or served in any kind of combination or mixture. For instance, Jews may not spread butter on their bread if they serve meat at the same meal. They may only drink a glass of milk after a lapse of several hours between their consumption of meat and their intake of milk.

In order to segregate these products even further, a 'kosher home', is equipped with two complete sets of cooking utensils, dishes, and cutlery. A third set for 'neutral' food, such as fruit, is not uncommon. The Passover Feast requires two additional complete sets of dishes (one for meat, one for dairy products) undefiled or untainted by any kind of fermented or leavened food, a characteristic of day-to-day diets, since the requirements for Passover call for unleavened food.

Trained rabbis supervise and rule on all decisions relating to kashrut, but all pious Jews share the responsibility for observing dietary laws, from the shochet and the retailing butcher to the housewife, cook, and ultimate consumers. They all accept their obligation to abide by prescribed dietary laws with the joyful conviction of performing the will of God in soul and body. This unremitting and unequivocal adherence day by day is considered a sacred duty, a *mitzvah*.

Circumcision

Every male among you shall be circumcised. You shall be circumised in the flesh of your foreskins, and it shall be a sign of the covenant between Me and you. He that is eight days old among you shall be circumcised . . .

Genesis 17:10-12

Brith millah, or circumcision, of a male child eight days after his birth is the oldest Jewish ritual to survive unchanged to the present day. The biblical justification for this rite is that it is 'a token of Covenant' between God and the Jews. By no means is it conceived as a 'sacrament' of induction into Judaism—his birth does that. Circumcision is the external symbol of the child's status representing the covenant of Abraham. In other words, circumcision is a mitzvah patterned on the example of Abraham, into whose covenant the child enters (Genesis 17:9-14).

The rite of circumcision is performed by a *mohel*, a pious Jew especially trained to undertake this surgical operation. Nowadays some Jewish parents prefer that the circumcision be performed by a Jewish surgeon in a hospital in the presence of a rabbi, instead of in a synagogue. Reform and Conservative Jews approve this latter method. Orthodox Jews tend to adhere to tradition, which calls for a quorum of ten to witness the rite in the synagogue.

The child is brought into the gathering by the godmother and held by the godfather. The mohel removes the foreskin of the penis with a quick stroke, wipes off the blood, and secures the skin to stop further growth. The father of the child recites the following blessing: 'Blessed are You, O Lord our God, ruling Spirit of the Universe, who has commanded us to enter our son into the Covenant of our father Abraham.' The response by the attendants is: 'As he entered the Covenant, so may he enter into the love of Torah, into the marriage canopy and into a life of good deeds.' Then the child is named, a blessing made over the cup of wine, and a drop of wine placed on the child's lips, the father drinking the rest. A festive celebration completes what everyone (except perhaps for the baby) regards as a joyful occasion.

In modern times, non-Orthodox Jews have initiated a rite for female children, who have a reduced status in Orthodox homes. There is no surgical operation, but otherwise the ritual follows the same pattern accorded male children.

Bar/Bath Mitzvah

When a child begins to speak, his father should speak with him in the holy tongue and teach him Torah. If he does not do so, it is as though he buries him.[1]

The training of a Jewish boy in applying the observances of his faith starts at a very early age. The Talmud declares: 'As soon as a child can speak, his father teaches him the Torah'.[2] The Shema and the commandment of Moses (Deuteronomy 33:4) are among the first texts to be memorized. On the completion of his thirteenth year he becomes a *Bar Mitzvah*, literally a Son of Duty or a Son of Commandment. From that date on he is, according to Jewish tradition, responsible for fulfilling his own religious obligations. The occasion is marked by a summons to read the Torah from the altar of the synagogue on the Sabbath preceding his thirteenth birthday.

Jewish historians consider this ceremony to be of recent origin—possibly since the fourteenth century AD. In many European Jewish communities, it was once customary for the Bar Mitzvah to deliver a thoughtful address on the intricacies of the Talmud, which would have been familiar to him by the age of thirteen. Today, it is simply a solemn pledge to live according to the dictates of the Torah.

Several Reform and Conservative congregations have recently introduced a *Bath Mitzvah*, an innovation representing a counterpart for girls reaching their thirteenth birthday. Whether the ceremony marks the end of childhood for a male or female, it is an occasion for family members, relatives and friends to celebrate after the formal observances.

Following the Christian custom of confirmation, Reform
Jews have introduced group confirmation for both sexes at the
age of fifteen or sixteen as a substitute for the Bar or Bath
Mitzvah. While the practice at first was to hold confirmation
services at various times of the year, nowadays they are
reserved for Shavuoth, the Festival, commemorating the giving
of the Torah. Some Conservative Jews, too, have opted for this
method.

Marriage

When a man is newly married . . . he shall be free at home one year, to
be happpy with his wife, whom he has taken.

Deuteronomy 24:5

The ideals of the sanctity of life are fostered and inculcated in
the home; and the home is founded upon the sacred character of
Jewish marriage. Traditionally, elaborate rituals solemnized a
Jewish betrothal, but today there is less uniformity, formality,
and rigidity associated with Jewish marriage ceremonies. Many
of the customs are largely a matter of local practice rather than
of Jewish law. Wherever Jews have settled they have adopted
the customs of the people of the country in which they resided.

And yet, there are still certain features of religious significance that characterize nearly all modern Jewish weddings.
These include taking vows under the canopy; tasting wine
together from a single cup or glass; signing the marriage
contract or document. In most Jewish ceremonies there is an
additional ritual: the shattering of the wine-cup at the conclusion of the ceremony. Each of these traditional rites has a
significant symbolic meaning.

The canopy symbolizes the couple's home in which their
vows are enshrined and fulfilled. Sharing from a cup of wine
symbolizes their common destiny, and the signing of the legal
document symbolizes marital stability and security. At the end
of the solemnization of the marriage the groom breaks a glass.
Some consider this custom to be a vestige of primitive magic,
presumably to frighten away evil spirits that would disrupt
human happiness. But Jewish tradition has held that the

shattering of a glass symbolizes the destruction of the Jewish Temple, as a reminder of the national pledge expressed by the Psalmist (Psalm 137:6), not to forget Jerusalem even in the midst of joy.

In the event that a marriage breaks down, Jewish tradition makes provision for divorce without requiring either partner to provide proof of guilt. A bill of divorce is written in accordance with certain regulations, only after the couple have obtained their final divorce from civil courts. Divorced persons are encouraged to remarry.

Death

My God and God of my fathers, accept my prayer; do not ignore my supplication. Forgive me for all the sins which I have committed in my lifetime . . .

May it be Your will to heal me. Yet, if You have decreed that I shall die . . . may my death atone for all sins and transgressions which I have committed before You. Shelter me in the shadow of Your wings and grant me a share in the world to come.

Father of orphans and Guardian of widows, protect my beloved family, with whose soul my soul is bound.

Into Your hands I commit my soul. You have redeemed me, O Lord God of truth.

Hear O Israel, the Lord our God, the Lord is One. The Lord, He is God. The Lord, He is God.[3]

This prayer is recited by pious Jews on their death beds. The utterance, in particular, of the last two lines with one's dying breath (i.e., the affirmation of faith) is regarded as a mark of particular mercy from God.

No rabbi or clergyman is required to officiate at the last rites. Tradition confers responsibility for performing the last acts of kindness to *hevrah kadishah* (holy fellowship), a group of men or women distinguished by their piety. Their voluntary act of free devotion on behalf of the dying is considered a true mitzvah. These attendants first place the corpse on the earth (symbolic of the place from which one comes and returns). Later, they wash and dress it in simple white linen garments, as a symbol of the equality of all people in the eyes of God. The body is then placed in a simple wooden coffin the head resting on earth brought especially from the Holy Land. Ostentation is further inhibited by a black shroud that is thrown over the casket.

Flowers and music, symbols of joy, have no place in Jewish funerals. Embalming is discouraged, unless required by law. Cremation is a rare form of committal among Jews on the grounds that it is an undignified method of disposing of a body. Only burial is considered appropriate. Friends lower the coffin into the earth.

The obligation to 'sit Shiva' follows burial. For seven days after the funeral the next of kin remain in the house to recite the *Kaddish* (sanctification of God's name) three times a day and to receive the consolation of friends and neighbours. As the name of the service implies, the theme of the Kaddish is the praise and glory of God, not the soul of the departed:

> Magnified and sanctified by the glory of God
> In the world created according to His will . . .
> May the glory of God be eternally praised,
> Hallowed and extolled, lauded and exalted,
> Honored and revered, adored and worshipped . . .
> He who ordains the order of the universe
> Will bring the peace to us and to all Israel.
> Let us say: Amen.[4]

The maximum period of mourning, however, ends after thirty days with one exception only: the death of parents. The mourning period for one's parents lasts eleven months during which the sons (or the eldest daughter in the absence of any son) attend public worship daily to recite the Kaddish, and occasionally to pray that the departed 'may be bound up in the bond of life with the Eternal.' At the end of this period a memorial stone commemorates the deceased at the graveside. The anniversary of each family death is observed annually by relatives who recite a prayer and light a candle in honour of the dead.

Nowadays, Jewish funerals and observances associated with mourning have been modified to conform with local customs and with variations among different Jewish groups. Some still adhere rigidly to ancient rituals and practices, but whatever the outward forms may take, Jewish mourning rites all serve the same purpose: national solidarity.

New Year (Rosh Hashanah)

In the seventh month, on the first day of the month, you shall observe a day of solemn rest, a memorial proclaimed with blast of trumpets, a holy convocation. You shall do no laborious work; and you shall present an offering by fire to the Lord.

Leviticus 23:23-25

The Jewish New Year, *Rosh Hashanah*, is considered one of the most solemn days in the Jewish calendar. It is celebrated in autumn, September-October (since the Judaic calendar is luni-solar), and ushers in a ten-day period of penitence. Orthodox and Conservative Jews follow ancient tradition and celebrate the occasion for two days; the Reform group, for one day only.

The main symbol associated with the New Year is the *shofar*, ram's horn. It calls the faithful to repent of their sins, and to return to God in humility and thanksgiving. Among the various meanings assigned to the New Year is the anniversary of 'Creation'. As such it represents a period of Judgement, when individuals are called to account by God to justify their creation and the time committed to their care. Rabbinic writings state that on New Year's Day three books are opened in which the deeds of every individual are inscribed and sealed.

On Rosh Hashanah, three books are opened in the heavenly court; one for the wicked, one for the righteous, and one for those in between. The fate of the righteous is inscribed and sealed then and there: Life. The fate of the wicked is inscribed and sealed then and there: Death. The fate of those in between remain undecided from Rosh Hashanah to Yom Kippur. If during those days, their deeds show their worthiness, they are inscribed and sealed for Life; if not, they are inscribed and sealed for Death.[5]

Jews greet each other accordingly each New Year: 'May you be inscribed and sealed for a good year.' New Year also fore-shadows the universal divine event towards which all creation is moving: the Messianic redemption of the Jews and the entire human race. In fact, the highest point in the day's liturgy is the prayer 'for God's universal sovereignty over humans and nature, for the arrival of God's kingdom in which mankind will be joined in universal brotherhood to do the divine will with a perfect heart.'

✳ Day of Atonement (Yom Kippur)

On the tenth day of this seventh month is the day of atonement; it shall be for you a time of holy convocation . . . and you shall do no work on this same day . . . it is a statute for ever throughout your generations.

Leviticus 23:27-32

Jewish tradition ranks *Yom Kippur*, the Day of Atonement, as the holiest day of the year. Starting after sunset on the ninth day after the New Year, it is marked by twenty-four hours of prayer and fasting in emulation of God's angels, who according to tradition neither eat nor drink but continuously praise God and live in His presence. So one day a year on Yom Kippur Jews attempt to serve God as if they were angels. 'Eating, drinking, washing, anointing with oil, wearing of sandals and sexual intercourse are forbidden,' according to Talmudic injunction.[6] All prayers during the twenty-four-hour period include the confession of sins, recited at times privately but often in unison to acknowledge collective guilt. The liturgy prescribes the prayer of 'Confession' which is recited several times (traditionally ten times) on Yom Kippur. Worshippers review the traditional catalogue of sins, shortcomings, and transgressions that cover human dereliction.

Our God and God of our fathers, let our prayer come before You. Hide not from our supplication . . . truly, we have sinned. We have trespassed, we have betrayed, we have robbed, we have spoken slander. We have perverted what is right, we have wrought wickedness, we have been presumptuous, we have done violence, we have forged lies. We have given evil counsel, we have spoken falsely, we have scoffed, we have revolted, we have blasphemed, we have been rebellious, we have been perverse, we have transgressed, we have oppressed, we have been stiff-necked. We have acted wickedly, we have acted corruptly, we have committed abomination, we have gone astray, we have led others astray . . .

You know all things, hidden and revealed. You know the mysteries of the universe, and the hidden secrets of all living . . . May it therefore be Your will, O Lord our God and God of our fathers, to forgive us for all our sins, to pardon us for all our iniquities, and to grant us atonement for all our transgressions.[7]

Prayer Book—High Holy Day

Tradition states that Satan can tempt and accuse the Jewish people every day of the year except on Yom Kippur. On that day God declares to Satan: 'You have no power over them today; nevertheless go and see what they are doing.' Then Satan finds them all fasting and praying clothed like angels in white garments. Returning to God in shame and confusion Satan replies: 'They are like angels and I have no power over them.' Whereupon God binds Satan in chains and declares to His people: 'I have forgiven you all.'[8]

Jews think of Yom Kippur as *the* day of forgiveness (i.e., the Day of Atonement). It represents the culmination of the ten-day penitential period following the New Year. Before Yom Kippur begins, Jews ask anyone they may have wronged, including family members, for forgiveness.

The evening service in the synagogue is introduced by the *Kol Nidre*, a haunting chant led by the cantor asking God for forgiveness of unfulfilled vows made to Him only. No prayers can absolve a person from unfulfilled promises to neighbours— only a forgiving neighbour may do so.

By the authority of the Heavenly Court and the earthly court, with the sanction of God and the sanction of the congregation, we hereby declare it permissible to pray together with those who have transgressed. Of all vows, bonds, promises, obligations and oaths wherewith we have avowed, sworn and bound ourselves from this Day of Atonement to the next Day of Atonement, may it come unto us for good—of all these vows we hereby repent. They shall be absolved, released, annulled, made void, and of no effect. They shall not be binding, nor shall they have any power. Our vows shall not be vows; our bonds shall not be bonds; and our oaths shall not be oaths.[9]

Prayer Book—**High Holy Day**

The service concludes with the sevenfold proclamation of God's unity and the sounding of the *shofar* (ram's horn). This signals the end of the fast and the beginning of new tasks for the coming year. A festive meal further celebrates the occasion.

Despite the solemnity of Yom Kippur, Jews feel a personal sense of familiarity or comfort with God. It is a relationship illustrated by an anecdote familiar to all Jews. Once, Rabbi Elimelekh of Lizhensk sent his disciples to watch the example of a humble tailor on Yom Kippur. The tailor took down from his shelf a book in which was written all the sins he had committed throughout the year, and addressed God: 'Today is the day of forgiveness for all Jews; the moment has come for You, God, and myself to settle our account. Here is the list of all my sins. But here also is another volume, the sins that You have committed: the pains, the woes, the heartaches that You have sent upon me and my family. Lord of the universe, if we were to total the accounts exactly, You would owe me much more than I would owe You! But it is the eve of the Day of Atonement, when everyone is commanded to make peace with his fellow being. Hence, I forgive You for Your sins if You will forgive me for mine.' Then the tailor poured himself a cup of wine, pronounced the blessing over it, and exclaimed: '*Lakhayyim* (to Life), Master of the world. Let there now be peace and joy between us, for we have forgiven each other, and our sins are now as if they never were.'[10]

The moral of the story is quite clear. As solemn as the day may be, there is still an element of joy in Yom Kippur—joy in the expectation of forgiveness. Jews trust implicitly in God's mercy and forgiveness. In the words of the Yom Kippur ritual: 'Thou, O God, desire not the death of the wicked, but that he return from his sin and live.'

Feast of Tabernacles (Sukkot)

On the fifteenth day of the seventh month, and for seven days, is the feast of the tabernacles to the Lord. On the first day shall be a holy convocation; you shall do no laborious work . . . on the eighth day you shall hold a holy convocation . . . it is a solemn assembly; you shall do no laborious work.

Leviticus 23:34-36

The Feast of *Sukkot* (singular *Sukkah*, meaning 'booth' or 'tabernacle') begins five days after Yom Kippur and continues for eight days, or seven for Reform Jews. It is an occasion for rejoicing since it marks the harvest festival of thanksgiving. Special services are held in the synagogue on the first two and last two days of the festival, except among Reform Jews, who observe only the first and last days.

The ritual in the synagogue is distinguished by four symbols: the citron; the branch of the date palm; myrtles and willows of the brook. These four plants are brought to the sanctuary in accordance with the commandment in Leviticus 23:40. Worshippers march around the interior of the synagogue in a processional circle bearing these four plants during the recitation of Psalms of Thanksgiving (Psalms 113-118).

Since the feast is associated with the ancient harvest festival, many families improvise a booth or tabernacle as a reminder of the temporary shelters that housed the ancient Jews during their wanderings in the Sinai desert. A table, chairs and fruits furnish the *sukkah*, where the family gather to have their meal during the entire week of the festival.

Glorification of Torah (Simchat Torah)

On the fifteenth day of the seventh month and for seven days is the feast of the tabernacles. . . . On the eighth day you shall hold a holy convocation to the Lord . . .

Leviticus 23:34-36

The last day of Sukkot is the celebration of yet another festival called *Simchat Torah*, the Glorification of the Torah. The annual cycle of Scripture readings from the Torah closes and the new cycle begins without a break. On this occasion, worshippers read the last chapters of the Book of Deuteronomy and the first chapter of the Book of Genesis, symbolizing the eternal continuity of the Torah.

During a festive service held in the synagogue, the Scrolls are carried in procession round the synagogue, and sometimes out into the streets as well, amidst exuberant singing and dancing. Children kiss the Scrolls, carry banners, and receive sweets or candies. Although the feast dedicated to the glorification of the

Torah is symbolized by solemn rituals, the festival has become the gayest day of the year.

Festival of Lights (Hannukah) ✳

And they built the sanctuary and the interior of the Temple and consecrated the courts. And they made new holy dishes and they brought the lampstand and the altar of incense and the table into the Temple. And they burned incense on the altar, and lighted the lamps on the lampstand, and they lighted the Temple . . . Then Judas and his brothers and all the congregation of Israel decreed that the days of the rededication of the altar should be observed at their season, every year, for eight days, beginning with the twenty-fifth of the month of Chislev, with gladness and joy.

I Maccabees 4:48-59

The festival of Hannukah (or Chanukah, literally meaning 'Dedication') lasts for eight days in the month of December. It used to be celebrated as a minor festival, but American Jews have transformed it into a major one mainly because of its proximity to Christmas. In fact, the festival of Hannukah has no biblical precedent. It is based on the story recorded in the book of Maccabees in the Apocrypha—a story of bloody political and military triumph which Jewish tradition was slow to accept as a religious celebration. The ancient rabbis emphasized the spiritual aspects of the incident rather than the victory of arms which gave them significance. The story goes as follows.

Jews living in Palestine after the conquest of Alexander the Great were so fascinated by Greek fashions and customs that they quickly embraced Greek ways of life. The observance of the Sabbath and other biblical ordinances gradually lapsed. Parents ignored the rite of circumcision. Jewish youth participated in Greek athletics in the Greek fashion—naked. People generally adopted Greek culture and religion in place of laws prescribed in the Torah, except for a small minority. Those Jews clung tenaciously to their ancestral customs and traditions.

Shortly after the accession of Antiochus IV (175-164 BC, also known as Antiochus Epiphanes), a large number of Jews, including their High Priest, made a determined effort to 'Hellenize' the Jews in Judea by force. Such a policy suited

Antiochus IV who was looking for some way to unify his Graeco-Syrian empire by imposing a national culture on his subjects. In 168 BC Antiochus IV imposed the death penalty on Jews who persisted in following traditional observances: keeping the Sabbath and festivals, possessing, the 'Book of the Law of Moses,' circumcising males, and offering religious sacrifices in the Jewish tradition. Adding insult to injury Antiochus IV converted the Jewish Temple to the worship of Zeus, the Olympian god, while sacrifices of swine were offered on the altars of the Temple.

The majority of Jews who refused to yield either perished as martyrs or fled to safety. A small band of heroic fighters led by Mattathias declared open rebellion. Mattathias, an old priest of the Hasmonean family who lived in Modin (north-west of Jerusalem), issued a call: 'Let every one who is zealous for the Torah and supports the Covenant come out with me' (I Maccabees 2:27). This battle-cry won the support of both those who wanted to defend the Jewish Covenant and those who wanted to throw off the yoke of foreign political rule.

The insurgents formed themselves into small groups and engaged in guerrilla activities. The troops of Antiochus IV retaliated, and on one occasion attacked on the Sabbath. Unwilling to desecrate the sacred day, the Jewish defenders perished without offering any resistance. This forced Mattathias to enact a decree, which has passed into Jewish law since then: Jews must defend themselves on the Sabbath if attacked.

After the death of Mattathias, the struggle continued for a few years under the leadership of Judas, one of the five sons of the dead priest. In a surprise night attack, he was able finally to repossess the Temple, cleanse it of foreign elements, and rededicate it to the God of the Jews on the twenty-fifth day of Kislev (December), in 165 BC. He then instituted the festival of Dedication, *Hannukah*, marked by the lighting of oil-lamps for eight days, as an annual celebration of the event.

Antiochus IV died shortly after the Jewish repossession of the Temple. Fighting continued sporadically, until, in 163 BC, the Jews won the right 'to live according to their ancient laws' (I Maccabees 6:59). But political freedom did not come for another twenty-two years. In 143 BC, Simon, the last of the surviving brothers, expelled the Syrian army from Jerusalem and made Judea an independent Jewish state. Then, by popular assembly, he was elected the civil ruler and the High Priest.

This is the background story of the observance of the festival of Hannukah, according to the author of the book of Maccabees. Rabbinic tradition emphasized or embroidered events selectively (Shabbat 21) in order to justify the celebration of freedom of worship even at the cost of human blood.

Tradition holds that when Judas and his supporters entered the Temple, they found the *menorah* (candelabrum) damaged beyond repair. They immediately improvised a makeshift menorah out of their spears unconsciously transforming their weapons into religious artefacts—symbols of peace. They found enough sacred oil to keep their menorah lit for one day. Miraculously, the oil lasted for eight days, the precise number of days it would take to secure and sanctify a new supply of sacred oil. Consequently, it was ordained that this miraculous event be celebrated annually in every Jewish home by the kindling of lights for eight days. Hence the term, Festival of Lights.

A nine-branched menorah is the form hallowed by tradition. Some types of menorah burn oil, but candles are also permissible. The centre light is used for kindling each of the other eight tapers—one taper on each successive evening. Matching the spirit of Christmas, Jewish homes are decorated with a variety of Hannukah symbols, Jewish schools commemorate the victory for freedom of worship with pageants and plays, and young and old exchange gifts.

Festival of Lots (Purim)

In the twelfth year of king Ahasuerus they cast *Pur*, that is the lot, before Haman, day after day; and they cast it month after month till the twelfth month, which is the month of Adar.

Esther 3:7

The feast of *Purim* (literally 'lots') is one of the most joyous observances of Judaism, celebrated on the fourteenth of Adar (February-March) commemorating the spectacular events recorded in the biblical book of Esther. The story, for which there is no historical evidence, features four characters: the Persian King, Ahasuerus, his commander-in-chief, Haman, the Jewess Queen, Esther, and her Jewish uncle, Mordecai.

Haman plots to destroy all the Jews living in Persia and by villainous recourse to devious deception, persuades the king to appoint him as agent of destruction. But the wisdom of Mordecai and the boldness of Queen Esther result in the evasion of catastrophy and the hanging of Haman. Because Haman cast 'lots' to determine the appropriate day for the Jewish massacre, the festival is known as Purim.

On this day, the book of Esther is read from a special handwritten parchment scroll, gifts are exchanged and, for once, drunkenness is accorded the status of mitzvah. In modern Israel, the reading from the scroll of Esther is broadcast on radio and television, streets are decorated with flags and bunting, and masquerading parties (like participants in the Christian carnival of Mardi Gras) carouse through the late hours of the night.

Passover (Pesach)

In the first month, on the fourteenth day of the month in the evening, is the Lord's passover. And on the fifteenth day of the same month is the feast of unleavened bread to the Lord; seven days you shall eat unleavened bread. On the first day you shall have a holy convocation . . . and on the seventh day is a holy convocation; you shall do no laborious work.

Leviticus 23:4-8

Pesach, or Passover, is the oldest and the most important family festival in Judaism. It begins on the eve of the fourteenth day of Nisan (March-April) and lasts for eight days, or seven days among Reform Jews and Jews who live in Palestine. Originally, Pesach was a spring festival, observed long before the Jews settled in Egypt. Today the festival commemorates the deliverance, or Exodus, of the Jews from Egypt. In fact, the observance of Pesach has evolved gradually from its origins in antiquity, yet it has retained one element from the very beginning: it is a family festival.

The major part of the ritual is celebrated at home. One day

before the festival begins, the entire house is examined in order to remove all traces of leavened bread, which is replaced during the entire period of the festival by unleavened bread, or *matzoth*. It symbolizes the haste in which Jews left Egypt, since the dough they had prepared with which to bake bread had no time to rise before it was placed in the oven.

On the first two nights of Pesach, (on only the first night among Reform Jews) each Jewish family holds a special banquet known as the *Seder* (order). The purpose is to commemorate the Exodus from Egypt by simulating at home the atmosphere associated with that ancient migration. The occasion is celebrated with an elaborate ritual. Special symbolic foods are spread on the table: hard-boiled eggs, symbolizing the sanctity of life; bitter herbs, symbolizing the bitter lot of their ancestors; a mixture of nuts and apples in remembrance of the mortar used by Jewish slaves to build cities for their Egyptian task-masters. In addition, unleavened bread and lamb are served, foods which are both associated with the Exodus.

Besides these implicit reminders to illustrate and dramatize the events associated with the Exodus, there is an explicit reminder. The youngest child at the table asks a series of predetermined questions about the proceedings: Why is this night so different from all other nights of the year? Why does one eat unleavened bread? What is the significance of the bitter herbs, of dipping food in salt-water, of leaning on a pillow at the Seder table? In reply, the head of the household retells the story of the Exodus by reading from the book known as *Haggadah* (Narration).

Another important custom associated with the Pesach is the sharing of blessings with the less fortunate. Consequently, guests are invited to the family table. These may be friends, or students away from their homes, or even travellers who are far away from their families.

Special synagogue services are also held to mark the occasion. Here the Torah is read, the story of the Exodus recounted and psalms of praise chanted.

Festival of Weeks (Shavuoth)

Count the seven weeks from the time you first put the sickle to the

standing grain. Then you shall keep the feast of the weeks to the Lord
your God with the tribute of a free-will offering . . .

Deuteronomy 16:9-10

Fifty days after Pesach is the festival of *Shavuoth* (Weeks).
Celebrated for two days (for one day by Reform Jews), on the
sixth and seventh day of Sivan (May-June), this festival
originally marked the wheat harvest, but now also commemorates the anniversary of the giving of the Torah by God to
Moses at Mount Sinai. Homes and synagogues are decorated
with fresh fruit, plants, and flowers. Readings from the Torah
include the books of Exodus and Ruth—a Moabite girl who
adopted the Jewish faith. In modern Israel, farmers carrying
baskets of fresh fruit join Shavuoth processions.

Additional Observances

In addition to these festivals, a number of Orthodox Jews
observe two traditional periods of mourning. One is the *Sefirah*
('counting' the days), the six weeks immediately following
Pesach in remembrance of the Roman persecutions, and the
other is the *Tishah b'Av* (literally meaning, 'the ninth of the
month of Av'), the three-week period during the summer in
commemoration of the destruction of ancient Jerusalem and the
Temple. Special synagogue services and fasting form part of
these observances. Pious Jews sit on the ground, to recite with
bowed head and tearful eyes the mournful odes of the book of
Lamentations. For East European Jews the restrictions imposed
during this observance are rigorous. They may not wash nor eat
meat for nine days. For others still, the observance is associated
with sleeping on a stone as a pillow or by visiting the cemetery.

Jewish tradition also prescribes the observance of *Rosh
Hodesh*, or the 'greeting of the new moon' each month, with a
special religious ceremony. In ancient days work was prohibited on the days of the 'new moon', but today, Rosh Hodesh is
a semi-holiday observed in a variety of ways depending on local
customs and the country in which the Jews live.

The observance of the new moon coincides with the first day
of the month according to the Jewish calendar, because the
Jewish calendar is luni-solar, which means that the months are

measured according to the moon's orbit around the earth (lunar), while the years are calculated by the earth's orbit around the sun (solar). Consequently, religious festivals calculated according to the Jewish calendar, always fall on the same date, whereas these dates vary from year to year on the Gregorian calendar, the cycle common to the Western world. Here are the names of the months, with the corresponding phase of the Gregorian calendar:

Tishri	(September-October)	Nisan	(March-April)
Heshran	(October-November)	Iyar	(April-May)
Kislev	(November-December)	Sivan	(May-June)
Tebet	(December-January)	Tamuz	(June-July)
Shebat	(January-February)	Av	(July-August)
Adar	(February-March)	Elul	(August-September)

The various groups within Judaism follow different styles of observances. Members of certain groups do not feel bound necessarily by traditional restrictions imposed on activities defined as work. In addition, various popular forms of celebration have emerged in modern Israel, sometimes replacing traditional ones. All of these variations reflect different expressions of Jewish faith.

6

REFLECTIONS

In these chapters I have attempted to present Judaism as it is understood by pious Jews based on their cosmic perspective of 'holiness' in five indivisible components: God, People, Land, Book, and Observances. In the past, Judaism influenced people and events and was in turn influenced by them. The purpose of this closing chapter therefore is to reflect briefly on the role and significance of Judaism in world religion.

Judaism numbers today some 13 million adherents. Compared to the 6 million Sikhs or the 1 million Jains, or the 150,000 Zoroastrians, Jews are numerous. Compared to the 1,000 million followers of Christianity, the 750 million of Islam, the 500 million of Hinduism, or the 400 million of Buddhism, Judaism is a small religion.

But if Judaism cannot claim superiority in numbers, it can at least claim longevity. Judaism is one of two ancient surviving religions in the world. The other is Hinduism. Their origins are too distant and their traces too indistinct to discern with any certainty but scholars speculate that their roots date back to around 1800 BC, Hinduism in India and Judaism in the Middle East. Both religions are indigenous—the products or reflections of native Indian and Jewish cultures respectively. Both have survived to this day as national religions serving the needs of each group. Both produced religious leaders of such stature that they changed the course of world civilization: Gautama the Buddha and Jesus the Christ. Judaism is the wellspring—the source—of Western as opposed to Eastern or oriental religion.

Scholars may argue that Judaism is not the only ancient source of Western religious traditions. The point is that it is the

only one that has survived. It survived the religious pogroms of
the Roman Empire following the Empire's zealous espousal of
Christianity after the fourth century. When Christians finally
surfaced in triumph from their hiding places among the
catacombs of Rome they, in turn, drove former detractors,
nonconformists, and rivals underground—but permanently.
Christianity and its agents and adherents were directly or
indirectly responsible for eradicating the religions of former
great civilizations such as the Egyptian, Babylonian, Greek,
Roman, European, Aztec, Mayan and Inca.

Judaism was the exception. What gave it immunity from
Christian proselytizing zeal and crusading fervour? Jews maintained no standing armies and their traditions mitigated against
the appearance of charismatic military leaders. They were
tough, resourceful, and dispersed, but they represented easy
targets. Chosen people do not blend into the background.
Closed societies stand out. Their sense of exclusivity and their
unique traditions combine to give them high profiles whether
they like it or not.

Jews in the Roman Empire presented visible and vulnerable
targets. Why did not Judaism follow Mithraism and all the rest
into oblivion? The reason is that Christianity is an offshoot of
Judaism and indissolubly bound to it.

There was a time when the religious movement which came
to be known as Christianity was viewed as another sectarian
form of Judaism to be distinguished only from variants
advocated by Pharisees, Sadducees, Essenes, and Zealots. The
occupying Roman government certainly thought so. Jesus
taught in the Jewish Temple as well as in the streets. The first
Christians were Jews. Jesus, the founder of Christianity, and
Paul, who formulated most, if not all, of Christian theology,
ethic, and practice were adherents of Judaism. Nobody felt
threatened by their unorthodoxy except the orthodox.

Christianity was the result of a split in Judaism over matters
of theology, institutions, and observances. The Jesus of history
(whatever other characteristics are attributed to him) was a
devout adherent of Judaism who became the founder of a Judaic
sectarian movement called Christianity in very much the same

way that Martin Luther (1483-1546) was a devout adherent of Roman Catholicism who became the founder of a Christian sectarian movement called Lutheranism which, in turn, spawned Protestantism.

It is not likely that Luther would have accepted the parallel, but Pilate and the priests who negotiated the crucifixion of Jesus might have. It is only the long perspective of time that gives Christians the illusion that they are anything other than non-conforming Jews.

Paul thought of Christianity as a 'branch' of Judaism comprising Jewish members, 'natural branches', and Gentiles, 'grafted branches'.

Now I am speaking to you Gentiles . . . If some of the branches were broken off, and you, a wild olive shoot, were grafted in their place to share the richness of the olive tree, do not boast over the branches. If you do boast, remember it is not you that support the root, but the root that supports you. You will say, 'Branches were broken off so that I might be grafted in'. That is true. They were broken off because of their unbelief, but you stand fast only through faith . . . For if you have been cut from what is by nature a wild olive tree, and grafted, contrary to nature, into a cultivated olive tree, how much more will these natural branches be grafted back into their own olive tree . . .

Romans 11:13-24

Christianity is, therefore, according to Paul, rooted in Judaism. At no time can Christianity cut off the root that sustains it. In fact, the Apostle Paul postulates a universal divine mystery: the rejection of God's plan of salvation in Christ by the Jews means the reconciliation of the Gentile world to God. But Paul wants Christians to understand clearly that the refusal of Jews to accept God's latest plan of redemption through Christ is a temporary condition requiring the redemption of the entire Gentile world before the Jews themselves can also be saved. Here are his words:

. . . a hardening has come upon part of Israel, until the full number of the Gentiles come in, and so all Israel will be saved . . . As regards the gospel they are enemies of God, for your sake; but as regards election they are beloved for the sake of their forefathers. For the gifts and the call of God are irrevocable. Just as you were once disobedient to God but now have received mercy because of their disobedience, so that they have now been disobedient in order that by the mercy shown to you they also may receive mercy.

Romans 11:25-31

Followers of this new Judaic sect, including Paul, believed and still believe, that Jesus the Jew was none other than the long awaited Messiah (*Christos* in Greek, abbreviated to *Christ*) of the Jews. It was natural, therefore, that though Jesus, Peter, Paul, and converts to this new Judaic sect, which came to be identified as Christianity, rejected orthodox Judaic tradition, they also retained major elements from Judaism. Admittedly, non-Jews (Gentiles) also joined this new sectarian movement, but the influence they brought to bear on Christianity from their own religious backgrounds was slight compared to the dominance of Judaic traditions retained by adherents of the new sect. Basic ideologies, solemn observances and important institutions of Judaism survived intact or were carefully modified. A few examples must suffice in a book of this deliberately limited scope.

Christians accepted and revered the same collection of materials that was regarded in Judaism as Scripture. This acceptance embraced all the stories and theological concepts (but not all of the observances) recorded in the Holy Book.

The Messianic prophecies were considered by Christians to have been fulfilled in Jesus. The concepts implied by the terms 'election' and 'covenant' were inherited or assumed from the Jews, 'the old Israel', by the Christians, 'the new Israel'. Henceforth, according to Christians, God renewed the covenant with the Jews (Hebrews 8:13; 10:9) and made a new covenant with the Christians through Jesus (Hebrews 9:15). In fact, Christians considered themselves now to be the sole interpreters of God's will.

In addition to appropriating the Judaic text of the Holy Book and the privilege of God's favour formerly bestowed on Israel, Christians, the 'new' Israel, retained the Judaic notion of God acting in world history. As evidence, Christians interpreted the destruction of the Jewish Temple and the city of Jerusalem by the Romans in AD 70 and AD 135 respectively, as God's act of punishment upon the Jews for committing the crime of deicide—killing the Son of God. Here are the words of Origen, a prominent third-century Christian theologian of towering renown:

We may thus assert in utter confidence that the Jews will not return to their earlier situation, for they have committed the most abominable of crimes [i.e. deicide] . . . Hence the city where Jesus suffered was necessarily destroyed, the Jewish nation was driven from its country, and another people was called by God to the blessed election.[1]

Origen's confident assertion is not at issue in the present context. It is simply cited here as a further illustration of the conviction held by Christians that they had assumed from the Jews the mantle, the burden, of carrying God's word to the people on earth.

There are, of course, numerous other elements from Judaism that are retained in Christianity in either their original or modified form. The Mosaic Decalogue (Ten Commandments) remains to this day the standard of Christian life and conduct. The Judaic injunction to set aside one day as the Lord's Day or the day of rest is still literally and rigorously maintained by many Christians. The Judaic Feasts of Passover (Christian Easter) and of Shavuoth (Christian Pentecost) are Christian observances in their modified forms. The Christian rite of baptism, the significance and sanctity of marriage, the proper order of burial represent characteristics of Christian worship and belief derived from the Judaic legacy. Again, the Judaic theologies of good and evil, sin and repentance, and the problem of reconciling human suffering with a loving, caring God are all major issues of Christian theology. The respect due to the Patriarchs, to Moses, to the Jewish monarchs, and to the prophets, is retained in Christianity as it is in Judaism proper.

Christianity has never acknowledged or sustained a common bond with any other world religion as it has with Judaism. It is this intimate relationship that motivates Christians to study the Jewish Bible, the rabbinic materials, the institutions, and the practices of Judaism. By studying and exploring the rich literary and institutional heritage of Judaism, Christianity has promoted understanding among non-Jews of what Judaism is all about. Today, Christians are more attracted to books written on any aspect of Judaism than they are on materials written about Shinto, Sikhism, the Baha'i Faith, Hinduism, Buddhism or any other world religion. The reason for this is that Christianity is indissolubly rooted in Judaism. In fact, Christians often refer to their religion as the 'Judaeo-Christian' tradition, acknowledging the common ancestral bond between Jews and Christians. There is no better evidence of this than the official statement issued by the Roman Catholic Church at Vatican II Council (1962-64):

As this sacred Synod searches into the mystery of the Church, it recalls the spiritual bond linking the people of the New Covenant with Abraham's stock. For the Church of Christ acknowledges that, according to the mystery of God's saving design, the beginnings of her faith and her election are already found among the patriarchs, Moses, and the prophets . . . The Church, therefore, cannot forget that she received the revelation of the Old Testament through the people with whom God in His inexpressible mercy deigned to establish the Ancient Covenant . . . The Church recalls too that from the Jewish people sprang the apostles, her foundation stones and pillars, as well as most of the early disciples who proclaimed Christ to the world.[2]

The relationship is quite clear. Christians consider Christianity to be an extension of biblical Judaism. Jews, too, consider Judaism to be an extension of biblical Judaism. Christians think of themselves as successors or inheritors of the 'Chosen People' recorded in the 'Old' Testament, of the Patriarchs, of Moses, and of the prophets. Jews consider themselves as direct descendants of the 'Chosen People' recorded in their Bible. Christians proclaim that God made a new Covenant with them. Jews proclaim that God never rejected nor annulled the Covenant He made with them.

From early times to Vatican II, Christians justified their acts of barbarism against the Jews as just retribution for the crime committed against Christ. Jews justified their cruel sufferings and persecutions at the hand of Christians as witness to the world of their continued trust and loyalty to the living God. Christians associated the Jews with the biblical Cain and the fate destined for him. Jews associated themselves with the destiny of the Suffering Servant, a symbolic representation of the biblical Isaiah. Christians insisted, and still do, that Jews should turn and accept Christ, their long unrecognized Messiah. Jews insist that no Messiah possessing extraordinary attributes and superior powers of leadership has arrived yet.

These are not the claims and rebuttals of alien and disparate religious movements. These examples, limited as they are, clearly illustrate common roots, common spiritual values, and common aspirations.

Until very recently, it is true, Christians inveighed against the Jews with a litany of charges, including ignorance, rebellion, repudiation of faith, and the death of the long heralded Messiah. There is no better evidence for this than the words of a fourth-century Christian theologian:

Murderers of the Lord, assassins of the prophets, rebels and detesters of God, they outrage the Law, resist grace, repudiate the faith of their fathers. Companions of the devil, race of vipers, informers, calumniators, darkeners of the mind, pharisaic leaven, Sanhedrin of demons, accursed, detested, lapidators, enemies of all that is beautiful . . .[3]

These charges were, of course, not original. The Apostle Peter expressed the same sentiments centuries earlier on the day of Pentecost to the Jews assembled in Jerusalem:

Men of Israel, hear these words: Jesus of Nazareth a man attested to you by God with mighty works and wonders and signs which God did through Him in your midst . . . this Jesus, delivered up according to the definite plan and foreknowledge of God, you crucified and killed by the hands of lawless men . . .

Let all the house of Israel therefore know assuredly that God has made Him both Lord and Christ, this Jesus whom you crucified.

Acts 2:22-23, 36

All through the intervening twenty centuries Christians compelled the Jews through philosophical persuasion, but basically
through physical force, to submit to the Christian faith. The
record of attempts to effect forcible conversion makes sad
reading. And yet, all through these bloody twenty centuries
Christians shrank from the wholesale eradication of Judaism
which characterized their confrontations with rival ideologies.
Were it not for the common bond between Judaism and
Christianity, Judaism would not have survived the determined
and often savage proselytizing zeal of the militant servants of
Christianity. For, until modern times, Christianity chose to
condemn all other religions. Its task was to convert the entire
human race, including Jews, to Christianity. Judaism paid, as it
were, a very high price for its survival.

A few typical instances will serve to show the official or
institutional policy of Christians towards Jews during the long
course of centuries.

Sidonius Apollinaris, fifth-century bishop of Averni, wrote
as follows:

This letter commends a Jew to your notice. Not that I am pleased with
the error in which that nation is involved, and which leads to
perdition, but because it becomes us not to call any one of them sure
of damnation while he yet lives, for there is still a hope that he may
turn and be forgiven.[4]

The following decree issued in 1199 by Pope Innocent III
reflects the view of medieval Christian society towards Jews:

Although in many ways the disbelief of the Jews must be reproved,
since nevertheless through them our own faith is truly proved, they
must not be oppressed grievously by the faithful, as the prophet says:
'Do not slay them, lest these be forgetful of Thy Law', [Ps. 58 (59):12]
as if he were saying more openly: Do not wipe out the Jews
completely, lest perhaps Christians might be able to forget Thy Law,
which the former, although not understanding it, present in their
books to those who do understand it.[5]

Pope Gregory IX (1227-1241) expressed his indignation of the

Crusades which resulted in the godless execution of French
Jews who refused to convert to Christianity:

The Crusades . . . executed godless judgement against the Jews. But
in so doing they had not considered that Christians must derive the
evidences of their faith from the archives of the Jews, and that the
Lord would not reject His people for ever, but a remnant of them
should be saved. Not considering this, they had acted as if they meant
to exterminate them from the earth and with unheard-of cruelty had
butchered 2,500 persons of all ages and sexes. And in extenuation of
this atrocious crime, they affirmed that they had done so, and
threatened to do worse, because the Jews would not be baptized.[6]

The feelings entertained by Christians towards the Jews are
succinctly expressed by Robert Grosseteste (1235-53), Bishop
of Lincoln:

As murderers of the Lord, as still blaspheming Christ and mocking
His Passion, they were to be in captivity to the Princes of the earth. As
they have the brand of Cain and are condemned to wander over the
face of the earth, so they were to have the privilege of Cain, that no
man was to kill them.[7]

This rationalization in order to justify some degree of respite to
Jews is also echoed by Peter, the celebrated twelfth-century
Abbot of Cluny:

If the Saracens, who, in respect to the faith of Christ, have so much
in common with us, are still to be abominated, how much more
should we detest the Jews who blaspheme and ridicule Christ and
cast aside all the sacraments of our redemption . . . We should let
them live like the fratricide Cain to their greater shame and
torment.[8]

The official attitude of the Roman Catholic Church since the
Council of Vatican II (1962-64) is best stated in the 'Declaration
on the Relationship of the Church to Non-Christian Religions':

As holy Scripture testifies, Jerusalem did not recognize the time of her
visitation (cf. Lk. 19:44), nor did the Jews in large numbers accept the

gospel; indeed not a few opposed the spreading of it (cf. Rom. 11:28). Nevertheless, according to the Apostle [Paul], the Jews still remain most dear to God because of their fathers . . . In company with the prophets and the same Apostle, the Church awaits that day, known to God alone, on which all peoples will address the Lord in a single voice and 'serve him with one accord' (Soph. 3:9; Is. 66:23; Ps. 65:4; Rom. 11:11-32).[9]

It is not difficult to isolate from all these quotations the phrases that precisely identify the reasons that prompted Christians throughout the centuries to resist their normal reaction to obdurate opposition from any group—in this case the complete extermination of Jews and hence the extinction of Judaism:

• there is still a hope that he may turn and be forgiven;
• do not wipe out the Jews completely, lest perhaps Christians might be able to forget Thy Law;
• the Lord would not reject His people for ever, but a remnant of them should be saved;
• as they have the brand of Cain and are condemned to wander over the face of the earth, so they were to have the privilege of Cain, that no man was to kill them;
• we should detest the Jews . . . and we should let them live like the fratricide Cain to their greater shame and torment;
• the Jews still remain most dear to God because of their fathers.

The exceptional if tentative and patronizing tolerance of Christianity for Judaism accounts for its survival from oblivion. In a sense, the spread of Christianity promoted Judaism. The triumph of Christianity is the triumph of Judaism. People all over the world came to know of Jews and Judaism *because* of Christianity. In other words, the survival of Jews and Judaism in the last twenty centuries has been, in my opinion, dependent upon Christianity, in spite of the frequent and brutal incidence of persecution perpetrated by Christians against Jews. Christianity can take no credit for their unflattering performance which history reveals as a game of cat-and-mouse with the Jews. There are now signs of radical change. 'No one has to hate the Jews in order to love Jesus'.[10]

And what is the future prospect of Judaism? Fortunately, the long era of Christian complacency and exclusiveness has come to an end. The traditional Christian missionary enterprise of proselytization is in profound crisis. India, China, Africa, and many other non-Christian countries around the world are openly resisting, if not legally prohibiting, Christian imperialism. In addition, the scientific and technological achievements of the twentieth century have heralded the end of religious isolation and have radically altered the pattern of everyday living. People all over the world who were previously isolated one from another by distance, culture, language, and religion are becoming increasingly aware of each other's customs and ways of thinking. This global consciousness, resulting from numerous factors, such as the development of efficient transportation, extensive trade, rapid means of communication, and economic interdependence has, inevitably, created the climate for 'dialogue' among people of differing religious traditions. And what significance does all this have for Judaism?

From the time of Jesus to the end of the eighteenth century Jewish interest in Christianity remained peripheral. During the Middle Ages Jews developed some interest in Christianity, but they understandably hesitated to expound critically and openly on the monolithic faith of their oppressors. However, emancipation from ghetto life in modern times gave Jews the courage of their strongly held convictions and the determination to frame rebuttals. Also, long-standing Christian religious imperialism finally condescended to listen and then to join in Christian-Jewish dialogue. Slowly and hesitatingly, a few Jewish thinkers were attracted to New Testament studies, the life of Jesus, and the teachings of Paul. Moses Mendelssohn (1729-1786) is considered to be the pioneer of serious, scholarly study of Christianity by Jews. This paved the way for future Jewish scholars who sought to attain an understanding of Christianity in Jewish terms. Among the dozen or more leading Jewish scholars in the area of Christianity are Abraham Geiger (1810-1874); Isaac Mayer Wise (1819-1900); Hermann Cohen (1842-1918); Claude G. Montefiore (1858-1938); Franz Rosenzweig (1886-1929); Leo Baeck (1873-1956); Martin Buber

(1878-1965); and, in modern times, Samuel Sandmel and Emil Fackenheim.

In spite of the well-intentioned efforts of these few, old fears and inhibitions about the good faith and intentions of Christians persist. Although the future path of Jewish-Christian dialogue is uncertain, one hopes that the present climate of religious toleration will lead Jews and Christians to a sense of brotherhood, to mutual understanding, and, above all, to mutual admiration, love, and respect.

REFERENCES

Chapter One: Holy God

1. *Hullin* 60a.
2. Moses Maimonides, *Guide of the Perplexed,* trans. by M. Friedlander (New York: Hebrew Publishing Co., 1881, Part I, chp. 57-58).
3. *The Zohar,* Gen. 10 3a-b; trans. by Sperling and Simon (London: Soncino Press, n.d.).
4. *Weekday Prayer Book,* New York: The Rabbinical Assembly of America, 1961, p. 42.
5. *Ibid.,* p. 141.
6. Israel Baal-Shem, in N. N. Glatzer, ed., *In Time and Eternity,* New York: Schocken Books, Inc., 1946, p. 87.
7. Saadia Gaon, *The Book of Beliefs and Opinions,* trans. by S. Rosenblatt, New Haven, Conn.: Yale University Press, 1948, Treatise II, chp. 12.
8. *Avodah Zarah* 36.
9. *Midrash Exodus Rabah,* ii, 9.
10. Jerusalem *Talmud Haggigah* 1:7.
11. As cited in I. Epstein, *Judaism* (England: Penguin Books Ltd., 1974, p. 215).
12. Hayyim ibn Musa, in N. N. Glatzer, ed., *op. cit.,* pp. 74-75.
13. L. Roth, *Judaism: A Portrait* (New York: The Viking Press Inc., 1961, p. 125).
14. *Genesis Rabbah* 12:15.
15. N. N. Glatzer, ed., *Franz Rosenzweig: His Life and Thought* (Philadelphia: Jewish Publication Society, 1953, p. 304).
16. S. R. Hirsch, *The Nineteen Letters of Ben Uziel,* New York: Bloch, 1942, Seventh Letter.
17. A. I. Kook, "The Rebirth of Israel", in A. Hertzberg, *The Zionist Idea,* Garden City, N.Y.: Doubleday & Co. Inc., 1959, p. 424.

18. *Weekday Prayer Book, op. cit.*
19. *Genesis Rabbah* 34:8.
20. *Nineteen Letters,* Sixteenth Letter, as cited in L. Trepp, *Judaism: Development and Life,* 3rd edit. (Belmont, California: Wadsworth Publishing Co., 1982, p. 8).
21. From a letter of Judah Ibn Tibbon to his son Samuel, as cited in F. Kobler, *A Treasury of Jewish Letters,* Vol. I, pp. 160-61.
22. Moses Luzatto, *Mesillot Yesharim,* chp. 5.
23. Cited in N. Kertzer, *What Is a Jew?* rev. edit. (New York: Macmillan Co., 1965, pp. 139-40).
24. Adapted from L. Roth (*op. cit.,* p. 207).
25. *Weekday Prayer Book, op. cit.,* pp. 56-67.
26. As cited in I. Epstein (*op. cit.,* p. 312).
27. *Ibid.,* p. 321.
28. *Mishnah Ediyot* 2:10.
29. Isaiah 26:19 may possibly be an earlier view than Daniel, though its date is disputable.
30. In N. H. Cohen, *Jüdische Schriften* III, p. 173ff., as cited in L. Trepp, *op. cit.,* p. 244.

Chapter Two: Holy People

1. H. Hess, *Rome and Jerusalem,* trans. by M. Waxman, as cited in I. Epstein, *Judaism* (England: Penguin Books, 1974, p. 305).
2. A. Schwarz-Bart, *The Last of the Just,* trans. by S. Becker (London: Secker & Warburg, 1961, p. 409).
3. E. Fackenheim, *The Jewish Return into History,* (New York: Schocken Press, 1978, p. 96).
4. E. Wiesel, *A Jew Today* (New York: Vintage Books, 1979, p. 234).
5. R. Rubenstein, *After Auschwitz* (Indianapolis: Bobbs Merrill, 1966, pp. 130,136).
6. N. N. Glatzer, ed., *Franz Rosenzweig: His Life and Thought,* 2nd edit. (New York: Schocken Press, 1961, p. 223).
7. Quoted in I. Epstein (*op. cit.,* p. 271).
8. I. Eisenstein and E. Kohn, ed., *Mordecai M. Kaplan: An Evaluation* (New York: Jewish Reconstructionist Foundation, 1952, p. 296).
9. M. M. Kaplan, *The Purpose and Meaning of Jewish Existence: A People in the Image of God* (Philadelphia: Jewish Publication Society, 1964, p. 299).

Chapter Three: Holy Land

1. Y. Kaufmann, *The Religion of Israel,* trans. and abr. by M. Greenberg (Chicago: University of Chicago Press, 1960).
2. M. Noth, *The History of Israel,* 2nd edit., trans. by P. R. Ackroyd (New York: Harper & Row, 1960, pp. 53-84).
3. J. Bright, *Early Israel in Recent History Writing,* Studies in Biblical Theology, No. 19 (London: SCM Press, 1956, pp. 79-110).
4. G. E. Mendenhall, in 'The Hebrew Conquest of Palestine', in E. F. Campbell and D. N. Freedman, eds., *The Biblical Archaeologist Reader,* No. 3 (Garden City, New Jersey: Doubleday, Anchor Books, 1970, pp. 100-120).
5. As cited in J. A. Brundage, *The Crusades: A Documentary Survey* (Milwaukee: The Marquette University Press, 1962, pp. 18-19).

Chapter Four: Holy Book

1. H. N. Bialik, 'Address at the Inauguration of the Hebrew University in Jerusalem, 1925' cited in A. D. Hertzberg, *The Zionist Idea,* Garden City, N.Y.: Doubleday & Co. Inc., 1959, p. 282.
2. K. Kohler, *Jewish Theology* (New York: The Macmillan Co., 1928, p. 352).
3. S. Schechter, *Studies in Judaism* (Philadelphia: Jewish Publication Society, 1896, pp. 248-49).
4. C. T. Fritsch, 'Pseudepigrapha', in *The Interpreter's Dictionary of the Bible,* vol. 3 (New York: Abingdon Press, 1962, pp. 961-62).

Chapter Five: Holy Observances

1. *Sifre Ekev.*
2. *Talmud Sukkah,* 42a.
3. *Weekday Prayer Book,* New York, N.Y.: The Rabbinical Assembly of America, 1961.
4. *Ibid.*
5. *Rosh Hashanah* 16b.
6. *Mishnah Yoma* 8:1.
7. As cited in A. Hertzberg (*op. cit.,* pp. 137-38).
8. *Midrash Tehillin* 27:4.
9. As cited in A. Hertzberg (*op. cit.,* p. 137).
10. S. Y. Agnon, *Yamin Noraim,* New York, N.Y.: Schocken Books, Inc., 1946, p. 230.

Reflections

1. *Contra Celsum*, 4.22. A striking parallel is found in *Oratio Catechetica Magna*, 18, by Gregory of Nyssa.
2. This statement was officially issued by the Roman Catholic Church during the Twenty-First Ecumenical Council, commonly known as Vatican II Council (1962-64); see W. M. Abbott, ed., *The Documents of Vatican II*, trs. by J. Gallagher (New York: Guild Press, 1966, pp. 663-64).
3. From the Treatise *Against the Jews, on the Trinity*, by Gregory of Nyssa (though the authorship is often disputed).
4. *Ep.* vii 11; as cited in C. H. Robinson, *The Conversion of Europe* (New York: Longman's, Green, 1917, pp. 539-40).
5. *Constitution for the Jews*, cited in E. A. Synan, *The Popes and the Jews in the Middle Ages*, New York, N.Y.: Macmillan Co., 1965, p. 230.
6. Raynaldi, *Annales*, anno 1236, 48, cited in C. H. Robinson (*op. cit.*, pp. 547-48).
7. *Epistle R. Grosstêste*, Rolls series, p. 36, cited in C. H. Robinson (*op. cit.*, p. 540).
8. *Epistoloe*, lib. iv. cap. 36. Migne P. L. clxxxix, col. 367, cited in C. H. Robinson (*op. cit.*, p. 540).
9. W. M. Abbott, ed. (*op. cit.*, pp. 664-65).
10. D. D. Runes, *The War Against the Jew* (New York: Philosophical Library, Inc., 1968, xxv).

BIBLIOGRAPHY

THE literature on Judaism is vast. The following list supplements that covered in the main body of the text as well as in the sources of quotations, and is limited to works written in English. Hence, it provides the next step for the interested reader who wishes to pursue further the individual subjects discussed under each chapter.

Chapter One: Holy God

Albright, W. F., *Yahweh and the Gods of Canaan* (Garden City, New York: Doubleday, 1968).

Baeck, L., *God and Man in Judaism,* trs. by A. K. Dallas (New York: Union of American Hebrew Congregations, 1958).

Baeck, L., *The Essence of Judaism,* trs. by I. Howe (New York: Schocken Books, 1948).

Bamberger, B. J. *The Search for Jewish Theology* (New York: Behrman, 1978).

Bergmann, S. H., *Faith and Reason: An Introduction to Modern Jewish Thought* (Washington, D. C.: B'nai Brith Hillel Foundations, 1961).

Berkowitz, E., *Faith After the Holocaust* (New York: Ktav Publications, 1973).

Borowitz, E. B., *How Can a Jew Speak of Faith Today?* (Philadelphia: Westminster Press, 1969).

Buber, M., *Israel and the World,* 2nd edit. (New York: Schocken Books, 1963).

Dimont, M., *Jews, God and History* (New York: New American Library, 1964).

Guttman, J., *Philosophies of Judaism* (New York: Schocken Books, 1973).

Herberg, W., *Judaism and Modern Man* (New York: Atheneum, 1970).

Heschel, A. J., *God in Search of Man* (New York: Farrar, Straus and Cudahy, 1956).

Jacobs, L., *Principles of the Jewish Faith: An Analytical Study* (London: Vallentine, Mitchell, 1964).

Kaplan, M. M., *The Meaning of God in Modern Jewish Religion* (New York: Jewish Reconstructionist Press, 1962).

Klausner, J., *The Messianic Idea in Israel* (New York: Macmillan, 1955).

Maimonides, M., *The Guide of the Perplexed,* 2 Vols. trs. by S. Pines (Chicago: University of Chicago Press, 1963).

Martin, B., *Great Twentieth Century Jewish Philosophers* (New York: Macmillan, 1970).

Rosenzweig, F., *Star of Redemption,* trs. by W. Hallo (Boston: Beacon Press, 1972).

Scholem, G., *The Messianic Idea in Judaism and Other Essays* (New York: Schocken Books, 1971).

Steinberg, M., *Basic Judaism* (New York: Harcourt, Brace and World, 1947).

Chapter Two: Holy People

Anderson, G. W., *The History and Religion of Israel* (Oxford: Oxford University Press, 1966).

Badi, J., *Religion in Israel Today* (New York: Bookman Associates, 1959).

Ben-Zvi, I., *The Exiled and the Redeemed* (Philadelphia: Jewish Publication Society, 1961).

Bickerman, E. J., *From Ezra to the Last of the Maccabees* (New York: Schocken Books, 1962).

Blau, J. L., *Modern Varieties of Judaism* (New York: Columbia University Press, 1966).

Davis, M., *The Emergence of Conservative Judaism* (Philadelphia: Jewish Publication Society of America, 1963).

Finkelstein, L., *The Jews: Their History, Culture and Religion,* 3rd edit. 2 Vols. (New York: Harper & Row Pub. Inc., 1960).

Glazer, N., *American Judaism,* 2nd edit. (Chicago: University of Chicago Press, 1972).

Hertzberg, A., *The Zionist Idea* (New York: Atheneum, 1970).

Kaddushin, M., *The Rabbinic Mind* (New York: Jewish Theological Seminary of America, 1952).

Kaufmann, Y., *The Religion of Israel,* abr. and trs. by M. Greenberg (Chicago: University of Chicago Press, 1960).

Lacks, R., *Women and Judaism* (New York: Doubleday, 1980).

Meiselman, M., *Jewish Woman in Jewish Law* (New York: Ktav Publications, 1978).

Nigosian, S. A., *Occultism in the Old Testament* (Philadelphia: Dorrance & Co., 1978).

Philipson, D., *The Reform Movement in Judaism*, rev. ed. (New York: Ktav Publications, 1967).

Ringgren, H., *Israelite Religion* (Philadelphia: Fortress Press, 1966).

Rudavsky, B., *Emancipation and Adjustment* (New York: Diplomatic Press, 1967).

Runes, D. D., *The War Against the Jew* (New York: Philosophical Library Inc., 1968).

Russell, D. S., *The Jews From Alexander to Herod* (Oxford: Oxford University Press, 1967).

Scholem, G., *Major Trends in Jewish Mysticism*, rev. ed. (New York: Schocken Books, 1946).

Silver, D. J., and Martin, B., eds., *A History of Judaism*, 2 Vols. (New York: Basic Books, 1974).

Singer, S. A., *Medieval Jewish Mysticism: The Book of the Pious* (Northbrook, Illinois: Whitehall Co., 1972).

Tcherikover, V., *Hellenistic Civilization and the Jews*, trs. by S. Applebaum (Philadelphia: Jewish Publication Society of America, 1959).

Zeitlin, S., *The Rise and Fall of the Judaean State: A Political, Social and Religious History of the Second Commonwealth*, 3 Vols. (Philadelphia: The Jewish Publication Society of America, Vol. 1, 1962; Vol. 2, 1969; Vol. 3, 1978).

Zimmels, H. J., *Ashkenazim and Sephardim* (Oxford: Oxford University Press, 1958).

Chapter Three: Holy Land

Abu-Lughod, I., ed., *The Transformation of Palestine* (Michigan: Northwestern University Press, 1971).

Aharoni, Y., *The Land of the Bible: A Historical Geography*, trs. by A. F. Rainey (Philadelphia: Westminster Press, 1967).

Aharoni, Y., and Michael, A., *The Macmillan Bible Atlas* (New York: Macmillan, 1968).

Baly, D., *The Geography of the Bible: A Study in Historical Geography*, rev. edit. (New York: Harper and Row, 1974).

Benvenisti, M., *The Crusades in the Holy Land* (New York: Macmillan, 1972).

Elston, D. R., *The Making of a Nation* (London: Anglo-Israel Association, 1963).

Hurewitz, J. C., *The Struggle for Palestine* (New York: Norton, 1950).

Joseph, D., *Faithful City: The Siege of Jerusalem* (New York: Simon and Schuster, 1964).

Parkes, J., *Whose Land?* (New York: Penguin, 1971).

Sacher, H., *Israel: The Establishment of a State* (London: Weidenfeld and Nicolson, 1952).

Chapter Four: Holy Book

Adler, M., *The World of the Talmud,* 2nd edit. (New York: Schocken Books, 1970).

Cassuto, U., *The Documentary Hypothesis and the Composition of the Pentateuch,* trs. by I. Abrahams (Jerusalem: Magness Press, 1961).

Charles, R. H., *The Apocrypha and Pseudepigripha of the Old Testament in English,* 2 Vols. (Oxford: Oxford University Press, 1913, reprint 1963).

Danby, H., *The Mishnah* (Oxford: Oxford University Press, 1933).

Epstein, I., ed., *The Babylonian Talmud in English,* 36 Vols. (London: Soncino Press, 1935-1953).

Hanson, P. D., *The Dawn of Apocalyptic* (Philadelphia: Fortress Press, 1975).

Metzger, B. M., *An Introduction to the Apocrypha* (New York: Oxford University Press, 1957).

Montgomery, R. M., *An Introduction to Source Analysis of the Pentateuch* (Nashville: Abingdon Press, 1971).

Noth, M., *A History of Pentateuchal Traditions,* trs. by B. W. Anderson (Englewood Cliffs, New Jersey: Prentice-Hall, 1972).

Sandmel, S., *The Hebrew Scriptures: An Introduction* (New York: Knopf, 1962).

Sperling, H., Simon, M., and Levertoff, P. trs. *Zohar,* Vol. I-V. (London: Soncino Press, 1931-1934).

Strack, H. L., *Introduction to the Talmud and Midrash* (New York: Harper and Row, 1965).

Chapter Five: Holy Observances

Agnon, S. Y., *Days of Awe* (New York: Schocken Press, 1948).

Cahnman, W. J., *Intermarriage and Jewish Life* (New York: Herzl Press, 1963).

Donin, H. H., *To Be A Jew* (New York: Basic Books, 1972).

Gaster, T. H., *Festivals of the Jewish Year* (London: Apollo, 1961).

Heschel, A. J., *The Sabbath: Its Meaning for Modern Man* (New York: Farrar, Strauss, and Young, 1951).

Klein, I., *A Guide to Jewish Religious Practice* (New York: Jewish Theological Society of America, 1979).

Lehrman, S. M., *The Jewish Festivals* (London: Shapiro, Vallentine, 1953).

Schauss, H., *Guide to Jewish Holy Days,* trs. by S. Jaffe (New York: Schocken Books, 1970).

Simpson, W. W., *Jewish Prayer and Worship: An Introduction for Christians* (Naperville, Illinois: SCM Press, 1965).

Trepp, L., *The Complete Book of Jewish Observance* (New York: Behrman House-Summit Books, 1980).

INDEX